1990 United Nations List of National Parks and Protected Areas

Liste des Nations Unies des Parcs Nationaux et des Aires Protégées 1990

LHBEC

Published by: IUCN, Gland, Switzerland and Cambridge, UK

Prepared and published with the support of Unesco

A contribution to GEMS – the Global Environment Monitoring System

Citation: IUCN (1990). *1990 United Nations List of National Parks and Protected Areas*. IUCN, Gland, Switzerland and Cambridge, UK. 284 pp.

ISBN: 2-8317-0032-9

Printed by: Avon Litho Limited, Stratford-upon-Avon, UK

Cover design by: IUCN Publications Services Unit

Cover photographs: Bartholomé Island, Galapagos; Namib Desert, Namibia; Wetland in Kakadu National Park, Australia – J.W. Thorsell: Baobab *Adansonia grandidieri*, Madagascar – Martin Nicoll

Produced by the IUCN Publications Services Unit on desktop publishing equipment purchased through a gift from Mrs Julia Ward.

Available from: IUCN Publications Services Unit,
219c Huntingdon Road, Cambridge, CB3 0DL, UK

The designations of geographical entities in this book, and the presentation of the material, do not imply the expression of any opinion whatsoever on the part of IUCN, Unesco or WCMC concerning the legal status of any country, territory, or area, or of its authorities, or concerning the delimitation of its frontiers and boundaries.

1990 United Nations List of National Parks and Protected Areas

Liste des Nations Unies des Parcs Nationaux et des Aires Protégées 1990

Prepared by the
World Conservation Monitoring Centre
and the
IUCN Commission on National Parks and Protected Areas

Préparée par
le Centre mondial de surveillance continue de la conservation de la nature
et
la Commission des parcs nationaux et des aires protégées de l'UICN

IUCN – THE WORLD CONSERVATION UNION
UICN – L'ALLIANCE MONDIALE POUR LA NATURE
1990

Publié par: l'UICN, Gland, Suisse et Cambridge, Royaume-Uni.

Préparée et publiée avec la contribution de l'Unesco.

Préparé dans le cadre du GEMS – Système mondial de surveillance continue de l'environnement.

WORLD CONSERVATION
MONITORING CENTRE

Citation: UICN (1990). *Liste des Nations Unies des Parcs Nationaux et des Aires Protégées 1990*. UICN, Gland, Suisse et Cambridge, Royaume-Uni. 284 pp.

ISBN: 2-8317-0032-9

Imprimé par: Avon Litho Limited, Stratford-upon-Avon, Royaume-Uni

Couverture conçue: Service des publications de l'UICN

Couverture photos: Ile Bartolomeo, Galápagos; Désert de Namib, Namibie; Zone humide dans le Parc national de Kakadu, Australie – J.W. Thorsell: Baobab *Adansonia grandidieri*, Madagascar – Martin Nicoll

Publication de l'UICN assistée par ordinateur et rendue possible grâce à un don de Madame Julia Ward.

Disponible auprès du: Service des publications de l'UICN
219c Huntingdon Road, Cambridge, CB3 0DL, Royaume-Uni

La terminologie géographique employée dans cet ouvrage, de même que sa présentation, ne sont en aucune manière l'expression d'une opinion quelconque de la part de l'UICN, de l'Unesco ou du CMSC en ce qui concerne le statut juridique ou l'autorité de quelque Etat, territoire ou région que ce soit ou en ce qui concerne la délimitation de leurs frontières.

IUCN – THE WORLD CONSERVATION UNION

Founded in 1948, IUCN – the World Conservation Union – is a membership organisation comprising governments, non-governmental organisations (NGOs), research institutions, and conservation agencies in 120 countries. The Union's objective is to promote and encourage the protection and sustainable utilisation of living resources.

Several thousand scientists and experts from all continents form part of a network supporting the work of its six Commissions: threatened species, protected areas, ecology, sustainable development, environmental law, and environmental education and training. Its thematic programmes include tropical forests, wetlands, marine ecosystems, plants, the Sahel, Antarctica, population and sustainable development, and women in conservation. These activities enable IUCN and its members to develop sound policies and programmes for the conservation of biological diversity and sustainable development of natural resources.

L'UICN – L'ALLIANCE MONDIALE POUR LA NATURE

Fondée en 1948, l'UICN, l'Alliance mondiale pour la nature, est une organisation qui compte parmi ses membres des Etats, des organisations non gouvernementales (ONG), des institutions de recherche, ainsi que des organismes de conservation, répartis dans 120 pays. L'UICN a pour objectif de promouvoir et d'encourager la protection et l'utilisation durable des ressources vivantes.

Plusieurs milliers de scientifiques et d'experts des cinq continents formant un réseau sur lequel s'appuient les six commissions de l'UICN: espèces menacées, aires protégées, écologie, développement durable, droit de l'environnement, et éducation et formation en matière d'environnement. Ses programmes spéciaux comprennent les forêts tropicales, les zones humides, les écosystèmes marins, les plants, le Sahel, l'Antarctique, la population et le développement durable, ainsi que les femmes et la conservation. Grâce à ces activités, l'UICN et ses membres sont en mesure d'établir des politiques et des programmes pour la conservation de la diversité biologique et l'utilisation durable des ressources naturelles.

WCMC – THE WORLD CONSERVATION MONITORING CENTRE

The World Conservation Monitoring Centre (WCMC) is a joint venture between the three partners in the World Conservation Strategy, IUCN – the World Conservation Union, the World Wide Fund for Nature (WWF), and the United Nations Environment Programme (UNEP). Its mission is to support conservation and sustainable development by collecting and analysing global conservation data so that decisions affecting biological resources are based on the best available information.

WCMC has developed a global overview database of the world's biological diversity that includes threatened plant and animal species, habitats of conservation concern, critical sites, protected areas of the world, and the utilisation and trade in wildlife species and products. Drawing on this database, WCMC provides an information service to the conservation and development communities, governments and United Nations agencies, scientific institutions, the business and commercial sector, and the media. WCMC produces a wide variety of specialist outputs and reports based on analyses of its data.

LE CMSC – LE CENTRE MONDIAL DE SURVEILLANCE CONTINUE DE LA CONSERVATION DE LA NATURE

Le Centre mondial de surveillance continue de la conservation de la nature (CMSC) est une entreprise commune des trois partenaires de la Stratégie mondiale de la conservation: l'Alliance mondiale pour la nature (UICN), le Fonds mondial pour la nature (WWF), et le Programme des Nations Unies pour l'environnement (PNUE). Ce centre a pour mission d'appuyer la conservation et le développement durable en recueillant et en analysant des données mondiales sur la conservation, afin que les décisions concernant les ressources biologiques reposent sur les meilleurs informations disponibles.

Le CMSC a établi une banque de données sur la diversité biologique mondiale, qui comprend des données sur les espèces animales et végétales menacées, les biotopes préoccupants du point de vue de la conservation, les sites critiques, les aires protégées, ainsi que l'utilisation et le commerce des espèces et produits de la faune et de la flore sauvages. S'appuyant sur cette banque de données, le CMSC fournit un service d'information aux communautés de la conservation et du développement, aux gouvernements, aux institutions des Nations Unies, aux instituts scientifiques, au monde du commerce et des affaires, et aux médias. Le CMSC publie de très nombreux rapports et documents spécialisés, fondés sur l'analyse de ses données.

CONTENTS

TABLE DES MATIERES

INTRODUCTION

Protected areas make a vital contribution to the conservation of the world's natural and cultural resources. Values range from retention of representative samples of natural regions and the preservation of biological diversity, to the maintenance of environmental stability of surrounding regions. Protected areas can provide opportunity for rural development and rational use of marginal lands, for research and monitoring, for conservation education, and for recreation and tourism. As a result most countries have developed systems of protected areas.

However, protected area systems vary considerably one country to another, depending on needs and priorities, and on differences in legislative, institutional and financial support. Also, the range of services and values that protected areas provide is such that some management objectives are not compatible with others. This has lead to the emergence of a wide range of protected area designations and definitions.

The aim of the *UN List* is to provide a definitive list of protected areas meeting certain criteria.

History of the UN List

The *United Nations List of National Parks and Equivalent Reserves* is drawn up at the request of the United Nations following a resolution adopted by the General Assembly at its Sixteenth Session in December 1962 on "Economic Development and Nature Conservation". This resolution served to endorse an earlier resolution (No. 713) of the 27th session of the UN Economic and Social Council held in 1959, which recognised National Parks and Equivalent Reserves as an important factor in the wise use of natural resources, and led to the compilation of the first *World List of National Parks and Equivalent Reserves*.

IUCN was instrumental in the preparation of the two resolutions, and has since had prime responsibility for the compilation and maintenance of the list. The *UN List* is now jointly compiled by the IUCN Commission on National Parks and Protected Areas, and by the Protected Areas Data Unit, part of the World Conservation Monitoring Centre. The version of the *UN List* immediately preceding this was published by IUCN in 1985; other versions were published in 1961/2, 1966 (English version 1971), 1972 (addendum to the 1966/71 list), 1973, 1974, 1975, 1980 and 1982.

The IUCN Commission on National Parks and Protected Areas

IUCN's Commission on National Parks and Protected Areas (CNPPA) is the leading international scientific and technical body concerned with the selection, establishment and management of national parks and other protected areas. Its membership includes protected areas professionals from more than 90 countries. CNPPA is responsible for that part of the IUCN Programme which promotes the establishment of a world-wide network of effectively managed terrestrial and marine protected areas.

During preparation of this edition of the *UN List*, CNPPA has been under the chairmanship of Harold Eidsvik, Senior Policy Advisor to the Canadian Parks Service, with Adrian Phillips, Director General of the Countryside Commission of England and Wales, as Deputy Chairman. During the same period, the work of the Commission has been coordinated by Dr James Thorsell, based at the IUCN headquarters in Gland, Switzerland. Organisation of the Commission is regional, with 12 regional Vice-Chairmen, and there are normally two Commission meetings a year. Since the last *UN List* was compiled, there have been meetings in Argentina, Niger, New Zealand, Costa Rica, Italy, Vanuatu and Czechoslovakia.

The WCMC Protected Areas Data Unit

The Protected Areas Data Unit (PADU) was established by CNPPA in 1981 to handle the increasing amount of information, and to assist the Commission in preparing publications on national parks and other protected areas around the world. The unit is now a part of the World Conservation Monitoring Centre, and is based in Cambridge in the United Kingdom. The objective of PADU's work is to be able to provide accurate up-to-date information on individual protected areas and protected area systems of the world to those who need it, or, failing that, to identify where such information can be quickly obtained.

In order to meet its objective, WCMC collaborates with the many agencies around the world managing protected areas, and with conservationists and scientists who work in this field. Many of the individuals involved are members of CNPPA. PADU also has a particular responsibility for managing information on Biosphere Reserves and World Heritage Sites (accorded by the MAB Secretariat and the World Heritage Committee respectively), and on sites listed under the Ramsar (Wetlands) Convention (accorded by the Convention Bureau).

Criteria for inclusion

There are three criteria which govern whether or not a protected area is included in the *UN List*: size, management objectives, and the authority of the management agency.

1. **Size:** Only protected areas of over 1,000 hectares are included, with the exception of offshore or oceanic islands of at least 100 hectares where the whole island is protected. One thousand hectares is equivalent to 10 square kilometres, 2,471 acres or 3.86 square miles.

2. **Management objectives:** A series of protected area management categories, defined by management objective, are identified by IUCN/CNPPA in the paper on *Categories, Objectives and Criteria for Protected Areas* published in the proceedings of the World National Parks Congress held in Bali. The definitions of each category are provided below. Nationally designated sites are allocated to the relevant IUCN Categories, on the basis of their legally defined management objectives, and implementation of those objectives.

    Where the available information suggests that management of the site is insufficient to implement nationally legislated objectives, the site may either be omitted from the list, or, where relevant, included under another category. Reasons for this might include inappropriate use, inadequate resources, severe encroachment or civil strife, and are often beyond the control of the management authority. It is anticipated that such omission or reclassification would be temporary, pending improvement in the information available, or in the actual on-site situation.

    The 1990 edition of the *UN List* includes sites in IUCN Management Categories I through V. Protected areas which are also designated Ramsar Sites, World Heritage Sites or Biosphere Reserves, are included both in the nationals lists and in the lists of areas of international significance.

3. **Authority of the management agency:** Only those sites managed by the "highest competent authority" are included within the *UN List*, i.e the highest appropriate level of government.

The 1990 *UN List* is the third to be prepared jointly by PADU and CNPPA, and, as with the previous two lists (published in 1982 and 1985), there has been a considerable expansion in the list – despite the fact that the criteria for inclusion have remained unchanged. While there have been some significant extensions to protected areas networks, much of the expansion of the list is due to improvements in available information, and improvements in our ability to collect and manage it. It is important to bear this in mind when using the list.

Layout of the UN List

Sites which meet the above-mentioned criteria are listed country by country (in alphabetic order of the English-language version of the country name). Within each country sites are presented in alphabetic order by national designation (for example national parks, nature reserves, wildlife sanctuaries). Three items of information are provided about each site: its IUCN management category, its size (in hectares), and the year it was established (or significantly altered in either size or designation). This format is different from lists produced in recent years, where sites were listed by IUCN Management Category and a biogeographic code was provided (see below). The present format should, however, be easier to use. Further information on each of these sites is held by PADU.

Compilation of the UN List

CNPPA and PADU have been collecting and managing information on protected areas for a number of years, and a large body of information is available, some of which has been published. New information is also constantly being received. In preparing the 1990 *UN List*, staff at PADU reviewed existing material, and revised and updated lists of protected areas (which included the appropriate IUCN Management Category for each site). Draft lists for each country were sent to national management agencies and to members of CNPPA, with a request that they be checked, updated, and returned. Based on the information received, PADU staff revised this draft, following up queries with contacts in the countries concerned, or officers of the CNPPA.

In Europe a new procedure was tested, where draft lists were sent to the CNPPA Regional Vice-Chairman for review, prior to being sent to the national management agencies.

Accuracy and quality of information

The world of protected areas is rapidly changing, new areas are created, boundaries of existing areas are revised and some sites are destroyed through industrial development, shifting agriculture, or natural disasters. To state emphatically that there has been any net gain for conservation in the amount of land and water protected in the last few years is very difficult. It is not simply a question of hectares protected or of the number of areas protected, but is more a question of management effectiveness. Are the protected areas achieving the objectives for which they were established?

The quality of the information available used to compile the *UN List* is very variable, and information on management effectiveness is still lacking for a number of countries. While the vast majority of the national parks which meet the relevant criteria are listed, information on the other categories of protected area is still incomplete, and much more information is necessary before we can be confident we are providing complete lists of areas in every management category. Some state or provincial parks have been included, but the data are still not wholly adequate, and again much more information still needs to be collected.

Introduction

The 1990 *UN List* undoubtedly includes mistakes and omissions, but it is hoped that these will stimulate ever more accurate information. The responsibility for errors and oversights rests with the compilers, and corrections or updates should be communicated to the:

Protected Areas Data Unit
World Conservation Monitoring Centre
219c Huntingdon Road, Cambridge CB3 0DL
United Kingdom

Telephone: (0223) 277314
Fax: (0223) 277136
Telex: 817036 scmu g

Acknowledgements

Compilation of the list has been carried out by all PADU staff, which currently comprises Graham Drucker (North Africa and the Middle East), Harriet Gillet (data entry), Michael Green (Indomalaya), Jeremy Harrison (Head of Unit), Zbigniew Karpowicz (Europe and the USSR), James Paine (Oceania) and Alison Suter (data entry). Graham Drucker has coordinated compilation of the list for those countries outside the areas of responsibility indicated.

Compilation has been actively supported by CNPPA, and in particular by the officers of the Commission, and Dr James Thorsell of the IUCN Secretariat.

The list was prepared for publication by Barbara Lambert of the IUCN Publication Services Unit.

Finally, many individuals in protected areas management agencies and elsewhere in each country have provided information which has been used in compiling this list. Without this input, the list could not have been completed.

INTRODUCTION

Les aires protégées apportent une contribution vitale à la conservation des ressources naturelles et culturelles de la planète. Elles ont aussi bien pour fonction de préserver des échantillons représentatifs de régions naturelles et la diversité biologique que de maintenir la stabilité écologique des régions qui les entourent. Elles sont un moteur pour le développement rural et l'utilisation rationnelle des terres marginales, la recherche et la surveillance continue, l'éducation à la conservation, les loisirs et le tourisme. Pour toutes ces raisons, la plupart des pays se sont dotés d'un réseau d'aires protégées.

Toutefois, les réseaux d'aires protégées varient énormément d'un pays à l'autre, selon les besoins et les priorités, selon les différences entre les moyens législatifs, institutionnels et financiers disponibles. En outre, la gamme des services et valeurs des aires protégées est telle que certains objectifs de gestion sont incompatibles avec d'autres. Une multitude de termes et définitions sont donc appliqués aux aires protégées.

La *Liste des Nations Unies* a pour objectif de donner une liste définitive d'aires protégées répondant à certains critères.

Histoire de la Liste des Nations Unies

La *Liste des Nations Unies des parcs nationaux et réserves analogues* a été établie selon le voeu des Nations Unies et dans l'esprit d'une résolution sur "le développement économique et la conservation de la nature", adoptée par l'Assemblée générale à sa 16e Session, en décembre 1962. Cette résolution entérinait une résolution précédente (No. 713) de la 27e Session du Conseil économique et social, tenue en 1959. Cette dernière résolution reconnaissait que les parcs nationaux et réserves analogues sont un instrument important de l'utilisation rationnelle des ressources naturelles et a débouché sur l'établissement de la première *Liste mondiale des parcs nationaux et réserves analogues*.

L'UICN a joué un rôle central dans la préparation des deux résolutions et, depuis lors, est responsable de la compilation et de la mise à jour de la Liste. La *Liste des Nations Unies* est aujourd'hui compilée conjointement par la Commission des parcs nationaux et des aires protégées de l'UICN et l'Unité de données sur les aires protégées qui fait partie du Centre mondial de surveillance continue de la conservation de la nature. La version précédente de la *Liste des Nations Unies* a été publiée par l'UICN en 1985. De plus anciennes versions datent de 1961/1962, 1966 (version anglaise 1971), 1972 (ajout à la Liste de 1966/1971), 1973, 1974, 1975, 1980, 1982.

La Commission des parcs nationaux et des aires protégées de l'UICN

La Commission des parcs nationaux et des aires protégées de l'UICN (CPNAP) est le principal organe international, scientifique et technique s'intéressant au choix, à la création et à l'aménagement des parcs nationaux et des aires protégées en général. Elle a des membres dans plus de 90 pays qui sont tous des spécialistes du domaine des aires protégées. La CPNAP est responsable de la partie du programme de l'UICN qui vise à encourager la mise en place et la gestion efficace d'un réseau mondial d'aires protégées terrestres et marines.

Durant la préparation de la présente édition de la *Liste des Nations Unies*, la CPNAP était placée sous la présidence de Harold Eidsvik, Conseiller principal auprès du Service canadien des parcs pour les politiques et sous la vice-présidence d'Adrian Phillips, directeur général de la *Countryside Commission of England and Wales*. Les travaux de la Commission étaient

5

coordonnés par James Thorsell, depuis le siège de l'UICN, à Gland, Suisse. La Commission est organisée sur une base régionale. Elle compte 12 vice-présidents pour les régions et tient normalement deux réunions par an. Depuis la compilation de la dernière *Liste des Nations Unies*, des réunions ont eu lieu en Argentine, au Niger, en Nouvelle-Zélande, au Costa Rica, en Italie, au Vanuatu et en Tchécoslovaquie.

L'Unité de données sur les aires protégées du CMSC

L'Unité de données sur les aires protégées (PADU) a été créée par la CPNAP en 1981, chargée de traiter la quantité croissante de données et d'aider la Commission à préparer des publications sur les parcs nationaux et aires protégées du monde entier. L'Unité est maintenant intégrée au Centre mondial de surveillance continue de la conservation de la nature et basée à Cambridge, au Royaume-Uni. Les travaux de PADU visent à fournir des informations précises et à jour sur chaque aire protégée, chaque réseau d'aires protégées, à ceux qui en ont besoin ou, à défaut, de trouver où obtenir rapidement cette information.

Afin d'atteindre son objectif, le CMSC collabore avec les nombreux organismes qui, dans le monde entier, sont chargés de gérer les aires protégées ainsi qu'avec des spécialistes de la conservation et des scientifiques actifs dans ce domaine. La plupart des personnes concernées sont membres de la CPNAP. PADU est également chargée de gérer l'information sur les réserves de la biosphère et les biens du patrimoine mondial (responsabilités qui lui sont confiées respectivement par le MAB et le Comité du patrimoine mondial) ainsi que sur les sites (zones humides) figurant sur la Liste de la Convention de Ramsar (responsabilité confiée par le Bureau de Ramsar).

Critères d'inscription

Trois critères gouvernent l'inscription d'une aire protégée sur la *Liste des Nations Unies*: ses dimensions, les objectifs de gestion et l'autorité de l'organe de gestion.

1. **Les dimensions:** Seules sont incluses les aires protégées de plus de 1000 hectares, à l'exception d'îles océaniques qui couvrent au moins 100 hectares, si elles sont entièrement protégées. Mille hectares équivalent à 10 kilomètres carrés.

2. **Les objectifs de gestion:** Dans le document *Categories, Objectives and Criteria for Protected Areas* (Catégories, objectifs et critères relatifs aux aires protégées) publié dans les procès-verbaux du Congrès des parcs nationaux tenu à Bali, la CPNAP et l'UICN ont défini une série de catégories de gestion pour les aires protégées. Les définitions en question sont données ci-après. Les sites désignés au plan national sont classés dans les catégories appropriées de l'UICN, en fonction de leurs objectifs de gestion définis juridiquement et de la façon dont ces objectifs sont mis en oeuvre.

    Lorsqu'il est apparent, à travers l'information disponible, qu'un site n'est pas géré de façon à appliquer les objectifs fixés par la législation nationale, ce site peut être omis de la Liste ou, le cas échéant, inclus dans une autre catégorie. Cela peut se produire dans le cas d'utilisation inappropriée du site, de ressources inadéquates, d'empiétement grave ou de guerre civile, événements sur lesquels l'organe de gestion n'a souvent aucune prise. Il est entendu que l'omission ou le reclassement sont temporaires, en attendant de meilleures informations ou une amélioration de la situation sur le terrain.

L'édition 1990 de la *Liste des Nations Unies* inclut les sites des catégories de gestion UICN de I à V. Les aires protégées qui sont également des sites Ramsar, des biens du patrimoine mondial ou des réserves de la biosphère figurent à la fois dans les listes nationales et dans les listes d'aires d'importance internationale.

3. **Autorité de l'organe de gestion**: Seuls sont inclus dans la *Liste des Nations Unies* les sites gérés par la "plus haute autorité compétente" c'est-à-dire le plus haut organe gouvernemental approprié.

La *Liste des Nations Unies 1990* est la troisième que préparent de concert PADU et la CPNAP et, comme dans le cas des deux précédentes (publiées en 1982 et 1985), cette Liste a été considérablement élargie bien que les critères d'inscription soient restés inchangés. Les réseaux d'aires protégées ont connu une forte expansion mais, en fait, celle de la Liste est due, en grande partie, à l'amélioration des informations disponibles et à une meilleure capacité mise en place pour les recueillir et les gérer. Il importe d'avoir cela présent à l'esprit pour bien utiliser la Liste.

Présentation de la Liste des Nations Unies

Les sites qui satisfont aux critères susmentionnés sont classés pays par pays (dans l'ordre alphabétique du nom anglais du pays). Pour chaque pays, les sites figurent par ordre alphabétique, selon l'appellation nationale (par exemple parcs nationaux, réserves naturelles, sanctuaires de faune sauvage). Pour chaque site, trois éléments d'information sont fournis: la catégorie de gestion selon l'UICN, les dimensions (en hectares) et l'année de création (ou de modification importante des dimensions ou de l'appellation). Cette présentation diffère de celle des années précédentes où les sites étaient classés selon les catégories de gestion de l'UICN et dotés d'un code biogéographique (voir ci-après). La présentation actuelle devrait cependant être plus facile à utiliser. PADU détient de plus amples informations sur tous les sites.

Compilation de la Liste des Nations Unies

La CPNAP et PADU rassemblent et traitent des informations sur les aires protégées depuis plusieurs années. Elles disposent donc d'un vaste capital de données dont certaines ont été publiées. Elles reçoivent, en permanence, de nouvelles informations. Pour préparer la *Liste des Nations Unies 1990*, le personnel de PADU a examiné le matériel existant, révisé et mis à jour des listes d'aires protégées (qui comprenaient la catégorie de gestion UICN appropriée pour chaque site). Des projets de listes de chaque pays ont été envoyés aux organes de gestion nationaux et aux membres de la CPNAP qui les ont vérifiés et mis à jour. Avec l'information reçue en retour, PADU a révisé les projets, résolvant les questions pendantes avec ses contacts dans les pays concernés ou des cadres de la CPNAP.

Une nouvelle procédure a été mise à l'épreuve en Europe où des projets de listes ont été envoyés pour examen aux vice-présidents régionaux de la CPNAP avant d'être transmis aux organes de gestion nationaux.

Exactitude et qualité de l'information

Le monde des aires protégées évolue rapidement: on crée de nouvelles aires, on modifie les limites de celles qui existent tandis que d'autres sont détruites par le développement industriel, l'agriculture ou les catastrophes naturelles. Dire franchement que la conservation a fait des progrès ces dernières années, du point de vue de l'augmentation de la superficie terrestre ou aquatique protégée, serait très difficile. Il ne s'agit pas simplement d'hectares protégés ou du nombre d'aires protégées mais plutôt de l'efficacité de la gestion. Les aires protégées remplissent-elles les objectifs qui ont présidé à leur création?

La qualité de l'information qui sert de base à la compilation de la *Liste des Nations Unies* est très variable et l'information sur l'efficacité de la gestion fait encore défaut pour un certain nombre de pays. Alors que la vaste majorité des parcs nationaux remplissant les critères appropriés figure sur la Liste, l'information sur les autres catégories d'aires protégées est encore incomplète et il faudra rassembler encore beaucoup de données avant d'avoir la certitude que les listes sont complètes pour chaque catégorie. Certains parcs d'Etat ou provinciaux ont été inclus mais les données ne sont pas encore totalement satisfaisantes. Là encore, il importe de rassembler beaucoup plus de données.

Il va de soi qu'il reste sans doute des erreurs ou des omissions dans la *Liste des Nations Unies 1990*. Nous espérons néanmoins que ces erreurs et omissions nous permettront de recevoir des informations encore plus précises. Les compilateurs assument l'entière responsabilité de ces erreurs ou omissions et toute correction ou mise à jour devrait leur être communiquée à l'adresse suivante:

Protected Areas Data Unit
World Conservation Monitoring Centre
219c Huntingdon Road, Cambridge CB3 0DL
Angleterre

Téléphone: (0223) 277314
Télécopieur: (0223) 277136
Télex: 817036 scmu g

Remerciements

La Liste a été compilée par l'ensemble du personnel de PADU qui comprend actuellement: Graham Drucker (Afrique du Nord et Moyen-Orient), Harriet Gillet (saisie de données), Michael Green (Indo-Malaisie), Jeremy Harrison (chef de l'Unité), Zbigniew Karpowicz (Europe et URSS), James Paine (Océanie) et Alison Suter (saisie de données). Graham Drucker a coordonné la compilation de la Liste pour les pays se trouvant hors des régions mentionnées.

La compilation a été activement soutenue par la CPNAP et, en particulier, par les cadres de la Commission et James Thorsell du secrétariat de l'UICN.

La Liste a été préparée pour la publication par Barbara Lambert du Service des publications de l'UICN.

Enfin, de nombreuses personnes, notamment des organes de gestion des aires protégées de chaque pays, ont fourni des informations utilisées pour compiler cette Liste. Sans elles, la Liste n'aurait pu être terminée.

CATEGORIES FOR CONSERVATION MANAGEMENT

The maintenance and development of the human habitat requires that some areas be retained in their wild state. The quality of water, the maintenance of genetic materials, the protection of scenic and aesthetic areas and the opportunity to enjoy and appreciate natural heritage, all depend upon the conservation of natural areas.

Other renewable natural resources include wood products, building materials, wild animal products (including fish), grazing from natural grasslands, and water for agriculture, industry, domestic use, and energy which can be produced on a sustained-yield basis.

Logically, some of these benefits can be received from natural areas or wildlands in perpetuity if management is properly designed and implemented. However, there are types of benefits which compete with one another; for example, it is physically and biologically difficult to remove wood products and study natural ecosystems on the same area. But the preservation of a sample ecosystem and research and monitoring can be readily done together if appropriately designed and controlled. Controlled tourism and species conservation can be compatible in both the terrestrial and marine environments.

Management categories can be designed and implemented so that each addresses a compatible set of benefits, without the pursuit of any one benefit ruling out the possibility of receiving other benefits. Commonly known categories which maintain the most options include the national park, wildlife sanctuary and forest reserve.

Even among generally compatible activities, conflicts may arise during particular seasons or on specific sites such as during nesting or calving periods or at critical habitats. These types of conflicts can be treated through a zoning system or a periodic restricted activity system.

Each benefit is related to specific objectives of management, such as the protection of rare or endangered species or habitats, the conservation of natural features of aesthetic value, and the conservation of areas where renewable resources can be utilised on a sustained-yield basis. Ideally all objectives and activities are related to environmental protection and to economic and social development.

Areas which are managed to meet specified compatible conservation objectives can be considered to be "protected areas"; they can be classified according to the objectives for which they are being managed. In contrast, however, the specific means required to meet the objectives of conservation will depend upon each particular situation and will vary with cultural, institutional, political and economic considerations.

Conservation categories provide the basis for clearly incorporating conservation into development (eco-development). Each category relates to one or several of the major goals of a nations's development plan: nutrition, education, housing, water, science, technology, defense and national identity. Viewed in this way, conservation categories become means for sustainable development.

Taken together, these categories can be administered as a unified national system of conservation areas. In practice, the categories are generally divided among various divisions of central government; some of the categories may be administered by state, provincial or even private or corporate institutions. Multiple use areas or international categories such as the Biosphere Reserve and the World Heritage Site will often require cooperative administration among several institutions. What is important, however, is that a specified institution is made responsible and empowered to provide for the appropriate management of the resources.

The ten categories of areas necessary to manage the wildland resources of any nation can be divided into three groups:

a) Those categories for which CNPPA and WCMC take responsibility to monitor the status of each conservation area and for which CNPPA takes a responsibility to provide technical advice as requested.

    I   Scientific Reserve/Strict Nature Reserve
    II   National Park
    III   Natural Monument/Natural Landmark
    IV   Nature Conservation Reserve/Managed Nature Reserve/Wildlife Sanctuary
    V   Protected Landscape or Seascape

b) Those categories which are of particular importance to IUCN as a whole and are generally found in most nations, but would not be considered exclusively within the scope of CNPPA. However, CNPPA and WCMC may wish to monitor, and CNPPA to provide expertise, on those areas which are of particular importance to nature conservation.

    VI   Resource Reserve
    VII   Anthropological Reserve/Natural Biotic Area
    VIII Multiple Use Management Area/Managed Resource Area

c) Those categories which form part of international programmes and which have specific relevance for nature conservation yet may, in many cases, already receive protection under a previous category. CNPPA and WCMC may be called upon to monitor these categories and to provide special expertise in cooperation with other institutions with which IUCN has consultative status.

    IX   Biosphere Reserves
    X   World Heritage Sites (Natural)

The following sections are abbreviated versions of the definitions/criteria provided in the IUCN/CNPPA paper on *Categories, Objectives and Criteria for Protected Areas* published in the Bali proceedings. Categories IX and X (Biosphere Reserves and World Heritage Sites) are not defined here as they are discussed in an earlier section.

Category I (Scientific Reserve/Strict Nature Reserve)

These areas possess some outstanding ecosystems, features and/or species of flora and fauna of national scientific importance or are representative of particular natural areas; they often contain fragile ecosystems of life forms, areas of important biological or geological diversity or areas of particular importance to the conservation of genetic resources. Size is determined by the area required to ensure the integrity of the area to accomplish the scientific management objective and provide for the protection of the area.

Natural processes are allowed to take place in the absence of any direct human interference; tourism, recreation, and public access are generally proscribed. Ecological processes may include natural acts that alter the ecological system or physiological features, such as naturally occurring fires, natural succession, insect or disease outbreaks, storms, earthquakes and the like, but necessarily exclude man-made disturbances. The educational function of the site is to serve as resource for studying and obtaining scientific knowledge.

Use of the reserve should in most cases be controlled by central government. Exceptions may be made where adequate safeguards and controls for long-term protection are ensured and where the central government concurs.

Category II (National Park)

The 10th General Assembly of IUCN, held in New Delhi in November 1969 approved a definition of the term "national park" in accordance with the following resolution:

> Considering the importance given by the United Nations to the national park concept, as a sensible use of natural resources, and considering the increasing use which has been made during these last few years in some countries of the term "national park" to designate areas with increasingly different status and objectives. The 10th General Assembly of IUCN meeting in New Delhi in November 1969 recommends that all governments agree to reserve the term "national park" to areas answering the following characteristics and to ensure that their local authorities and private organisations wishing to set aside nature reserves do the same:

> A national park is a relatively large area where:

> 1) one or several ecosystems are not materially altered by human exploitation and occupation, where plant and animal species, geomorphological sites and habitats are of special scientific, educative and recreative interest or which contains a natural landscape of great beauty;
> 2) the highest competent authority of the country has taken steps to prevent or eliminate as soon as possible exploitation or occupation in the whole area and to enforce effectively the respect of ecological, geomorphological or aesthetic features which have led to its establishment; and
> 3) visitors are allowed to enter, under special conditions, for inspirational, educative, cultural and recreative purposes.

> Governments are accordingly requested not to designate as "national park":

> 1) A scientific reserve which can be entered only by special permission (strict nature reserve).
> 2) A natural reserve managed by a private institution or a lower authority without some type of recognition and control by the highest competent authority of the country.
> 3) A "special reserve" as defined in the African Convention on the Conservation of Nature and Natural Resources of 1968 (fauna or flora reserve, game reserve, bird sanctuary, geological or forest reserve, etc.).
> 4) An inhabited and exploited area where landscape planning and measures taken for the development of tourism have led to the setting up of "recreation areas" where industrialisation and urbanisation are controlled and where public outdoor recreation takes priority over the conservation of ecosystems (parc naturel régional, nature park, Naturpark, etc.). Areas of this description which may have been established as "national parks" should be redesignated in due course.

This resolution was subsequently adopted by the Second World Conference on National Parks held in Yellowstone and Grand Teton National Parks, 1972.

In general, exploitation of natural resources must be prohibited in an area which is to be included within Category II. Exploitation is taken to include agricultural and pastoral activities, hunting, fishing, lumbering, mining, public works construction (transportation, communications, power, etc.), and residential, commercial or industrial occupation.

It is recognised that within the boundaries of certain national parks there are existing villages, towns, communication networks, and the on-going activities connected with them. Provided that these areas do not occupy a significant part of the land and are *de facto* zoned and so arranged that they do not disturb the effective protection of the remaining area, they will not be considered as a basis for exclusion from this category.

It is also recognised that management activities may be necessary and desirable for maintenance of the desired flora and fauna, to maintain public access and facilities, and for the purposes of administration and management of the area.

Effective zoning is an important tool for avoidance of conflict of interests within protected areas. At the 11th General Assembly of IUCN at Banff in 1972 it was agreed by CNPPA that sites designated as national parks should include areas here designated as "strict natural zones", "managed natural zones", and "wilderness zones", and that they could in addition appropriately contain areas of the kind here designated as "protected anthropological zones", or "protected historical" or "archaeological zones".

However, national parks must be available for public visitation. This use, it was agreed, could be combined with the primary function of nature conservation through a system of zoning. In this, one zone would be established in which roads or other access ways may be constructed, buildings or other structures to accommodate tourism and park administrative functions may be located, and in which appropriate recreational facilities may be placed. This special tourism/administrative zone would not be one designated primarily for nature conservation, but would be so delimited and located as to create minimum interference with the nature conservation function of the park. National parks can also satisfy the public visitation function by establishment of wilderness areas over all or part of the national park, thus providing for limited tourism of a special kind.

To qualify as a national park in the IUCN sense therefore, an area may consist of various combinations of zones as follows:

– Wilderness zone only.
– Wilderness zone combined with strict natural zone, managed natural zone or both.
– Any or all of the above zones combined with a tourist/administrative zone.
– Any or all of the above zones combined with one or more zones classified as anthropological, archaeological or historical.

Category III (Natural Monument/Natural Landmark)

This category normally contains one or more of several specific natural features of outstanding national significance which, because of uniqueness or rarity, should be protected. The specific feature to be protected ideally has little or no evidence of man's activities. These features are not of the size nor do they contain a diversity of features or representative ecosystems which would justify their inclusion as a national park. Size is not a significant factor; the area only needs to be large enough to protect the integrity of the site.

Although Category III areas may have recreational and touristic value, they should be managed to remain relatively free of human disturbance. These areas may be owned and managed by either central or other government agencies or non-profit trusts or corporations as long as there is assurance that they will be managed to protect their inherent features for the long term.

Category IV (Nature Conservation Reserve/Managed Nature Reserve/Wildlife Sanctuary)

A Category IV area is desirable when protection of specific sites or habitats is essential to the continued well-being of resident or migratory fauna of national or global significance. Although a variety of areas fall within this category, each would have as its primary purpose the protection of nature; the production of harvestable, renewable resources may play a secondary role in the management of a particular area. The size of the area is dependent upon the habitat requirements of the species to be protected; these areas could be relatively small, consisting of nesting areas, marshes, or lakes, estuaries, forest, or grassland habitats, or fish spawning areas, or seagrass feeding beds for marine mammals.

The area may require habitat manipulation to provide optimum conditions for the species, vegetative community, or feature according to individual circumstances. For example, a particular grassland or heath community may be protected and perpetuated through a limited amount of livestock grazing; a marsh for wintering waterfowl may require continual removal of excess reeds and supplementary planting of waterfowl food; or a reserve for an endangered animal may need protection against predators. Limited areas may be developed for public education and appreciation of the work of wildlife management.

Ownership may be by the central government or, with adequate safeguards and controls, by lower levels of government, non-profit trusts or corporations or private individuals or groups.

Category V (Protected Landscape or Seascape)

The scope of areas that fall within this category is necessarily broad because of the wide variety of semi-natural and cultural landscapes that occur within various nations. This may be reflected in two types of areas: those whose landscapes possess special aesthetic qualities which are a result of the interaction of man and land; and those that are primarily natural areas managed intensively by man for recreational and tourism uses.

In the former case, these landscapes may demonstrate certain cultural manifestations such as: customs, beliefs, social organisation, or material traits as reflected in land use patterns. These landscapes are characterised by either scenically attractive or aesthetically unique patterns of human settlement. Traditional land use practices associated with agriculture, grazing, and fishing are dominant. The area is large enough to ensure the integrity of the landscape pattern.

The latter case often includes natural or scenic areas found along coastlines and lake shores, in hilly or mountainous terrain, or along the shores of rivers, often adjacent to tourist highways or population centres; many will have the potential to be developed for a variety of outdoor recreational uses with national significance.

In some cases the area may be privately held and the use of either central or delegated planning control would be necessary to ensure the perpetuation of both the land use and life style. Means of government assistance might be required to improve the standard of living while maintaining the natural quality of the site through appropriate management practices. In other instances, the areas are established and managed under public ownership, or a combination of public and private ownership.

Category VI (Resource Reserve – Interim Conservation Unit)

Category VI areas will normally comprise an extensive and relatively isolated and uninhabited area having difficult access, or regions that are lightly populated yet may be under considerable pressure for colonisation and greater utilisation. In many cases, there has been little study or evaluation of these areas, so the consequences of converting these areas to agriculture, mineral or timber extraction, the construction of roads, or intensive fishing, dredging or mariculture is unclear. Similarly, use of the resources may not be appropriate because of the lack of technology, human or financial resource restrictions, or alternative national priorities. Consequently, natural, social, and economic values are not sufficiently identified to permit the area to be managed for specific objectives or to justify its conversion to other uses. On land, restricted access is implied so areas will normally require control, depending upon the pressures to enter and utilise the area. Areas may be owned or administered by government or public corporations.

Maintenance of existing conditions to allow for studies on the potential use for the designated areas is a prerequisite. No exploitation should occur with the exception of use of resources by indigenous inhabitants; ongoing ecologically sound activities are acceptable.

This category might also be used for those areas which are protected by legislation, but which have not been implemented, for whatever reason.

Category VII (Natural Biotic Area/Anthropological Reserve)

Category VII areas are characterised by natural areas where the influence or technology of modern man has not significantly interfered with or been absorbed by the traditional ways of life of the inhabitants. These areas may be remote and isolated and their inaccessibility may be maintained for a considerable period of time. The societies are of particular significance to the maintenance of cultural diversity; there is a strong dependence of man upon the natural environment for food, shelter, and other basic material to sustain life. Extensive cultivation or other major modifications of the vegetation and animal life is not permitted.

Management is oriented towards the maintenance of habitat for traditional societies so as to provide for their continuance within their own cultural mores.

Category VIII (Multiple Use Management Areas/Managed Resource Areas)

A Category VIII area is large, containing considerable territory suitable for production of wood products, water, pasture, wildlife, marine products and outdoor recreation; parts of the area may be settled and may have been altered by man. The area may possess nationally unique or exceptional natural features, or may as a whole represent a feature or area of international or national significance.

Planning programmes to ensure the area is managed on a sustained yield basis is a prerequisite. Land ownership is under government control. Through proper zoning, significant areas can be given specific additional protection. For instance, the establishment of wilderness-type areas is consistent with the purpose of these areas as would be establishing nature reserves. Multiple use, in the context of Category VIII, is considered to be the management of all renewable resources, utilised in some combination to best meet the needs of the country. The major premise in the management of these areas is that they will be managed to maintain the overall productivity of the areas and their resources in perpetuity.

CATEGORIES DE GESTION DES ESPACES NATURELS POUR LA CONSERVATION

Le maintien et la mise en valeur de l'habitat humain exigent que certains espaces demeurent à l'état sauvage. La qualité de l'eau, la sauvegarde du patrimoine génétique, la protection des paysages et la beauté de certaines régions, enfin la possibilité d'apprécier le patrimoine naturel et d'en profiter: tout cela dépend de la conservation des zones naturelles.

Au nombre des ressources naturelles renouvelables, il faut compter le bois et ses dérivés, les matériaux de construction, les produits d'animaux sauvages (y compris le poisson), les parcours naturels utilisés pour le pâturage, l'eau destinée à l'agriculture, à l'industrie et à la consommation domestique ainsi que l'énergie renouvelable.

En principe, certaines de ces ressources peuvent être obtenues de façon permanente, dans la mesure où la gestion des zones naturelles ou sauvages est conçue et mise en oeuvre de façon appropriée. Cependant, certaines activités entreront nécessairement en conflit et sont par conséquent incompatibles. Ainsi, il est difficile, d'un point de vue physique et biologique, de prélever les produits du bois dans un écosystème naturel et, simultanément, d'étudier le fonctionnement naturel de cet écosystème; en revanche, il est possible de préserver un écosystème échantillon et d'y mener des recherches et un programme de surveillance continue si la zone est aménagée et contrôlée de façon appropriée. Le tourisme organisé et la conservation des espèces peuvent être compatibles dans un milieu, qu'il soit terrestre ou marin.

Des catégories de gestion des espaces naturels peuvent être conçues et attribuées de façon à répondre à un ensemble d'objectifs compatibles, la poursuite d'un objectif particulier n'excluant pas la possibilité de tirer d'autres profits. Les catégories les plus connues et qui présentent le plus de possibilités sont le parc national, le sanctuaire de faune et la réserve forestière.

Il arrive que, même entre des activités généralement compatibles, des conflits se produisent à certaines périodes (nidification, périodes de mise bas) ou en des endroits particuliers (biotopes critiques). De tels conflits peuvent normalement être réglés en ayant recours à la zonation ou à des périodes d'activités limitées.

Toute ressource appelle des objectifs de gestion spécifiques tels que la protection d'espèces ou d'habitats rares ou menacés, la conservation de paysages exceptionnels ou d'éléments naturels présentant une valeur esthétique, la conservation de zones où les ressources naturelles peuvent être prélevées et utilisées de façon durable. Dans l'idéal, tous les objectifs et activités devraient s'inscrire dans une perspective de protection de l'environnement et de développement socio-économique.

On considère comme "aires protégées" les zones qui sont aménagées de façon à répondre à des objectifs de conservation spécifiques et compatibles. Ces zones peuvent être classées en fonction des objectifs pour lesquels elles sont gérées. En revanche, les moyens à mettre en oeuvre pour réaliser ces objectifs de conservation dépendront de chaque cas particulier et varieront en fonction de considérations culturelles, institutionnelles, politiques et économiques.

Les catégories de zones de conservation permettent d'incorporer nettement les principes de conservation dans le développement (éco-développement). Chacune d'elles se rattache à un ou plusieurs objectifs du plan de développement d'un pays: nutrition, éducation, logement, eau, science et technologie, défense et identité nationale. Considérées sous cet angle, les diverses catégories de gestion des zones naturelles deviennent des instruments au service d'un développement durable.

Ces catégories, prises toutes ensembles, peuvent être gérées dans le cadre d'un système national harmonisé d'aires de conservation. Dans la pratique, les diverses catégories sont en général gérées par différents services gouvernementaux. Certaines catégories sont administrées par des organismes d'état, provinciaux ou même par des institutions privées ou des associations. L'administration d'aires aménagées à des fins d'utilisation multiple ou des catégories internationales telles que les réserves de la biosphère ou les biens du patrimoine mondial, nécessite souvent la coopération de plusieurs institutions. L'important toutefois est qu'une institution donnée soit responsable et qu'elle ait le pouvoir d'assurer la gestion appropriée des ressources.

Les dix catégories nécessaires à la gestion des ressources naturelles d'un pays peuvent être divisées en trois groupes:

a)   Les catégories pour lesquelles la CPNAP et le Centre mondial de surveillance continue de la conservation de la nature se chargent d'assurer la surveillance continue de chaque zone de conservation et pour lesquelles la CPNAP donnera ses avis techniques sur demande.

   I   Réserves scientifiques/Réserves naturelles intégrales
   II   Parcs nationaux
   III   Monuments naturels/Eléments naturels marquants
   IV   Réserves de conservation de la nature/Réserves naturelles dirigées/Sanctuaires de faune
   V   Paysages terrestres ou marins protégés

b)   Les catégories qui ont une importance particulière pour l'UICN en général et que l'on rencontre dans la plupart des pays, mais qui ne sont pas considérées comme étant exclusivement du ressort de la CPNAP. Néanmoins la CPNAP et le Centre peuvent souhaiter en assurer la surveillance continue et la CPNAP apporter son expertise sur les zones qui présentent une importance particulière pour la conservation de la nature.

   VI   Réserves de ressources naturelles
   VII   Réserves anthropologiques/Régions biologiques naturelles
   VIII Régions naturelles aménagées à des fins d'utilisation multiple/Zones de gestion des ressources naturelles

c)   Les catégories qui relèvent des programmes internationaux et qui intéressent par certains aspects la conservation de la nature, mais qui dans des cas particuliers, bénéficient déjà d'une protection au titre d'une des catégories énoncées précédemment. La CPNAP peut être appelée à surveiller ces catégories et à apporter une expertise particulière en coopération avec d'autres institutions auprès desquelles l'UICN jouit d'un statut consultatif.

   IX   Réserves de la biosphère
   X   Biens (naturels) du patrimoine mondial.

Les paragraphes suivants sont des versions abrégées des définitions/critères figurant dans le document de la CPNAP et de l'UICN, *Categories, Objectives and Criteria for Protected Areas*, publié dans les procès-verbaux de Bali. Les catégories IX et X (réserves de la biosphère et biens du patrimoine mondial) ne sont pas définies ici car elles sont traitées dans un paragraphe antérieur.

Catégorie I (Réserves scientifiques/Réserves naturelles intégrales)

Ces espaces comportent des écosystèmes remarquables, des éléments ou des espèces animales et végétales présentant une importance scientifique nationale, ou sont représentatifs de régions naturelles particulières. Ils renferment souvent des écosystèmes ou des formes de vie fragiles, des zones présentant une diversité remarquable du point de vue biologique ou géologique ou qui sont particulièrement importantes pour la conservation des ressources génétiques. Leur dimension est déterminée par la superficie requise pour assurer l'intégrité du territoire permettant d'atteindre les objectifs de gestion scientifique et de protection.

Les processus naturels peuvent s'y dérouler en l'absence de toute intervention directe de l'homme: le tourisme, les activités de loisir et l'accès du public sont généralement interdits. Ces processus peuvent être des phénomènes naturels qui altèrent le système écologique ou l'élément physique à un moment donné, tels que les feux spontanés, les successions végétales naturelles, les épidémies ou infestations d'insectes, les orages, les tremblements de terre, etc., mais excluent les perturbations artificielles. Le site a pour fonction éducatrice de servir de sujet d'étude, permettant de faire avancer la connaissance scientifique.

L'utilisation de la plupart de ces réserves devrait être placée sous la responsabilité du gouvernement central. On peut envisager des exceptions dans le cas de régions où la protection à long terme est garantie par des mesures adéquates de sauvegarde et de contrôle auxquelles le gouvernement participe.

Catégorie II (Parcs nationaux)

La 10e Assemblée générale de l'UICN qui s'est réunie à New Delhi en novembre 1969 a adopté une résolution définissant le terme "parc national":

> Vu l'importance reconnue aux parcs nationaux par les Nations Unies en tant qu'aspect de l'emploi judicieux des ressources naturelles, et vu l'utilisation croissante depuis quelques années qui est faite dans certains pays de l'expression "parc national" pour désigner des territoires à statut et à objectifs de plus en plus différents, la 10e Assemblée générale de l'UICN, réunie à la Nouvelle-Delhi en novembre 1969 recommande que les gouvernements de tous les pays acceptent de réserver la dénomination "parc national" aux territoires répondant aux caractéristiques ci-après et d'assurer que les pouvoirs locaux et les organisations privées désireux de constituer des réserves naturelles fassent de même:

Un parc national est un territoire relativement étendu:

1) qui présente un ou plusieurs écosystèmes, généralement peu ou pas transformés par l'exploitation et l'occupation humaine, où les espèces végétales et animales, les sites géomorphologiques et les habitats offrent un intérêt spécial du point de vue scientifique, éducatif et récréatif, ou dans lesquels existent des paysages naturels de grande valeur esthétique et,

2) dans lequel la plus haute autorité compétente du pays a pris des mesures pour empêcher ou éliminer dès que possible, sur toute sa surface, cette exploitation ou cette occupation, et pour y faire effectivement respecter les entités écologiques, géomorphologiques ou esthétiques ayant justifié sa création et

3) dont la visite est autorisée, sous certaines conditions, à des fins récréatives, éducatives et culturelles.

En conséquence, il est demandé aux gouvernements de ne plus désigner sous le nom de "parc national":

1) Une réserve scientifique dont l'accès exige une autorisation spéciale (réserve naturelle intégrale).

2) Une réserve naturelle gérée par une institution privée ou par un pouvoir subordonné, en dehors de toute reconnaissance et de tout contrôle de la plus haute autorité compétente du pays.

3) Une "réserve spéciale" désignée aux termes de la Convention africaine de 1968 sur la conservation de la nature et des ressources naturelles (réserves de faune, de flore, de chasse, sanctuaire ornithologique, réserve géologique, forestière, etc.).

4) Une zone peuplée et exploitée, où un plan régional d'aménagement du territoire et de développement touristique vise à créer, en retardant l'industrialisation et l'urbanisation, une zone destinée plus à la récréation du public qu'à la conservation des écosystèmes (parc naturel régional, nature park, Naturpark, etc.). Des territoires répondant à cette description qui ont été appelés "parcs nationaux" devraient voir leur dénomination modifiée le moment venu.

Cette résolution a été adoptée ultérieurement par la deuxième Conférence mondiale sur les parcs nationaux (parcs nationaux de Yellowstone et de Grand Teton, 1972).

En général, l'exploitation des ressources naturelles doit être interdite dans un territoire susceptible de figurer dans la catégorie II. On entend par exploitation les activités agro-pastorales et minières, la chasse, la pêche, la sylviculture, la construction d'ouvrages d'intérêt public (transport, communications, énergie, etc.) ainsi que les activités immobilières, commerciales ou industrielles.

On sait qu'à l'intérieur des limites de certains parcs nationaux, il existe des villages, des petites villes, des réseaux routiers et toutes les activités qui y sont liées. A condition que ces établissements et équipements n'occupent pas une partie trop importante de la surface totale, qu'ils fassent partie *de facto* d'une zone définie et qu'ils soient conçus de manière à ne pas entraver la protection efficace de l'espace restant, ils ne constitueront pas un motif suffisant pour justifier l'exclusion de la catégorie.

On sait également que les activités d'aménagement peuvent être nécessaires, voire souhaitables, pour l'entretien de la faune et de la flore, des voies d'accès et locaux prévus pour les touristes, de même que pour les besoins de l'administration et de la gestion de l'aire.

La zonation est un outil efficace qui permet d'éviter les conflits d'intérêt à l'intérieur des aires protégées. Lors de la 11e Assemblée Générale de l'UICN à Banff, la CPNAP a convenu que les territoires désignés sous l'appellation de parcs nationaux devraient inclure des espaces désignés ici sous le nom d'espaces naturels de "protection intégrale", "espaces naturels dirigés" et "zones de nature sauvage" et qu'ils pouvaient en outre contenir, le cas échéant, des aires dénommées "zones anthropologiques protégées" ou "zones historiques" ou "archéologiques protégées".

Cependant, les parcs nationaux doivent être ouverts au public. Cette fonction peut parfaitement être combinée avec le rôle fondamental de protection de la nature par un système de zonation. Ainsi on pourrait établir une zone où serait autorisée la construction de routes ou d'autres voies d'accès, de bâtiments ou autres édifices nécessaires à l'accueil des touristes et aux services administratifs du parc, ainsi que d'éventuelles installations récréatives de type approprié. Cette zone spéciale à vocation touristique et administrative n'aurait pas pour rôle principal la conservation de la nature mais serait implantée et délimitée de manière à produire le moins d'interférences possibles avec la fonction du parc, qui est d'assurer la conservation de la nature. Les parcs nationaux peuvent aussi remplir leur fonction d'accueil du public par la création sur la totalité ou partie de leur territoire, de zones de nature sauvage où un tourisme limité de type particulier est autorisé.

Pour prétendre à l'appellation de parc national telle que la conçoit l'UICN, le zonage de ces espaces peut être modulé selon les combinaisons suivantes:

–   Zone de nature sauvage uniquement.
–   Zone de nature sauvage combinée avec un espace naturel intégral ou un espace naturel dirigé, ou encore avec l'un ou l'autre.
–   L'une ou l'autre ou l'ensemble des zones énumérées ci-dessus, combinées avec une zone à vocation touristique/administrative.
–   L'une ou l'autre ou l'ensemble des zones énumérées ci-dessus combinées avec une ou plusieurs zones classées comme zones anthropologiques, archéologiques ou historiques.

Catégorie III (Monuments naturels/Eléments naturels marquants)

Cette catégorie contient normalement un ou plusieurs éléments naturels particuliers d'importance nationale exceptionnelle qui, par leur caractère unique ou rare devraient être protégés. Dans le meilleur des cas, l'élément particulier à protéger ne comporte pas ou pratiquement pas de traces de l'activité de l'homme. Ces éléments n'occupent pas des superficies étendues et ne contiennent pas la variété de caractéristiques ou d'écosystèmes représentatifs qui justifierait leur inclusion dans la catégorie des parcs nationaux. La superficie n'est pas un facteur important: le territoire doit être suffisamment étendu pour assurer l'intégrité du site.

Bien que les sites de la catégorie III puissent présenter un intérêt sur le plan des loisirs et du tourisme, leur gestion doit les préserver dans toute la mesure du possible des perturbations artificielles. Ils peuvent appartenir à des organismes publics - nationaux ou autres - ou être gérés par eux, ou des organisations ou associations sans but lucratif, pour autant que leur gestion assure la protection à long terme des éléments intéressants.

Catégorie IV (Réserves de conservation de la nature/Réserves naturelles diriges/Sanctuaires de faune)

Il est souhaitable d'inclure un territoire dans la catégorie IV lorsque la protection de sites ou d'habitats particuliers est essentielle au maintien du bon état d'une faune sédentaire ou migratrice d'importance nationale ou mondiale. Bien que différents types de territoires entrent dans cette catégorie, ils devraient tous avoir pour objectif premier la protection de la nature; la production de ressources exploitables et renouvelables peut jouer un rôle secondaire dans la gestion d'une aire donnée. Les dimensions de la zone dépendent des exigences vis-à-vis de l'environnement de l'espèce à protéger. Ces aires peuvent être relativement limitées et comprennent des zones de nidification, des biotopes de marais ou lacs, estuaires, forêts ou prairies, des aires de frai pour le poisson ou des herbiers marins pour les mammifères marins.

Une intervention pourra s'avérer nécessaire dans de tels sites afin d'assurer des conditions optimales aux espèces, communautés végétales ou éléments physiques du milieu, selon le cas. Ainsi un groupement végétal particulier de prairie ou de lande à bruyère peut être protégé et perpétué par un pâturage limité. Un marais où hivernent les oiseaux d'eau peut nécessiter l'enlèvement continu des excédents de roseaux et la plantation de végétaux servant à l'alimentation des oiseaux; une réserve créée pour un animal menacé peut exiger l'adoption de mesures de protection contre les prédateurs. Des secteurs limités peuvent être équipés de matériel pédagogique et destinés à faire connaître le travail de gestion de la faune sauvage.

Ces territoires peuvent être propriété de l'Etat ou d'autres instances à un niveau moins élevé, d'organisations ou associations sans buts lucratifs ou de personnes ou groupes privés, à condition que des mesures de sauvegarde et de contrôle soient en place.

Catégorie V (Paysages terrestres ou marins protégés)

La vocation des zones qui s'inscrivent dans cette catégorie est nécessairement assez large du fait de la grande diversité des paysages semi-naturels et culturels qui existent de par le monde. On peut dégager deux grands types d'espaces de ce genre: ceux dont le paysage présente des qualités esthétiques particulières résultant de l'interaction de l'homme et de la nature, et ceux qui sont avant tout des zones naturelles que l'homme aménage de façon intensive dans un but de loisirs et de tourisme.

Dans le premier cas, les paysages peuvent être l'expression de faits culturels tels que coutumes, croyances, organisation sociale ou d'éléments physiques tels qu'ils s'expriment à travers les modes d'utilisation du sol. De tels paysages sont caractérisés par des formes d'occupation du sol qui sont soit attrayantes visuellement, soit uniques sur le plan esthétique. Les formes traditionnelles d'utilisation de l'espace liées à l'agriculture, au pâturage, à la pêche en sont l'élément dominant. La zone considérée est suffisamment étendue pour assurer l'intégrité du paysage en question.

Le second type comprend souvent des sites naturels ou panoramiques situés le long des côtes, au bord des lacs, dans des régions de collines et de montagnes, le long de rivières et souvent, près des grandes routes touristiques ou aux alentours de centres habités. Nombre de ces zones sont susceptibles d'être aménagées de façon à satisfaire toute une gamme de loisirs de plein air d'importance nationale.

Dans certains cas, le territoire est propriété privée et il est nécessaire qu'un contrôle de la planification de cet espace soit prévu à l'échelon le plus élevé ou à des niveaux inférieurs, afin d'assurer la pérennité de l'utilisation du territoire et du mode de vie de ses habitants. Certaines formes d'aide publique peuvent être nécessaires pour améliorer les conditions de vie tout en maintenant la qualité du paysage par une gestion appropriée. Dans d'autres cas, les aires sont désignées et gérées comme bien public ou comme propriété à la fois publique et privée.

Catégorie VI (Réserves de ressources naturelles)

Les espaces entrant dans la catégorie VI devront normalement comprendre des zones étendues et relativement isolées et inhabitées, d'accès difficile, ou des régions peu peuplées mais sur lesquelles s'exercent des pressions considérables de colonisation et d'utilisation accrue. Dans bien des cas, ces régions ont été peu étudiées ou évaluées et l'on connaît mal les conséquences possibles de leur mise en culture, de l'exploitation minière ou forestière, de l'ouverture de routes ou d'une pêche intensive, du dragage ou de la mariculture. D'autre part, l'utilisation des ressources peut ne pas être opportune, en raison d'obstacles humains, financiers ou technologiques, ou parce qu'il existe d'autres priorités nationales. De ce fait, la valeur naturelle, sociale et économique n'a pas été suffisamment bien définie pour permettre d'aménager la région considérée, en fonction d'objectifs spécifiques ou pour justifier le passage à d'autres types d'utilisation. L'accès en étant limité, de telles régions doivent normalement être soumises à un contrôle en fonction des pressions qui s'exercent pour s'installer dans ce territoire et l'utiliser.

Les terres peuvent être administrées par l'Etat ou par des associations publiques ou même leur appartenir.

Pour permettre l'étude des utilisations possibles de la région considérée, le maintien des conditions existantes est un préalable indispensable. Aucune exploitation ne devrait être permise, à l'exception de l'utilisation des ressources par la population indigène. Les activités fondées du point de l'écologie sont acceptables.

Cette catégorie est également utilisée dans la banque de données du Centre mondial de surveillance continue de la conservation de la nature pour les aires qui sont protégées par la législation mais qui, pour diverses raisons, ne disposent pas d'infrastructure et dont la protection est reconnue inadéquate.

Catégorie VII (Régions biologiques naturelles/Réserves anthropologiques)

Les régions qui entrent dans cette catégorie se caractérisent par le fait que l'influence de la technologie moderne ne s'y est pas exercée de façon importante ou que cette dernière n'a pas été incorporée dans le mode de vie traditionnel de ses habitants. Ces régions peuvent être reculées et isolées et peuvent rester inaccessibles pendant longtemps encore. Les sociétés humaines qui y vivent sont considérées comme particulièrement importantes pour le maintien de la diversité culturelle de l'humanité; l'homme dépend étroitement du milieu naturel pour subsister (nourriture, abri, etc.). Les cultures extensives ou d'autres modifications importantes de la végétation ou de la vie animale ne sont pas autorisées.

La gestion est orientée vers le maintien du milieu au bénéfice des sociétés traditionnelles afin d'assurer la permanence de leur culture.

Catégorie VIII (Régions naturelles aménagées à des fins d'utilisation multiple/Zones de gestion des ressources naturelles)

Une aire de la catégorie VIII est vaste. Elle contient des territoires étendus convenant à la production de produits forestiers, d'eau, de pâturages, de faune sauvage, produits marins et à l'organisation de loisirs de plein air. Certaines parties de ces régions peuvent être occupées par l'homme et avoir été transformées. L'aire peut posséder des éléments naturels uniques ou exceptionnels d'importance nationale ou, dans son ensemble, représenter un élément ou une région d'importance nationale ou internationale.

La planification de l'utilisation de tels territoires pour assurer un rendement permanent des ressources est une condition préalable indispensable. Le gouvernement est propriétaire. Une zonation appropriée devrait permettre d'assurer une protection supplémentaire de ces territoires. Ainsi, l'établissement de zones de nature sauvage (wilderness areas) est compatible avec les objectifs de telles régions, de même que la création de réserves naturelles. Dans le cadre de la catégorie VIII, la formule d'utilisation multiple d'un territoire constitue le mode de gestion de toutes les ressources renouvelables utilisées en les combinant d'une manière ou d'une autre, pour répondre au mieux aux besoins du pays. La principe essentiel d'un tel type de gestion est d'assurer le maintien à perpétuité de la productivité globale des ressources du territoire considéré.

UNITED NATIONS LIST OF NATIONAL PARKS
AND PROTECTED AREAS

LISTE DES NATIONS UNIES DES PARCS NATIONAUX
ET DES AIRES PROTEGEES

Name of Area/Nom de l'aire	Category/ Catégorie	Area/Super- ficie (ha)	Year/ Année
AFGHANISTAN			

Summary/Sommaire		
Category/Catégorie IV	4	142,438
Total	**4**	**142,438**

Name of Area/Nom de l'aire	Category/ Catégorie	Area/Super- ficie (ha)	Year/ Année
Waterfowl Sanctuaries/Sanctuaires d'oiseaux d'eau			
Ab-i-Estada	IV	27,000	1977
Dashte-Nawar	IV	7,500	1977
Wildlife Reserves/Réserves de ressources sauvages			
Ajar Valley	IV	40,000	1978
Wildlife Sanctuaries/Sanctuaires de ressources sauvages			
Pamir-i-Buzurg	IV	67,938	1978

AFRIQUE DU SUD
Voir paragraphe SOUTH AFRICA

ALBANIA/ALBANIE

Summary/Sommaire		
Category/Catégorie II	6	23,000
Category/Catégorie IV	7	31,500
Total	**13**	**54,500**

Name of Area/Nom de l'aire	Category/ Catégorie	Area/Super- ficie (ha)	Year/ Année
National Parks/Parcs nationaux			
Daji	II	4,000	1966
Divjaka	II	4,000	1966
Llorgara	II	3,500	1966
Lura	II	4,000	1966
Thethi	II	4,500	1966
Tomori	II	3,000	1956
Nature Reserves/Réserves de nature			
Berzan	IV	1,000	
Cangonj	IV	3,000	
Fushe-Senje (Kuqe Negel Patok)	IV	4,200	
Karaburum	IV	12,000	
Kuturman (Senisht Qerret Mirake)	IV	4,000	
Pishe Poro	IV	5,500	
Prushkull (Potull)	IV	1,800	

ALGERIA/ALGERIE

Summary/Sommaire		
Category/Catégorie I	4	26,200
Category/Catégorie II	8	11,761,150
Category/Catégorie IV	6	33,899
Category/Catégorie V	1	76,438
Total	**19**	**11,897,687**

National Parks/Parcs nationaux

Ahaggar	II	4,500,000	1987
Belezma	II	8,500	1985
Chrea	II	26,500	1983
Djurdjura	II	18,550	1983
El Kala	V	76,438	1983
Gouraya	II	1,000	1983
Tassili N'Ajjer	II	7,200,000	1972
Taza	II	3,000	1985
Theniet el Had	II	3,600	1983

Nature Reserves/Réserves de nature

Akfadou	IV	2,115	1925
Babor	I	1,700	1985
Beni-Salah	I	2,000	1985
La Macta	I	10,000	1985
Mergueb	I	12,500	1985

Hunting Reserves/Réserves de chasse

Djelfa	IV	20,000	1974
Lac Tonga	IV	2,392	1983
Mascara	IV	6,000	1985
Moulay Ismail	IV	1,000	
Tonga	IV	2,392	1983

ALLEMAGNE, REPUBLIQUE FEDERALE D'
Voir paragraphe GERMANY, FEDERAL REPUBLIC OF

ANDORRA/ANDORRE

No Areas Listed/pas de sites

ANGOLA

Summary/Sommaire		
Category/Catégorie II	1	790,000
Category/Catégorie IV	3	891,170
Category/Catégorie V	2	1,011,000
Total	**6**	**2,692,170**

National Parks/Parcs nationaux

Bikuar	II	790,000	1964
Kangandala	IV	63,000	1970
Kisama	V	996,000	1957

Integral Nature Reserves/Réserves naturelles intégrales

Ilheu dos Passaros	IV	170	1973
Luando	IV	828,000	1955

Regional Nature Parks/Parcs naturels régionaux

Chimalavera	V	15,000	1974

ANTARCTIC TREATY TERRITORY/TERRITOIRE DU TRAITE DE L'ANTARCTIQUE

Summary/Sommaire		
Category/Catégorie I	5	3,062
Category/Catégorie IV	4	194,487
Total	**9**	**197,549**

Special Protection Areas/Aires spécialement protégées

Ardery and Odbert Island	I	220	1966
Beaufort Island	I	1,865	1966
Litchfield Island	I	250	1975
Moe Island	I	117	1966
Southern Powell and adjacent islands	I	610	1966

Sites of Special Scientific Interest/Sites d'intérêt scientifique spécial

Barwick Valley	IV	29,120	1975
Byers Peninsular	IV	3,027	1975
Marine Plain Mule Peninsula	IV	2,340	1987
Western Shore, Admiralty Bay	IV	160,000	1979

ANTIGUA AND BARBUDA/ANTIGUA-ET-BARBUDA

National Parks/Parcs nationaux

Nelson's Dockyard	II	4,128	1984

ARABIE SAOUDITE
Voir paragraphe SAUDI ARABIA

ARGENTINA/ARGENTINE

Summary/Sommaire		
Category/Catégorie I	15	420,333
Category/Catégorie II	17	1,810,310
Category/Catégorie III	2	38,000
Category/Catégorie IV	48	5,255,840
Category/Catégorie V	31	5,114,250
Total	**113**	**12,638,733**

National Parks/Parcs nationaux

Baritu	II	72,439	1974
Calilegua	II	76,000	1980
Chaco	II	15,000	1954
El Palmar	II	8,500	1966
El Rey	II	44,162	1948
Iguazu	II	49,395	1934

Lago Puelo	II	14,220	1971
Laguna Blanca	II	8,213	1940
Lanin	II	200,870	1937
Lihuel Calel	II	9,900	1977
Los Alerces	II	186,730	1937
Los Arrayanes	II	1,000	1974
Los Glaciares	II	450,000	1937
Nahuel Huapi	II	475,781	1934
Perito Moreno	II	85,100	1937
Rio Pilcomayo	II	50,000	1951
Tierra del Fuego	II	63,000	1960

Integral Nature Reserves/Réserves naturelles intégrales

La Piramide	I	11,619	

Scientific Reserves/Réserves scientifiques

Aguaray-Mi	I	4,050	1988
Bahia San Blas	I	1,000	1937
Campos del Tuyu	I	3,500	1978
Copo	I	118,000	1968
Costa de la Bahia de Samborombon	I	9,380	1982
El Payen	I	192,996	1982
Fuerte Esperanza	I	11,619	
Laguna de Llancanelo	I	40,000	1980
Los Andes	IV	1,440,000	1980
Mocona	I	1,000	1989
Nacunan	I	11,900	1961

Natural Reserves/Réserves naturelles

Acambuco	IV	8,266	1979
Batea Mahuida	IV	1,286	1968
Cabo Virgenes	IV	1,230	1986
Cabo dos Bahias	IV	1,183	1973
Chacharameni	IV	2,500	1974
Chancani	IV	3,444	1986
Chany	IV	2,039	1986
Dunas de Atlantico Sur	IV	3,000	1989
El Rico	IV	2,600	1968
Formosa	IV	10,000	1968
General Manuel Belgrano	IV	87,000	1977
Guasamayo	IV	9,000	1963
Ibera	IV	1,200,000	1982
La Humada	IV	5,000	1974
La Loca	I	2,169	1968
La Reforma	I	9,500	1973
Laguna Brava	IV	405,000	1980
Laguna la Felipa	IV	1,307	1986
Las Lagunas de Epulafquen	IV	7,450	1973
Lihue Calel	I	2,600	1974
Limay Mahuida	IV	5,000	1974
Los Palmares	IV	6,000	1979
Olaroz-Cauchari	IV	180,000	1981
Parque Luro	IV	7,608	1975

Peninsula San Julian	IV	10,400	1986
Peninsula de Valdes	IV	360,000	1983
Pichi Mahuida	IV	4,119	1974
Punta Loma	IV	1,707	1967
Quebracho de la Legua	IV	2,242	1979
Ria de Puerto Deseado	IV	10,000	1977
Salitral Levalle	IV	9,501	1974
Santa Ana	IV	18,500	1951
Talampaya	IV	215,000	1975
Telteca	IV	20,400	1986
National Reserves/Réserves nationales			
El Palmar	IV	1,200	1966
Iguazu	IV	6,105	1970
Lago Puelo	IV	9,480	1937
Laguna Blanca	IV	3,038	1940
Lanin	IV	178,130	1937
Los Alerces	IV	76,270	1937
Los Glaciares	IV	150,000	1937
Nahuel Huapi	IV	282,219	1934
Perito Francisco P. Moreno	IV	29,900	1937
Fauna and Flora Reserves/Réserves de faune et de flore			
Valle de Acambuco	IV	8,266	1979
Forest and Faunal Reserves/Réserves forestières et fauniques			
Los Palmares	IV	6,000	1979
Faunal Reserves/Réserves fauniques			
Laguna Brava	IV	405,000	1980
Punta Leon	I	1,000	1988
Natural Monuments/Monuments naturels			
Bosques Petrificades	III	10,000	1954
Laguna de los Pozuelos	III	28,000	1979
Natural Parks/Parcs naturels			
Banados del Rio Dulce y Laguna de Mar	V	50,000	1966
Cerro Colorado	V	3,000	1974
Costero del Sur	V	74,000	
Ischigualasto	V	62,916	1971
La Florida	V	2,882	1936
Protected Landscapes/Paysages protégés			
Ichigualasto	V	62,916	1971
Laguna Blanca	V	770,000	1979
Monte de Las Barrancas	V	7,656	1974
Parque La Quebrada	V	4,200	1987
Parque Pereira Iraola	V	10,248	1949
Pozuelos O Carahuasi	V	20,000	1980
San Guillermo	V	981,000	1972
Sierra de la Ventana	V	6,718	1958
Valle Fertil	V	800,000	1971
Resource Reserves/Réserves de ressources			
Arroyo Feliciano	V	786,378	1969

Provincial Parks/Parcs provinciaux

Aconcagua	V	70,000	1983
Chancani	V	4,920	1986
Copahue	V	28,300	1962
El Tromen	V	24,000	1971
Franja de 1000m paralela costa rios Parana	V	17,000	1970
Islas Malvinas	V	10,036	1982
Laguna de los Pozuelos o Carahuasi	V	20,000	1980
Monte de las Barrancas	V	7,656	1974
Pampa del Indio	V	8,633	1957
Parque Ernesto Torquinst	V	6,097	1958
Pento Moreno	V	84,500	1937
Pereyra Iraola	V	1,400	1949
Sierra de San Javier	V	14,174	1973
Urugua-I	V	84,000	1988
Volcan Tupungato	V	110,000	1985

Provincial Nature Reserves/Réserves naturelles provinciales

Isla del Cerrito	IV	12,000	1970
Laguna Blanca	V	981,620	1979

Tourist and Forest Reserves/Réserves forestières et touristique

Epu-Lauquen o las Lagunas	IV	7,450	1973

Fish Reserves/Réserves ichtyologiques

Corpus	IV	30,000	1979

AUSTRALIA/AUSTRALIE

Summary/Sommaire		
Category/Catégorie I	16	2,024,213
Category/Catégorie II	339	27,551,131
Category/Catégorie IV	309	11,141,670
Category/Catégorie V	64	4,937,415
Total	**728**	**45,654,429**

Australian Capital Territory/Territoire de la capital australienne

National Parks/Parcs nationaux

Namadgi	II	94,000	

Nature Reserves/Réserves de nature

Jervis Bay	II	4,921	1971
Tidbinbilla	II	5,500	1964

Other areas/Autres aires

Lanyon	II	1,300	
Other reserves	II	6,000	

Australian External Territories/Territoires exterieurs australiens

National Parks/Parcs nationaux

Christmas Island	II	2,370	1980

National Nature Reserves/Réserves naturelles nationales

Ashmore Reef	I	58,300	1983
Coringa-Herald	I	885,600	1982
Elizabeth and Middleton Reefs	I	188,000	
Lihou Reef	I	843,600	1982

New South Wales/Nouvelles-Galles du sud

National Parks/Parcs nationaux

Bald Rock	II	5,451	1969
Barrington Tops	II	39,121	1969
Ben Boyd	II	9,455	1971
Blue Mountains	II	245,716	1959
Boonoo Boonoo	II	2,692	
Border Ranges	II	31,368	1979
Bouddi	II	1,167	1937
Brisbane Water	II	11,369	1959
Broadwater	II	3,737	1974
Budawang	II	16,102	
Budderoo	II	5,700	
Bundjalung	II	17,545	
Cathedral Rock	II	6,529	
Cocoparra	II	8,358	1969
Conimbla	II	7,590	
Crowdy Bay	II	8,005	1972
Deua	II	81,625	
Dharug	II	14,834	1967
Dorrigo	II	7,885	1967
Gibraltar Range	II	17,273	1963
Goulburn River	II	67,897	
Guy Fawkes River	II	35,630	1972
Hat Head	II	6,445	1973
Heathcote	II	2,251	1963
Kanangra-Boyd	II	68,276	1969
Kingchega	II	44,182	1969
Kings Plains	II	3,140	
Kosciusko	II	646,911	1944
Ku-Ring-Gai Chase	II	14,614	1894
Macquarie Pass	II	1,064	1969
Mallee Cliffs	II	57,969	
Marramarra	II	11,727	1979
Mimosa Rocks	II	5,181	
Mootwingee	II	68,912	
Morton	II	154,195	1938
Mount Imlay	II	3,808	1972
Mount Kaputar	II	36,817	1960
Mount Warning	II	2,210	
Mungo	II	27,847	
Murramarang	II	1,609	
Myall Lakes	II	31,493	1972

Nalbaugh	II	3,764	1972
Nangar	II	3,492	
New England	II	29,881	1931
Nightcap	II	4,945	1983
Nungatta	II	6,100	
Nymboida	II	1,368	
Oxley Wild Rivers	II	38,890	
Royal	II	15,020	1879
Sturt	II	310,634	1972
Tarlo River	II	6,759	
Wadbilliga	II	76,675	
Wallaga Lake	II	1,237	1972
Warrabah	II	2,635	
Warrumbungle	II	20,914	1961
Washpool	II	27,715	1983
Weddin Mountains	II	8,361	1971
Werrikimbe	II	35,178	1975
Willandra	II	19,386	1972
Woko	II	8,285	
Wollemi	II	487,289	1979
Yengo	II	140,000	
Yuraygir	II	18,285	1973
State Recreation Areas/Aires de loisirs publiques			
Booti Booti	V	1,488	
Bournda	V	2,305	
Bungonia	V	3,836	
Burrendong	V	1,227	
Burrinjuck	V	1,714	
Davidson Park	V	1,200	
Illawarra Escarpment	V	1,266	
Munmorah	V	1,007	
Parr	V	38,000	
Wyangala	V	2,034	
Nature Reserves/Réserves de nature			
Avisford	IV	2,437	
Banyabba	IV	12,560	1969
Barren Grounds	IV	2,024	1956
Bimberi	IV	7,100	
Binnaway	IV	3,699	
Bournda	IV	5,831	1972
Burrinjuck	IV	1,300	
Camerons Gorge	IV	1,280	
Cocoparra	IV	4,647	1963
Coolbaggie	IV	1,793	1963
Copperhannia	IV	3,494	1972
Coturaundee	IV	6,688	
Curumbenya	IV	9,380	1964
Dananbilla	IV	1,855	
Egan Peakes	IV	2,145	1972
Georges Creek	IV	1,190	1967

Ingalba	IV	4,012	1970
Ironbark	IV	1,604	
Kajuligah	IV	13,660	
Kemendok	IV	1,043	
Kooragang	IV	2,926	1983
Lake Innes	IV	3,510	
Limeburners Creek	IV	8,892	1971
Limpinwood	IV	2,443	1963
Macquarie Marshes	IV	18,211	1971
Mann River	IV	5,640	
Manobalai	IV	3,733	1967
Mount Hyland	IV	1,636	1984
Mount Neville	IV	2,666	
Mount Seaview	IV	1,704	1974
Mundoonen	IV	1,374	1970
Munghorn Gap	IV	5,934	1961
Muogamarra	IV	2,274	1960
Nadgee	IV	17,116	1957
Narran Lake	IV	4,527	
Nearie Lake	IV	4,347	1973
Nocoleche	IV	74,000	1979
Nombinnie	IV	70,000	
Pantoneys Crown	IV	3,230	1977
Pilliga	IV	69,595	1968
Razorback	IV	2,595	
Round Hill	IV	13,630	1960
Rowleys Creek Gulf	IV	1,659	1962
Scabby Range	IV	3,449	
Severn River	IV	1,947	1968
Sherwood	IV	2,444	1966
The Basin	IV	2,318	1964
The Hole Creek	IV	5,587	
Tinderry	IV	11,559	
Tollingo	IV	3,232	
Ulandra	IV	3,931	
Wallabadah	IV	1,132	1971
Watsons Creek	IV	1,260	
Winburndale	IV	9,396	1967
Wingen Maid	IV	1,077	
Woggoon	IV	6,565	1972
Yanga	IV	1,773	1972
Yathong	IV	107,241	1971

Flora Reserves/Réserves de flore

Banda Banda	IV	1,400	1984
Gilgai	IV	2,400	
Moira Lakes	IV	1,435	
Mt Dromedary	IV	1,259	
Nunnock Swamp	IV	1,020	
The Castles	IV	2,360	

Toolum Scrub	IV	1,665	
Waihou	IV	1,800	

Northern Territory/Australie du Nord

National Parks/Parcs nationaux

Finke Gorge	II	45,856	1967
Gurig	II	220,700	
Kakadu	II	1,755,200	1979
Katherine Gorge (Nitmiluk)	II	180,352	1963
Keep River	II	59,700	
Ormiston Gorge and Pound	II	4,655	
Simpsons Gap	II	30,950	1970
Uluru (Ayers Rock-Mount Olga)	II	132,538	1974

Conservation Reserves/Réserves de conservation

Connells Lagoon	IV	25,890	
Devils Marbles	IV	1,828	
Fogg Dam	IV	1,569	
Mac Clark (Acacia place)	IV	3,042	

Nature Parks/Parcs naturels

Cutta Cutta Caves	V	1,499	
Douglas Hot Springs	V	3,107	
Ellery Creek Big Hole	V	1,766	
Red Bank	V	1,295	
Ruby Gap	V	9,257	
Trephina Gorge	V	1,771	

Marine Parks/Parcs marins

Cobourg	II	229,000	1983

Queensland

National Parks/Parcs nationaux

Archer Bend	II	166,000	1977
Barron Gorge	II	2,784	1940
Bellenden Ker	II	31,000	1921
Blackdown Tableland	II	23,800	1979
Bladensburg	II	33,700	
Bowling Green Bay	II	55,300	1950
Bunya Mountains	II	11,700	1908
Burrum River	II	1,618	
Byfield	II	4,090	
Camooweal Caves	II	13,800	
Cania Gorge	II	2,000	
Cape Melville	II	36,000	1977
Cape Palmerston	II	7,160	1977
Cape Tribulation	II	16,965	
Cape Upstart	II	5,620	1967
Carnarvon	II	223,000	1979
Castle Tower	II	4,980	1975
Cedar Bay	II	5,650	1967
Conondale (2)	II	1,740	1931

Conway	II	23,800	
Cooloola	II	40,900	1975
D'Aguilar	II	1,328	1938
Dagmar Range	II	1,585	
Daintree	II	56,450	1977
Deepwater	II	4,090	
Dipperu	II	11,100	1967
Dunk Island	II	730	1936
Edmund Kennedy	II	6,200	1977
Ella Bay	II	3,430	
Endeavour River	II	1,840	1970
Epping Forest	II	3,160	1971
Eubenangee Swamp	II	1,520	
Eungella	II	50,800	1950
Eurimbula	II	7,830	1977
Flinders Group	II	2,962	
Forty Mile Scrub	II	4,500	1970
Girraween	II	11,399	1932
Gloucester and Middle Islands	II	3,970	
Graham Range	II	2,930	
Great Sandy	II	52,400	1977
Haslewood Island Group	II	1,210	
Herbert River Falls	II	2,428	
Herbert River Gorge	II	18,900	1963
Hinchinbrook Channel	II	5,585	
Hinchinbrook Island	II	39,350	1968
Hook Island	II	5,180	
Hull River	II	1,250	1968
Iron Range	II	34,600	1977
Isla Gorge	II	7,800	1964
Jardine River	II	235,000	1977
Jourama Falls	II	1,070	
Kroombit Tops	II	2,360	
Lakefield	II	537,000	1979
Lamington	II	20,200	1915
Lawn Hill	II	12,200	
Littabella	II	2,420	
Lizard Island	II	990	1939
Lonesome	II	3,367	
Magnetic Island	II	2,720	1954
Maiala	II	1,140	
Main Range	II	11,500	
Mazeppa	II	4,126	1972
Mitchell & Alice Rivers	II	37,100	1977
Moreton Island	II	15,400	
Mount Aberdeen (1)	II	1,667	
Mount Aberdeen (2)	II	1,242	1952
Mount Barney	II	11,400	1947
Mount Blackwood	II	1,060	
Mount Mistake	II	5,560	

Mount Spec	II	7,224	1952
Mount Walsh	II	2,987	1947
Orpheus Island	II	1,300	1960
Palmerston	II	14,200	1941
Porcupine Gorge	II	2,938	1970
Possession Island	II	510	1977
Pumicestone	II	1,930	
Robinson Gorge	II	77,300	1953
Rokeby	II	291,000	
Royal Arch Caves	II	1,514	
Scawfell	II	1,090	
Shaw Island	II	1,659	
Simpson Desert	II	555,000	1967
Snake Range	II	1,209	1972
South Island	II	1,619	
Southwood	II	7,120	1970
Springbrook	II	2,159	1956
Starcke	II	7,960	1977
Sundown	II	11,200	1941
West Hill Island	II	398	1938
Whitsunday Island	II	10,930	1977
Wild Duck Island	II	207	
Woodgate	II	5,490	1974
Woody Island	II	660	
Yamanie Falls	II	9,712	
Scientific Reserves/Réserves scientifiques			
Mariala	IV	27,300	
Palm Grove	IV	2,550	
Taunton	IV	11,470	1980
Scientific Areas/Aires scientifiques			
No 33 (Hurdle Gully Scrub)	IV	1,674	
No 39 (North Bargoo Creek)	IV	1,000	
No 40 (West Spencer Creek)	IV	3,700	
No 46 (Platypus Creek)	IV	1,200	
Faunal Reserves/Réserves fauniques			
Palmgrove	I	25,617	1967
Faunal Refuges/Refuges fauniques			
Taunton	IV	5,346	
Marine Parks/Parcs marins			
Green Island Reef	II	3,000	1974
National Park sections within GBRMP	II	4,700,314	1979
Pumicestone Passage	II	8,000	
Environmental Parks/Parcs environnementaux			
Goneaway	V	24,800	1974
Lake Broadwater	V	1,220	
Mount Archer	V	1,990	
Mount Zamia	V	1,140	
Townsville Town Common (1)	V	2,920	
Wilandspey	V	5,200	1977

South Australia/Australie du sud

National Parks/Parcs nationaux

Canunda	II	9,358	1966
Coffin Bay	II	30,380	
Coorong	II	39,904	1966
Flinders Chase	II	73,662	1919
Flinders Ranges	II	94,908	1970
Gammon Ranges	II	128,228	1970
Innes	II	9,141	1970
Lake Eyre	II	1,228,000	
Lincoln	II	17,423	1962
Mount Remarkable	II	8,649	1965
Nullarbor	II	231,900	
Witjira	II	776,900	

Aquatic Reserves/Réserves aquatiques

American River	IV	1,525	1971
Barker Inlet-St Kilda	IV	2,055	1973
Blanche Harbour-Douglas Bank	IV	3,160	1980
Seal Beach-Bales Bay	IV	1,140	1971
Whyalla-Cowleds Landing	IV	3,230	1980
Yatala Harbour	IV	1,426	1980

Native Forest Reserves/Réserves de forêts indigènes

Headquarters (Penola Forest Reserve)	IV	1,700	
Mount Gawler North (Mt Crawford Forest Reserve)	IV	1,013	
Murtho Forest Reserve	IV	1,910	
The Bluff Range (Wirrabara Forest Reserve)	IV	2,633	

Conservation Parks/Parcs de conservation

Bakara	II	1,022	
Barwell	II	4,561	
Bascombe Well	II	32,200	1970
Big Heath	II	2,351	1964
Billiatt	II	59,148	1963
Brookfield	II	6,333	
Calpatanna Waterhole	II	3,630	1974
Carcuma	II	2,881	1969
Clinton	II	1,958	1970
Cocata	II	6,876	
Danggali	II	253,480	1976
Deep Creek	II	4,184	1971
Dudley	II	1,122	1970
Dutchmans Stern	II	3,532	
Elliot Price	II	64,570	1967
Fairview	II	1,398	1960
Franklin Harbor	II	1,334	
Gum Lagoon	II	6,589	1970
Hambidge	II	37,992	1962
Hincks	II	66,285	1962
Isles of St Francis	II	1,320	1967

Karte	II	3,565	1969
Kellidie Bay	II	1,780	1962
Kelly Hill	II	7,374	1971
Kulliparu	II	13,536	
Lake Gilles	II	45,114	1971
Lathami	II	1,190	
Little Dip	II	1,977	1975
Martin Washpool	II	1,883	
Messent	II	12,246	1964
Mount Boothby	II	4,045	1967
Mount Rescue	II	28,385	1962
Mount Scott	II	1,238	1972
Mount Shaugh	II	3,460	1971
Munyaroo	II	12,385	1977
Ngarkat	II	207,941	1979
Nuyts Archipelago	II	5,420	1967
Pandappa	II	1,057	1973
Peebinga	II	3,371	1962
Pinkawillinie	II	127,164	1970
Pooginook	II	2,852	1970
Scorpion Springs	II	30,366	1970
Simpson Desert	II	692,680	1967
Swan Reach	II	2,016	1970
Telowie Gorge	II	1,946	1970
Unnamed	II	2,132,600	1970
Venus Bay	II	1,460	1976
Warrenben	II	4,061	1969
Western River	II	2,364	1971
Whyalla	II	1,011	
Yumbarra	II	106,189	1968
Regional Reserves/Réserves régionales			
Innamincka	V	1,381,765	
Simpson Desert	V	2,964,200	
Recreation Parks/Parcs de loisirs			
Onkaparinga River	V	1,680	
Para Wirra	V	1,409	

Tasmania/Tasmanie

National Parks/Parcs nationaux

Asbestos Range	II	4,281	1976
Ben Lomond	II	16,527	1947
Cradle Mountain-Lake St Clair	II	131,920	1922
Franklin-Lower Gordon Wild Rivers	II	181,075	1981
Freycinet	II	10,010	1916
Hartz Mountains	II	6,470	1939
Macquarie Island	II	12,785	1972
Maria Island	II	9,672	1964
Mount Field	II	16,257	1916
Mount William	II	13,899	1973

Rocky Cape	II	3,064	1967
Southwest	II	442,240	1968
Strzelecki	II	4,215	1967
Walls of Jerusalem	II	11,510	1981

Nature Reserves/Réserves de nature

Betsey Island	IV	181	1928
Big Green Island	IV	270	1983
Chappell Islands	IV	1,350	1975
East Kangaroo Island	IV	200	1984
Lavinia	IV	6,800	1975
Lime Bay	IV	1,310	1976
Three Hummock Island	IV	7,284	1977

Game Reserves/Réserves de faune

Bruny Island Neck	IV	1,450	1979
New Year Island	IV	112	1981

Victoria/Victoria

National Parks/Parcs nationaux

Alfred	II	3,050	1925
Baw Baw	II	13,300	1979
Bogong	II	81,200	1981
Brisbane Ranges	II	7,517	1975
Burrowa-Pine Mountain	II	17,600	1978
Cobberas-Tingaringy	II	116,600	
Coopracambra	II	35,100	1979
Croajingolong	II	87,500	1979
Dandenong Ranges	II	1,920	
Errinundra	II	25,100	
Fraser	II	3,750	1957
Grampians	II	167,000	
Hattah-Kulkyne	II	48,000	1960
Kinglake	II	11,430	1928
Lind	II	1,365	1926
Little Desert	II	132,000	1968
Lower Glenelg	II	27,300	1969
Mitchell River	II	11,900	
Mount Buffalo	II	31,000	1898
Mount Eccles	II	5,470	
Mount Richmond	II	1,733	1960
Otway	II	12,750	1981
Point Nepean	II	2,200	
Port Campbell	II	1,750	1965
Snowy River	II	95,400	1979
Tarra-Bulga	II	1,230	
The Lakes	II	2,390	1927
Wilsons Promontory	II	49,000	1898
Wonnangatta-Moroka	II	107,000	
Wyperfeld	II	100,000	1909

Reference Areas/Aires de référence

Benedore River (Croajingolong NP)	I	1,200	
Bungil (Mt Lawson SP)	I	1,300	
Burnside	I	1,190	
Cudgewa Creek	I	1,130	
Disappointment	I	1,090	
Roseneath	I	2,226	
Ryan Creek	I	1,570	
Seal Creek	I	1,000	
Sunset	I	8,400	
Toorour	I	1,750	

Wildlife Reserves/Réserves de ressources sauvages

Bronzewing	IV	11,200	
Dowd Morass	IV	1,501	
Ewing Morass	IV	7,300	
Jack Smith Lake	IV	2,781	
Kings Billabong	IV	2,166	
Koorangie	IV	2,853	
Lake Coleman	IV	2,055	
Lake Connewarre	IV	3,300	
Lake Murdeduke	IV	1,500	
Lake Timboram	IV	2,060	
Nooramunga	IV	9,996	1964
Red Bluff	IV	8,800	
Reedy Lake	IV	1,400	
Rocky Range	IV	4,453	NA
Tooloy-Lake Mundi	IV	2,416	
Wandella Forest	IV	1,060	
Wandown	IV	1,591	NA
Wathe	IV	5,763	
Westernport	IV	1,650	1979

Flora and Fauna Reserves/Réserves de faune et de flore

Bull Beef Creek	IV	1,490	
Crinoline Creek	IV	1,550	
Deep Lead	IV	1,240	
Fryers Ridge	IV	2,000	
Jilpanger	IV	8,290	
Lake Timboram	IV	2,060	
Lansborough	IV	1,800	
Mount Bolangum	IV	2,930	
Mullungdung	IV	1,520	1979
Providence Ponds	IV	1,650	
Stradbroke	IV	2,660	
Sweetwater Creek	IV	1,240	
Timberoo	IV	1,230	
Turtons Track	IV	1,525	
Wilkin	IV	3,600	
Wychitella	V	3,780	
Yarrara	IV	2,200	

Coastal Parks/Parcs côtiers			
Discovery Bay	V	8,590	1979
Gippsland Lakes	V	17,200	1979
Marine and Coastal Parks/Parcs marins et côtiers			
Corner Inlet	V	18,000	
Nooramunga	V	15,000	
Shallow Inlet	V	2,000	
Parks/Parcs			
Reef Hills	V	2,040	
Tyers	V	1,810	
Historic Parks/Parcs historiques			
Beechworth	V	1,130	
State Parks/Parcs publics			
Angahook-Lorne	V	21,000	
Barmah	V	7,900	
Black Range	V	11,700	
Carlisle	V	5,600	
Cathedral Range	V	3,577	1979
Chiltern Park	V	4,255	
Eildon	V	24,000	
French Island	V	8,300	1979
Holey Plains	V	10,576	1978
Kamarooka	V	6,300	
Kara Kara	V	3,840	
Kooyoora	V	3,593	
Lake Albacutya	V	10,700	
Lerderberg	V	13,340	
Moondarra	V	6,470	
Mount Arapiles-Tooan	V	5,050	
Mount Lawson	V	13,150	
Mount Napier	V	2,800	
Mount Samaria	V	7,600	1979
Mount Worth	V	1,040	
Pink Lakes	V	50,700	1979
Terrick Terrick	V	2,493	
Wabonga Plateau	V	21,200	1980
Warby Ranges	V	3,540	
Whipstck	V	2,300	
Other areas/Autres aires			
Avon Wilderness	V	40,000	
Big Desert Wilderness	V	113,500	1979
Langi Ghiran	V	2,695	
Murray Kulkyne	V	1,550	

Western Australia/Australie occidentale

National Parks/Parcs nationaux			
Alexander Morrison	II	8,501	1970
Avon Valley	II	4,366	1970
Badgingarra	II	13,121	1973

Beedelup	II	1,530	
Boorabbin	II	26,000	1977
Bungle Bungle	II	208,723	
Cape Arid	II	279,415	1969
Cape Le Grand	II	31,390	1948
Cape Range	II	50,581	1965
Collier Range	II	277,841	
D'Entrecasteaux	II	57,722	1967
Drovers Cave	II	2,681	1972
Drysdale River	II	435,906	1974
Eucla	II	3,342	1979
Fitzgerald River	II	242,804	1954
Frank Hann	II	61,420	1970
Geikie Gorge	II	3,136	1967
Goongarrie	II	60,356	
Hamersley Range	II	617,602	1969
Hassell	II	1,265	1971
Hidden Valley	II	1,817	
John Forrest	II	1,508	1957
Kalbarri	II	186,071	1963
Leeuwin-Naturaliste	II	16,172	1970
Millstream-Chichester	II	199,730	1969
Moore River	II	17,543	1969
Nambung	II	17,491	1968
Neerabup	II	1,082	1945
Peak Charles	II	39,959	1979
Pemberton	II	3,141	1977
Porongurup	II	2,572	1957
Rudall River	II	1,569,459	1977
Scott	II	3,273	1959
Shannon	II	52,598	
Sir James Mitchell	II	1,087	1969
Stirling Range	II	115,661	1913
Stockyard Gully	II	1,406	
Stokes	II	9,509	1974
Tathra	II	4,322	1970
Torndirrup	II	3,919	1968
Tuart	II	1,785	
Walpole-Nornalup	II	15,877	1957
Walyunga	II	1,812	1972
Warren	II	1,355	
Watheroo	II	44,512	1969
West Cape Howe	II	3,517	
William Bay	II	1,739	1971
Windjana Gorge	II	2,134	1971
Wolf Creek Crater	II	1,460	
Yalgorup	II	11,819	1968
Yanchep	II	2,799	1905

Nature Reserves/Réserves de nature

25 Mile Brook	IV	1,020	
Arthur River	IV	3,234	
Ascot	IV	1,861	
Austin Bay Reserve	IV	1,305	
Bakers Junction	IV	1,090	
Barlee Range	IV	104,544	1963
Barrow Island	IV	23,483	1910
Basil Road	IV	1,162	
Bendering	IV	1,602	1970
Bernier and Dorre Islands	IV	9,720	1970
Beynon	IV	3,323	
Billyacatting Hill	IV	2,063	
Boyagin	IV	4,804	1960
Buntine	IV	3,289	1963
Burngup	IV	1,289	1970
Burrma Road	IV	6,890	
Cairlocup	IV	1,577	
Camel Lake	IV	3,215	1962
Capamauro	IV	3,588	
Carlyarn	IV	2,723	1974
Cheadanup	IV	6,813	
Chiddarcooping	IV	5,217	
Chinocup	IV	19,821	
Coblinine	IV	4,033	1958
Cooloomia	IV	50,350	
Corackerup	IV	4,334	1970
Corneecup	IV	1,952	
Dobaderry	IV	4,005	
Dolphin Island	IV	3,203	
Dongolocking	IV	1,312	
Dragon Rocks	IV	32,219	
Duladgin	IV	1,619	
Dumbleyung Lake	IV	3,958	
Dunn Rock	IV	24,819	
Durokoppin	IV	1,030	1971
Gibson Desert	IV	1,859,286	1977
Gingilup Swamps	IV	2,807	
Goodlands	IV	1,349	
Great Victoria Desert	IV	2,495,777	1970
Haddleton	IV	1,161	
Harris	IV	3,610	
Jebarijup Lake	IV	1,016	1962
Jilbadji	IV	208,866	1972
Joverdine	IV	1,754	
Kathleen	IV	1,190	
Kondinin Salt Marsh	IV	2,208	
Kooljerrenup	IV	1,050	
Kundip	IV	2,170	
Lacepede Islands	IV	160	

41

Lake Ace	IV	2,392	
Lake Bryde	IV	1,454	
Lake Campion	IV	10,752	
Lake Cronin	IV	1,016	
Lake Gounter	IV	3,328	1955
Lake Hurlstone	IV	5,002	
Lake Liddelow	IV	1,133	
Lake Logue	IV	4,835	
Lake Magenta	IV	94,170	1958
Lake Muir	IV	11,310	
Lake Shaster	IV	10,756	
Lake Varley	IV	2,197	1970
Lakeland	IV	3,315	
Lowendal Islands	IV	245	1976
Mill Brook	IV	1,484	
Moondyne	IV	1,991	
Mt Manypeaks	IV	1,328	
Mungaroona Range	IV	105,842	1972
Namming	IV	5,432	
Nilgen	IV	5,507	
No 01058	IV	1,036	
No 01059	IV	1,861	
No 07634	IV	1,926	
No 08029	IV	1,020	
No 08434	IV	2,259	
No 10129	IV	2,509	
No 14429	IV	6,637	
No 16305	IV	1,235	
No 18583	IV	1,156	
No 19210	IV	5,262	
No 19881	IV	1,072	
No 20262	IV	1,019	
No 23825	IV	1,917	
No 24486	IV	12,622	
No 24496	IV	69,066	
No 26442	IV	1,400	
No 26792	IV	1,039	
No 26885	IV	5,200	
No 27386	IV	1,417	
No 27388	IV	4,467	
No 27487	IV	1,468	
No 27768	IV	1,106	
No 27872	IV	2,075	
No 27888	IV	4,341	
No 27985	IV	6,065	
No 28323	IV	1,180	
No 28940	IV	4,377	
No 29012	IV	1,403	
No 29027	IV	1,252	
No 29184	IV	1,309	

No 29920	IV	1,036	
No 30583	IV	5,418	
No 31424	IV	2,936	
No 31742	IV	1,651	
No 31799	IV	3,618	
No 31967	IV	23,945	
No 32129	IV	1,752	
No 32130	IV	2,481	
No 32131	IV	1,058	
No 32776	IV	4,732	
No 32777	IV	8,551	
No 32779	IV	1,046	
No 32780	IV	1,485	
No 32783	IV	7,082	
No 32784	IV	1,709	
No 32864	IV	1,437	
No 32995	IV	1,886	
No 33113	IV	8,860	
No 33466	IV	5,131	
No 33475	IV	1,735	
No 34604	IV	3,636	
No 34605	IV	308,990	
No 34720	IV	723,072	
No 34776	IV	2,249	
No 35659	IV	1,049	
No 35752	IV	20,925	
No 35918	IV	14,182	
No 36003	IV	1,113	
No 36053	IV	10,850	
No 36203	IV	6,612	
No 36208	IV	153,293	
No 36271	IV	321,946	
No 36419	IV	1,406	
No 36913	IV	6,090	
No 36915	IV	4,435	
No 36918	IV	13,750	
No 36936	IV	309,678	
No 36957	IV	780,883	
No 37083	IV	1,099	
No 38450	IV	1,009	
No 38545	IV	1,671	
No 39422	IV	40,105	
No 40156	IV	6,620	
No 40161	IV	1,170	
No 40628	IV	405,424	
North Karlgarin	IV	5,186	
North Sister	IV	1,008	
North Tarin Rock	IV	1,416	
Nuytsland	IV	625,343	1965
Pallarup	IV	4,191	

Palm Springs	IV	2,154	
Parry Lagoons	IV	12,370	
Pinjarrega	IV	18,221	
Point Coulomb	IV	28,676	1969
Prince Regent	IV	634,952	1964
Quarram	IV	3,825	
Queen Victoria Spring	IV	272,598	NA
Rock View	IV	1,733	
Roe	IV	1,246	
Seagroatt	IV	1,149	
Sheepwash Creek	IV	1,111	
Silver Wattle Hill	IV	1,660	
South Buniche	IV	1,298	
South Eneabba	IV	5,979	
South Stirling	IV	1,710	
Taarblin Lake	IV	1,285	
Tarin Rock	IV	2,391	1960
Tutanning	IV	2,090	1970
Two Peoples Bay	IV	4,745	1966
Unicup Lake	IV	3,290	1960
Wanagarran	IV	11,069	
Wandana	IV	25,976	
Wanjarri	IV	53,248	1971
Welsh	IV	1,717	
Wotto	IV	2,892	
Yenyening Lakes	IV	2,435	
Marine Parks/Parcs marins			
Marmion	II	10,500	
Ningaloo (Commonwealth Waters)	II	200,000	1987
Ningaloo (State waters)	II	230,000	1987

AUSTRIA/AUTRICHE

Summary/Sommaire		
Category/Catégorie IV	32	94,834
Category/Catégorie V	97	1,499,060
Total	**129**	**1,593,894**

National Parks/Parcs nationaux			
Hohe Tauern	V	25,000	1983
Nature Conservation Reserves/Réserves de conservation			
de la nature			
Altausseersee	V	1,050	1959
Arnspitze	IV	1,250	1942
Auhirschen	IV	1,400	
Bazora	IV	1,146	1959
Blockheide Eibenstein	V	1,400	1964
Dachsteingebiet	V	20,000	1964
Eisenerzer Reichensteine Krumpensee	IV	1,000	1973
Gesause und anschliessendes Ennstal	V	23,800	1958

Grossglockner-Pasterze mit Gamsgrube	IV	3,698	1935
Grundlsee	IV	9,700	1959
Grundlsee, Toplitzsee, Kammersee	V	9,700	1966
Gurkursprung	IV	1,497	1981
Hochifen u. Gottesackerwande	IV	2,956	1964
Hohe Kugel	IV	1,050	1973
Hohe Kugel-Hoher Freschen-Mellental	IV	7,500	1979
Inneres Pollatal	IV	3,200	1973
Kaisergebirge	V	10,200	1963
Karwendel	V	72,000	1933
Keutschacher See-Tal	V	2,532	1970
Lainzer Tiergarten	V	2,300	1941
Leiser Berge	IV	4,500	1969
Marchauen-Marchegg	IV	1,150	1973
Muttersberg	IV	1,146	1959
Nasskohr	IV	1,000	1971
Nenzinger Himmel	IV	1,051	1958
Neusiedlersee-Seewinkel	V	40,000	1932
Neydhartinger Moor	IV	1,238	1979
Niedere	IV	1,283	1974
Otscherland-Tormauer	IV	9,000	1969
Patscherkofel	IV	1,200	1947
Rellstal u. Lunerseegebiet	IV	3,328	1966
Rheindelta	IV	1,959	1976
Rosanin	IV	1,100	1977
Schobergruppe-Nord	IV	10,380	1964
Sengsengbirge	IV	3,400	1976
Sonntag	IV	6,313	1968
Tiefenwald-Staffel	IV	1,156	1974
Valsertal	V	3,300	1941
Vandans-Tschagguns	IV	4,062	
Villacher Alpe	IV	1,902	1967
Vilsalpsee	V	1,510	1957
Wildapenar Salzatal	V	51,460	1958

Landscape Protected Areas/Aires de paysages protégés

Amering-Stubalpe	V	22,000	1956
Ausseres Pollatal	V	1,730	1973
Autobahn	V	2,000	1958
Bisamberg	V	2,000	1965
Bohmerwald	V	96,000	
Bundschuhtal	V	2,250	1973
Dachstein-Salzkammergut	V	54,000	1956
Dobersberg	V	1,600	1978
Ennstaler Alpen-Eisenerzer Alpen	V	47,740	1956
Enzerfeld-Lindabrunn-Hernstein	V	7,000	1967
Friesingwand u. Enge v. StPeter-Freienstein	V	1,360	1956
Furtnerteich-Grebenzen	V	6,600	1956
Gaskiner Tal	V	13,860	1978
Geras und Umgebung	V	3,250	1970
Gleichenberger Kogel	V	5,280	1956

Goll	V	20,500	1958
Grossfragant	V	1,115	1973
Grossglochner Hochalpenstr.	V	1,650	1957
Habachtal	V	20,000	1960
Haltschlger Talschlusse	V	6,350	1978
Herberstein Klamm, Freienberger Klamm	V	2,160	1956
Hochalpe	V	7,140	
Hochschwab-Zeller Staritzen	V	37,080	1956
Hohe Wand-Durre Wand	V	12,800	1955
Kamptal	V	35,000	1955
Katselberg-Budesstrasse	V	1,710	1959
Konigsleitea	V	3,600	1964
Koralpe	V	3,200	1956
Lantschfeldtal	V	18,600	1958
Leiser Berge	V	7,000	1970
Lobau	V	1,000	1954
Mariazell-Seeberg	V	23,460	1956
Millstatter See-Sud	V	1,984	1970
Mittleres Ennstal	V	5,120	1956
Murauen Graz - Werndorf	V	1,480	1956
Murauen im Leibnitzer Feld	V	1,380	1956
Murauen-Mureck-Radkersberg	V	11,280	1956
Nordliches u. ost.Hugelland v.Graz	V	11,670	1956
Oberes Ennstal	V	7,400	1956
Oberes Pulkautal	V	3,500	1973
Otscher-Durrenstein	V	80,000	1955
Pack-Reinischkogel-Rosenkogel	V	23,480	1956
Palten-u.Liesingtal	V	7,820	1956
Peggauer Wand-Lurgrotte	V	1,140	1956
Plesch-Walzkogel	V	6,600	1956
Pleschaitz-Puxberg	V	2,400	1956
Pollauer Tal	V	12,100	1979
Postalm	V	1,405	1975
Rax-Schnecberg	V	71,500	1955
Reiting-Eisenerzer Reichenstein	V	10,280	
Rottenmanner-Triebener u. Seckauer Alpen	V	53,260	1957
Salzberg-Sud	V	1,030	1975
Sausal	V	6,200	1974
Schladminger Tauern bis Solker Pass	V	58,480	1956
Schlossberg b. Leutschach	V	2,120	1956
Schockl-Weizklamm-Hochlantsch	V	30,660	1956
Schonberg-Gfollerriegel	V	1,680	1956
Sierningtal	V	3,100	1978
Soboth-Radlpass	V	10,660	1956
Strudengau u. Umgeburg	V	12,600	1955
Stuhleck-Pretul	V	9,180	1956
Tennengebirge	V	6,800	1965
Thayatal	V	2,900	1955
Turracherhohe-Eisenhut Frauenalpe	V	26,620	1956
Untersberg	V	5,000	1953

Veitsch-Schneealpe-Raxalpe	V	23,560	
Villacher Alpe	V	3,904	1970
Vornbacher Enge	V	3,000	
Waldbach-Vorau-Hochwechsel	V	20,120	1956
Waldheimat	V	5,640	1956
Warscheneck-Gruppe	V	13,880	1956
Weissensee	V	7,648	1970
Westliches Berg-U. Hugelland	V	5,792	1956
Wienerwald	V	105,000	1955
Wildegg-Speikkogel	V	9,000	1956
Wildgerlostal	V	28,800	1958
Wollanig-Oswaldiberg	V	1,120	1970
Wolzertauern v. Solkerpass b. Gr.Windlucke	V	22,880	1956
Zirbitzkogel	V	9,200	1956
Lake Protection Areas/Aires lacustres protégées			
Aber oder Wolfgangsee	IV	1,904	1971
Grabensee und Trumersee	IV	1,953	1971
Waller oder Seekirchrer See	IV	1,412	1971
Nature Parks/Parcs naturels			
Fohrenberge	V	7,500	1974
Hohe Wand	V	2,000	1973
Leiser Berge	V	4,300	1970
Otscher-Tormauer	V	1,600	1978

BAHAMAS

Summary/Sommaire		
Category\Catégorie II	4	121,577
Category\Catégorie IV	1	1,813
Total	**5**	**123,390**

National Parks/Parcs nationaux			
Conception Island	II	810	1971
Exuma Cays	II	45,584	1958
Inagua	II	74,333	1965
Pelican Cays	II	850	1981
Managed Nature Reserves/Réserves naturelles gérées			
Union Creek (within Inagua NP)	IV	1,813	1965

BAHRAIN/BAHREIN

No Areas Listed/pas de sites

BANGLADESH

Summary/Sommaire		
Category\Catégorie IV	6	83,332
Category\Catégorie V	2	13,458
Total	**8**	**96,790**

National Parks/Parcs nationaux

Bhawal	V	5,022	1982
Madhupur	V	8,436	1982

Wildlife Sanctuaries/Sanctuaires de ressources sauvages

Chunati	IV	7,764	1986
Pablakhali	IV	42,087	1983
Rema-Kalenga	IV	1,095	1981
Sundarbans East	IV	5,439	1977
Sundarbans South	IV	17,878	1977
Sundarbans West	IV	9,069	1977

BARBADOS/BARBADE

No Areas Listed/pas de sites

BELGIUM/BELGIQUE

Summary/Sommaire		
Category\Catégorie IV	1	3,975
Category\Catégorie V	1	67,854
Total	**2**	**71,829**

State Nature Reserves/Réserves naturelles publiques

Hautes Fagnes	IV	3,975	1957

Nature Parks/Parcs naturels

Hautes-Fagnes-Eifel	V	67,854	1985

BELIZE

Summary/Sommaire		
Category\Catégorie II	1	4,144
Category\Catégorie IV	7	70,170
Total	**8**	**74,314**

National Parks/Parcs nationaux

Cayo Half Moon Bay	II	4,144	1982

Nature Reserves/Réserves de nature

Rio Grande	IV	2,340	1968
Shipstern	IV	9,000	1987

Wildlife Sanctuaries/Sanctuaires de ressources sauvages

Cockscomb Basin	IV	1,456	1986
Crooked Tree	IV	1,174	1981

Marine Reserves/Réserves marines

Hol Chan	IV	1,200	1987

Reserves/Réserves

Caracol	IV	20,000

Wilderness Sanctuaries/Sanctuaires de nature sauvage

Upper Bladen	IV	35,000

BENIN

Summary/Sommaire		
Category\Catégorie II	2	843,500
Total	**2**	**843,500**

National Parks/Parcs nationaux
Boucle de la Pendjari	II	275,500	1961
W du Benin	II	568,000	1954

BHUTAN/BHOUTAN

Summary/Sommaire		
Category\Catégorie II	2	67,976
Category\Catégorie IV	5	856,338
Total	**7**	**924,314**

National Parks/Parcs nationaux
Doga	II	2,176	1974
Royal Manas	II	65,800	1988

Wildlife Reserves/Réserves de ressources sauvages
Dungsum	IV	18,000	1984
Mochu	IV	27,843	1984
Shumar	IV	16,000	1984

Wildlife Sanctuaries/Sanctuaires de ressources sauvages
Jigme Dorji	IV	790,495	1974
Neoli	IV	4,000	1984

BOLIVIA/BOLIVIE

Summary/Sommaire		
Category\Catégorie I	2	136,500
Category\Catégorie II	6	2,541,020
Category\Catégorie IV	13	4,066,769
Category\Catégorie V	2	29,876
Total	**23**	**6,774,165**

National Parks/Parcs nationaux
Amboro	II	180,000	1983
Carrasco Ichilo	II	300,000	1988
Isiboro Secure	II	1,100,000	1965
Noel Kempf Mercado	II	914,000	1979
Sajama	II	29,940	1939
Santa Cruz la Vieja	II	17,080	1989
Torotoro	V	16,576	1989

Biological Stations/Stations biologiques
Beni	I	135,000	1982

National Reserves/Réserves nationales
Eduardo Avaroa	IV	714,000	1973
Lagunas del Beni y Pando	IV	275,000	1961

Manuripi Heath Amazonica	IV	1,884,000	1973
Noel Kempff Mercado	IV	21,900	1988
Tariquia	IV	246,870	1989
Ulla Ulla	IV	250,000	1972
Wildlife Refuges/Refuges de ressources sauvages			
Huancaroma	IV	11,000	1975
National Faunal Reserves/Réserves fauniques nationales			
Sajama	IV	153,570	1945
Reserves/Réserves			
Altamachi	IV	100,000	1977
Huancaroma	IV	140,429	1975
Sanctuaries/Sanctuaires			
Cavernas de Repechon	I	1,500	1986
Regional Parks/Parcs régionaux			
Lomas Arena	V	13,300	1989
Private Reserves/Réserves privées			
El Dorado	IV	180,000	1988
Estancias Elsner Espirita	IV	70,000	1978
Estancias Elsner San Rafael	IV	20,000	1978

BOTSWANA

Summary/Sommaire		
Category\Catégorie II	4	8,787,000
Category\Catégorie IV	5	1,238,000
Total	**9**	**10,025,000**

National Parks/Parcs nationaux			
Chobe	II	1,057,000	1968
Gemsbok	II	2,400,000	1971
Nxai Pan	II	150,000	1971
Wildlife Sanctuaries/Sanctuaires de ressources sauvages			
Maun	IV	8,500	
Game Reserves/Réserves de faune			
Central Kgalagdi	II	5,180,000	1961
Khutse	IV	260,000	1971
Mabuasehube	IV	166,500	1971
Makgadikgadi Pans	IV	413,000	1970
Moremi	IV	390,000	1965

BRAZIL/BRESIL

Summary/Sommaire		
Category\Catégorie I	27	3,054,514
Category\Catégorie II	63	10,851,950
Category\Catégorie IV	40	3,384,117
Category\Catégorie V	32	3,234,743
Total	**162**	**20,525,324**

National Parks/Parcs nationaux

Amazonia (Tapajos)	II	994,000	1974
Aparados da Serra	II	10,250	1959
Araguaia	II	562,312	1959
Brasilia	II	28,000	1961
Cabo Orange	II	619,000	1980
Caparao	II	26,000	1961
Chapada Diamantina	II	152,000	1985
Chapada dos Guimaraes	II	33,000	1989
Chapada dos Veadeiros	II	60,000	1961
Emas	II	131,868	1961
Fernando de Noronha (Marinho)	II	11,270	1988
Grande Sertao Veredas	II	84,000	1989
Iguacu	II	170,086	1939
Itatiaia	II	30,000	1937
Jau	II	2,272,000	1980
Lagoa do Peixe	II	34,400	1986
Lencois Maranhenses	II	155,000	1981
Marinho dos Abrolhos	II	91,300	1983
Monte Pascoal	II	22,500	1961
Pacaas Novos	II	765,801	1979
Pantanal Matogrossense	II	135,000	1981
Pico da Neblina	II	2,200,000	1979
Sao Joaquim	II	49,300	1961
Serra da Bocaina	II	100,000	1971
Serra da Canastra	II	71,525	1972
Serra da Capivara	II	97,933	1979
Serra do Cipo	II	33,800	1984
Serra do Divisor	II	605,000	1989
Serra dos Orgaos	II	11,000	1939
Sete Cidades	II	6,221	1961
Superagui	II	21,400	1989
Tijuca	II	3,200	1961

Federal Biological Reserves/Réserves biologiques fédérales

Abufari	I	288,000	1982
Atol das Rocas	I	36,249	1979
Augusto Ruschi (Nova Lombardia)	I	4,000	1982
Caracara	I	61,126	1971
Corrego Grande	I	1,604	1989
Corrego do Viado	I	2,392	1982
Guapore	I	600,000	1982
Gurupi	I	341,650	1988
Jaru	I	268,150	1979
Lago Piratuba	I	395,000	1980
Poco das Antas	I	5,000	1974
Rio Trombetas	I	385,000	1979
Santa Isabel	I	2,766	1988
Serra Negra	I	1,100	1982
Sooretama	I	24,000	1982
Tapirape Aquiri	I	190,000	1989

Parcs nationaux et aires protégées

Tingua	I	26,000	1989
Una	I	11,400	1980
Federal Ecological Reserves/Réserves écologiques fédérales			
Jutai-Solimoes	I	288,187	1983
Raso de Catarina	I	99,772	1984
Federal Ecological Stations/Stations écologiques fédérales			
Aiuba	IV	11,525	1981
Anavilhanas	IV	350,018	1981
Babitonga	IV	7,833	1987
Caracarai	IV	394,560	1982
Carijos	IV	11,296	1987
Coco-Javaes	IV	37,000	1981
Cunia	IV	104,000	1982
Foz do Sao Francisco	IV	5,322	1981
Guaraquecaba	IV	13,638	1982
Ique	IV	200,000	1981
Itabaina	IV	1,100	1987
Jari	IV	227,126	1981
Juami-Japura	IV	745,850	1985
Jureia	IV	24,065	1986
Mamiraua	IV	217,500	1985
Maraca	IV	101,312	1981
Maraca-Jipioca	IV	101,376	1981
Niquia	IV	286,600	1985
Pirai	IV	4,000	1982
Pirapitinga	IV	1,090	1987
Rio Acre	IV	77,500	1981
Serido	IV	1,116	1982
Serra das Araras	IV	28,700	1982
Taim	IV	33,818	1986
Taima	IV	14,325	1981
Urucui-Una	IV	135,000	1981
Federal Environment Protection Areas/Aires fédérales de protection de l'environnement			
Cairucu	V	33,800	1983
Cananeta - Iguape e Peruibe	V	202,832	1984
Guapi-Mirim	V	14,340	1984
Guaraquecaba	V	291,500	1985
Icarape Gelado	V	21,600	1989
Jericoacoara	V	6,800	1984
Mantiqueira	V	402,517	1985
Petropolis	V	44,000	1982
Piacabucu	V	8,600	1983
State Parks/Parcs publics			
Alto Ribeira	II	37,712	1958
Bacanga	II	3,075	1980
Campos do Jordao	II	8,286	1941
Carlos Botelho	II	37,797	1982
Delta do Jacui	II	4,322	1976
Espigao Alto	II	1,319	1946

Ibitipoca	II	1,488	1973
Ilha Anchieta	II	1,000	1977
Ilha Bela	II	27,025	1958
Ilha Grande	II	15,000	1978
Ilha do Cardoso	II	22,500	1962
Itacolomi	II	7,000	1967
Jacupiranga	II	150,000	1969
Jaiba	II	6,211	1973
Mananciais da Serra	II	2,249	
Mirador	II	385,000	1980
Morro do Chapeu	II	6,000	1973
Morro do Diabo	II	34,441	1986
Nonode	II	17,498	1949
Pedra Branca	II	12,500	1974
Pedra Talhada	II	1,800	1985
Rio Doce	II	35,973	1944
Rondinha	II	1,000	1982
Serra Caldas Novas	II	12,315	1970
Serra Furada	II	1,329	1980
Serra do Mar	II	314,800	1969
Serra do Tabuleiro	II	90,000	1975
Tainhas	II	4,824	
Turvo	II	17,491	1965
Vascununca	II	1,484	1970
Vila Velha	II	3,345	1953

State Biological Reserves/Réserves biologiques publiques

Araras	I	2,068	1972
Mata Acaua	I	5,000	1974
Parauna	I	3,490	1979
Praia do Sul	I	3,600	1981
Serra Geral	I	1,700	1982

State Ecological Reserves/Réserves écologiques publiques

Canela-Preta	I	1,844	1980
Sassafraz	I	5,416	1977

State Ecological Stations/Stations écologiques publiques

Aguas Emendades	IV	9,768	1968
Angatuba	IV	1,394	1985
Bracinho	IV	4,606	1984
Caetetus	IV	2,188	1987
Chauas	IV	2,700	1987
Ilha do Mel	IV	2,240	1982
Itirapina	IV	2,300	1984
Jataı	IV	4,532	1982
Jureia-Itatins	IV	82,000	1987
Mamanguape	IV	9,992	1982
Monte Roraima	IV	116,000	1989
Paraiso	IV	4,920	1987
Santa Barbara	IV	2,712	1984
Xitue	IV	3,095	1987

State Environment Protection Areas/Aires publiques
de protection de l'environnement

Abaete	V	1,800	1987
Bacia dos Rios Piracicaba e Juqueri - Mirim	V	390,000	1987
Bacias do Gama e Cabeca do Veado	V	25,000	1986
Cabreuva	V	26,100	1984
Cafuringa	V	30,000	1988
Cajamar	V	13,400	1987
Campos do Jordao	V	26,900	1984
Corumbatai-Botucatu-Tejupa	V	641,000	1984
Descoberto	V	39,100	1983
Desengano	V	22,500	1983
Fernando de Noronha-Rocas-S.Pedro e S.Paul	V	2,700	1986
Floresta do Jacaranda	V	2,700	1983
Gruta dos Brejoes/Vereda do Romao Gramacho	V	11,900	1985
Ibitinga	V	64,900	1987
Ilha Comprida	V	19,375	1987
Jundiai	V	43,200	1984
Mangaratiba	V	22,936	1987
Sao Bartolomeu	V	84,100	1983
Serra das Mangabeiras	V	96,743	1983
Serra do Mar	V	548,100	1984
Silveiras	V	42,700	1984
Tiete	V	45,100	1983
Varzea do Alto Tiete	V	8,500	1987

BRUNEI DARUSSALAM

Summary/Sommaire		
Category\Catégorie IV	4	122,367
Total	**4**	**122,367**

Forest Reserves/Réserves forestières

Andulau	IV	1,309	1940
Batu Apoi	IV	46,210	1950
Labi Hills	IV	64,283	1947
Ladan Hills	IV	10,565	1950

BULGARIA/BULGARIE

Summary/Sommaire		
Category\Catégorie I	23	42,892
Category\Catégorie II	4	66,119
Category\Catégorie III	2	4,424
Category\Catégorie IV	10	15,690
Total	**39**	**129,125**

National Parks/Parcs nationaux

Chumensko plato	IV	3,930	1980
Melnishki pyramidi	III	1,165	1960

Pirin	II	27,400	1963
Roussenski Lom	III	3,259	1970
Sinite kamani	II	6,685	1981
Steneto	II	5,487	1963
Vitosha	II	26,547	1934
Zlatni pyassatzi	IV	1,320	1943
Botanical Reserves/Réserves botaniques			
Tchervenata stena	IV	1,142	1962
Tissata (Tissova Bartchina)	IV	1,200	1949
Reserves/Réserves			
Alibotouch	I	1,628	1951
Atanassovsko ezero	IV	2,020	1980
Baevi doupki-Djindjiritza	I	2,873	1934
Bistrichko Branichte	I	1,177	1935
Boatin	I	1,281	1948
Djendema	I	3,291	1953
Doupkata	I	1,211	1956
Goliam Skakavetz	I	4,180	1985
Ibar	I	1,701	1985
Kamenchtitza	I	1,018	1984
Kongura	I	1,312	1988
Koupena	I	1,086	1961
Maritchini ezera	I	1,509	1951
Oreliar	IV	1,050	1985
Parangalitza	I	1,508	1933
Peechti skali	I	1,465	1979
Severen Djendem	I	1,610	1983
Sokolna	I	1,250	1979
Srebarna	IV	1,143	1988
Stara reka	I	1,906	1981
Steneto	I	2,636	1980
Tajansko jdrelo	IV	1,290	1985
Tchouprene	I	1,440	1974
Tzaritchina	I	1,420	1949
Uzdini ezera	IV	1,150	1985
Vratchanski karst	I	1,409	1983
Forest Reserves/Réserves forestières			
Kamtchia	IV	1,445	1951
Ouzounboudjak	I	2,535	1956
Rila Monastery	I	3,446	1986

BURKINA FASO

Summary/Sommaire		
Category\Catégorie II	3	440,400
Category\Catégorie IV	4	298,500
Total	**7**	**738,900**

National Parks/Parcs nationaux

Deux Bales	II	56,000	1967

Kabore-Tambi	II	149,400	1976
W du Burkina Faso	II	235,000	1954
Total Faunal Reserves/Réserves fauniques intégrales			
Arly	IV	76,000	1954
Bontioli	IV	12,700	1957
Madjoari	IV	17,000	1955
Singou	IV	192,800	1950

BURUNDI

Summary/Sommaire		
Category\Catégorie V	1	37,870
Total	**1**	**37,870**

National Parks/Parcs nationaux
Kibira	V	37,870	1980

BYELORUSSIAN SOVIET SOCIALIST REPUBLIC/REPUBLIQUE SOCIALISTE SOVIETIQUE BIELORUSSIE

Summary/Sommaire		
Category\Catégorie I	2	138,414
Category\Catégorie IV	2	98,524
Total	**4**	**236,938**

Zapovedniki/Zapovednik
Berezinskiy	I	76,201	1925
Prypyatskiy	I	62,213	1969
Hunting Reserves/Réserves de chasse			
Belovezhskaya Pushcha	IV	87,577	1940
Telekhanskoye	IV	10,947	1977

CAMBODIA/CAMBODGE

No Areas Listed/pas de sites

CAMEROON, UNITED REPUBLIC OF/REPUBLIQUE-UNIE DU CAMEROUN

Summary/Sommaire		
Category\Catégorie I	2	527,400
Category\Catégorie II	6	1,030,500
Category\Catégorie IV	5	541,805
Total	**13**	**2,099,705**

National Parks/Parcs nationaux
Benoue	II	180,000	1968
Bouba Ndjidah	II	220,000	1968
Faro	II	330,000	1980
Kalamaloue	II	4,500	1972
Korup	II	126,000	1986

Mozogo-Gokoro	I	1,400	1968
Waza	II	170,000	1968
Faunal Reserves/Réserves fauniques			
Dja	I	526,000	1950
Douala-Edea	IV	160,000	1932
Kimbi	IV	5,625	1964
Mbam et Djerem	IV	353,180	1968
Nanga-Eboke	IV	16,000	
Santchou	IV	7,000	1932

CANADA

Summary/Sommaire		
Category\Catégorie I	57	501,147
Category\Catégorie II	80	26,309,148
Category\Catégorie III	1	3,090
Category\Catégorie IV	162	18,506,762
Category\Catégorie V	126	4,132,136
Total	**426**	**49,452,283**

National Parks/Parcs nationaux

Auyuittuq	II	2,147,110	1972
Banff	II	664,109	1984
Bruce Peninsular	II	27,000	1987
Cape Breton Highlands	II	95,053	1936
Elk Island	II	19,425	1913
Forillon	II	24,040	1970
Fundy	II	20,590	1948
Glaciers	II	134,939	1886
Grasslands	II	90,000	1988
Gros Morne	II	194,250	1970
Jasper	II	1,087,800	1984
Kejimkujik	II	38,151	1968
Kluane	II	2,201,500	1972
Kootenay	II	137,788	1920
Kouchibouguac	II	22,533	1969
La Mauricie	II	54,390	1971
Mount Revelstoke	II	26,263	1914
Nahanni	II	476,560	1972
Northern Ellesmere Island	II	3,950,000	1986
Northern Yukon	II	1,016,865	1984
Pacific Rim	II	38,850	1970
Point Pelee	II	1,554	1918
Prince Albert	II	387,464	1927
Prince Edward Island	II	2,590	1937
Pukaskwa	II	187,775	1971
Riding Mountain	II	297,591	1927
South Moresby	II	147,000	1988
St Lawrence Islands	II	414	1914
Terra Nova	II	39,653	1957

Waterton Lakes	II	52,597	1911
Wood Buffalo	II	4,480,700	1922
Yoho	II	131,313	1886
National Park Reserves/Réserves de parc national			
Mingan Archipelago	II	15,074	1984
National Marine Parks/Parcs marins nationaux			
Fathom Five	II	13,028	1989
Ecological Reserves/Réserves écologiques			
Athabasca Dunes	I	3,770	1987
Baralzon Lake	I	39,000	1989
Byers/Conroy/Harvey/Sinnett Islands	I	12,205	1971
Cape St Mary's Seabird Sanctuary	IV	1,210	1963
Checleset Bay	I	34,650	1971
Dewdney and Glide Islands	I	3,845	1971
East Copper/Jeffrey/Rankine Islands	I	121	1971
East Redonda Island	I	6,212	1971
Gannet Islands Seabird Sanctuary	IV	202	1983
Gingietl Creek	I	2,873	1971
Gladys Lake	I	48,560	1971
Goose Mountain	I	1,246	1987
Goosegrass Creek	I	2,185	1971
Hands Hill	I	2,229	1988
Hare Bay Islands Seabird Sanctuary	IV	442	1983
Ile-Brion	I	670	1987
Ilgachuz Range	I	2,914	1971
Kennedy Coulee	I	1,068	1987
King George VI	IV	1,900	1984
Kingfisher Creek	I	1,441	1971
Kootenay Plains	I	3,204	1987
Lac Malakisis	I	2,000	1978
Lasqueti Island	I	201	1971
Long Point	I	1,600	1987
Mount Griffin	I	1,376	1971
Narcosli Lake	I	1,098	1971
Ningunsaw River	I	2,046	1971
Reindeer Island	I	14,200	1976
Saturna Island	I	131	1971
Sikanni Chief River	I	2,401	1971
Silver Valley	I	1,805	1987
Smith River	I	1,326	1971
Table Point	IV	1,160	1986
Tantare	I	1,491	1978
The Grass	IV	1,100	
Tow Hill	I	1,571	1971
Upper Bob Creek	I	6,427	1989
V.J. Krajina (Port Chanal)	I	9,834	1971
Wainwright Dunes	I	2,821	1988
Watt's Point	III	3,090	1986
Witless Bay	IV	141	1983

Nature Reserves/Réserves de nature			
Salmonier	IV	1,160	1972
Nature Reserves (Bird Reserves)/Réserves de nature			
(Réserves ornithologiques)			
Grand Manan	IV	250	1931
Shebody Bay	IV	13,200	
National Wildlife Areas/Aires nationales de faune			
et de flore sauvages			
Boot Island	IV	144	1979
Cap Tourmente	IV	2,230	1978
Chignecto	IV	1,020	1978
Iles de Contrecoeur	IV	202	1981
Iles-de-la-Paix	IV	121	1977
Lac Saint-Francois	IV	1,166	1978
Long Point	I	3,250	1984
Polar Bear Pass	I	81,000	1986
Portage Island	IV	439	1979
Portobello Creek	IV	2,097	1988
Prairie	IV	2,933	1978
Stalwart	IV	1,460	1978
Tintamarre	IV	1,990	1978
Wildlife Sanctuaries/Sanctuaires de ressources sauvages			
Bowman Bay	IV	107,900	1957
Thelon	IV	2,396,000	1927
Twin Islands	IV	142,500	1939
Bird Sanctuaries/Sanctuaires ornithologiques			
Akimiski Island	IV	336,700	1941
Anderson River Delta	IV	108,300	1961
Banks Island No 1	IV	2,051,800	1961
Banks Island No 2	IV	14,200	1961
Basin and Middle Lakes	IV	8,702	1925
Boatswain Bay	IV	17,900	1941
Bonoventure Island and Perce Rock	IV	1,340	1919
Botswain Bay	IV	17,700	1941
Bylot Island	IV	1,087,800	1965
Cape Dorset	IV	25,900	1958
Dewer Soper	IV	815,900	1941
Duncairn Reservoir	IV	1,550	1948
East Bay	IV	116,600	1959
Fielding	IV	1,300	1952
Fog Island	IV	4,450	1925
Hanna Bay (Ontario)	IV	29,800	1939
Hannah Bay (NWT)	IV	29,500	1939
Harry Gibbons	IV	149,000	1959
Iles aux Basques	IV	1,000	
Iles de la Paix	IV	1,100	1972
Kendall Island	IV	60,600	1961
Lake St Francis	IV	1,335	1978
Last Mountain Lake	IV	4,740	
Lenore Lake	IV	8,830	1925

Long Point	IV	3,250	1978
McConnell River	IV	33,000	1960
Mont St Hilaire	IV	5,550	1978
Moose River	IV	1,450	1958
Murray Lake	IV	1,170	1948
Nicolet	IV	2,850	
Old Wives Lake	IV	26,060	1925
Opuntia Lake	IV	1,400	1952
Queen Maud Gulf	IV	6,278,200	1961
Redberry Lake	IV	6,400	1925
Richardson Lake	IV	12,700	1953
Sable Island	IV	2,350	1977
Saskatoon Lake	IV	1,140	1948
Seymour Island	IV	800	1975
St Augustin	IV	55,300	1925
St Mary Islands	IV	4,500	1925
Upper Canada	IV	2,660	1961
Victoria	IV	1,700	1923
Watshishu	IV	11,200	1925
Wolf Bay	IV	4,000	1925
Wilderness Areas/Aires de nature sauvage			
Ghost River	II	15,317	1967
Siffleur	II	41,214	1961
White Goat	II	44,457	1961
Wildcat Hill	I	18,200	1971
Wilderness Reserves/Réserves de nature sauvage			
Avalon	I	107,000	1986
Bay du Nord	IV	289,500	1987
Natural Areas/Aires naturelles			
Beehive	IV	6,700	1987
Milk River Canyon	IV	5,400	1987
Park Reserves/Parcs-Réserves			
Grand Lake	IV	2,100	
Sepoy Hill	IV	7,284	
Winter Tickle Lake	IV	1,457	
Territorial Parks/Parcs territoriaux			
Herschel Island	I	10,100	1987
Marine Parks/Parcs marins			
Desolation Sound	IV	2,550	1973
Parks/Parcs			
Elk Lakes	IV	11,620	1986
Niagara Escarpment	V	1,900	1985
Wildlife Management Areas/Aires de gestion des ressources sauvages			
Alonsa	IV	10,536	
Assiniboine Corridor	IV	2,200	
Basket Lake	IV	7,175	
Broad Valley	IV	3,361	
Cape Churchill	IV	1,874,043	
Cape Tatnam	IV	521,160	

Cayer	IV	1,519	
Clematis	IV	5,365	
Dog Lake	IV	32,320	
Grahamdale	IV	1,487	
Gypsumville	IV	2,456	
Hilbre	IV	1,258	
Inwood	IV	2,268	
Langruth	IV	1,782	
Last Mountain Lake Cooperative	IV	15,602	
Lauder Sandhills	IV	3,135	
Lee Lake	IV	6,968	
Little Birch	IV	21,902	
Lundar	IV	1,102	
Mantagao	IV	50,357	
Marshy Point	IV	1,490	
Narcisse	IV	11,712	
Oak Hammock Marsh	IV	3,526	
Pembina Valley	IV	2,271	
Peonan Point	IV	2,341	
Point River	IV	3,370	
Portage Sandhills	IV	1,328	
Proulx	IV	3,304	
Proven Lake	IV	1,979	
Rat River	IV	1,004	
Rembrandt	IV	1,231	
Sandridge	IV	1,166	
Saskeram	IV	95,942	
Sharpewood	IV	1,814	
Sleeve Lake	IV	14,969	
Souris River Bend	IV	2,074	
Steeprock	IV	1,892	
Tom Lamb	IV	214,618	
Upper Assiniboine	IV	1,326	
Watson P. Davidson	IV	5,832	
Westlake	IV	5,739	
Whitemud Watershed	IV	4,764	
Whitewater Lake	IV	9,049	
Fish and Game Reserve Sanctuaries/Sanctuaires-Réserves de faune et de poissons			
Botswain Bay	II	17,700	
National Historic Parks/Parcs historiques nationaux			
Fortress of Louisbourg	V	5,224	1940
L'Anse aux Meadows	V	7,997	1978
Provincial Parks/Parcs provinciaux			
Abitibi-de-Troyes	V	11,068	1985
Agassiz Peatlands	I	2,315	1985
Aiguebelle	V	24,170	1985
Akamina-Kishinema	II	10,915	1986
Albany River	V	95,100	1989
Algonquin	IV	765,345	1893

Atikaki	V	406,841	1985
Atlin Park	II	271,138	1973
Aubrey Falls	IV	4,860	1985
Awenda	IV	2,917	1975
Babine Mountains	V	32,400	1984
Barachois Pond	V	3,497	1961
Bic	V	3,320	1984
Bigwind Lake	IV	1,970	1985
Birkenhead Lake	V	3,642	1963
Biscotasi Lake	V	1,238	1989
Blackstone Harbour	IV	11,976	1989
Bon Echo	IV	6,644	1971
Bonnechere River	V	1,198	1989
Bow Valley	II	1,261	1959
Bowron Lake	II	123,117	1961
Boya Lake	V	4,597	1965
Brightsand River	V	41,250	1989
Brooks Peninsula	V	28,780	1986
Bugaboo Alpine	IV	24,912	1969
Butler Lake	I	3,400	1985
Butter Pot	V	1,752	1966
Cabot Head	I	4,514	1985
Cape Scott	V.	15,054	1918
Carillon	V	1,417	1966
Carp Lake	II	19,334	1973
Carson Pegasus	V	1,177	1982
Cascade	V	16,680	1987
Castle Creek	I	1,075	1985
Cathedral	II	33,272	1968
Champion Lakes	V	1,425	1955
Chance Cove	V	2,068	1974
Chapleau-Nemegosenda River	V	8,165	1973
Clearwater River	V	224,035	1986
Coquilla Summit	II	5,750	1987
Cranberry Lake	I	2,800	1985
Crimson Lake	V	3,443	1955
Crooked River	V	1,016	1963
Cross Lake	V	2,076	1955
Cypress Hills (Alberta)	II	20,451	1951
Cypress	V	2,849	1975
Dana-Jowsey Lakes	V	2,538	1989
Darke Lake	V	1,470	1943
Dillberry Lake	V	1,012	1957
Dinosaur	II	6,622	1955
Douglas	V	4,434	1973
Dry Islands Buffalo Jump	II	1,180	1970
E.C. Manning	V	71,400	1941
Elk Falls	V	1,087	1940
Elk Island	V	1,000	1975
Elk Lakes	V	5,625	1973

Eneas Lakes	V	1,036	1968
Esker Lakes	IV	3,237	1957
Eskers	V	1,603	1987
Fawn River	V	12,140	1989
Fiordland	V	91,000	1987
French River	V	51,120	1989
Frontenac	IV	5,130	1974
Fushimi Lake	V	5,294	1979
Garibaldi	II	21,290	1964
Gaspesie	II	80,200	1981
Gitnadoix	V	58,000	1986
Golden Ears	V	55,594	1967
Goodspirit Lake	V	1,901	1931
Grands-Jardins	V	31,000	1977
Greenwater Lake	V	20,720	1932
Greenwater	IV	5,350	1957
Grindstone	V	25,841	1969
Grundy Lake	IV	2,554	1959
Ha Kai	V	122,998	1987
Halfway Lake	IV	4,730	1980
Hamber	II	24,518	1941
Hilliard's Bay	V	2,329	1978
International Ridge	V	1,905	1969
Ivanhoe Lake	IV	1,589	1957
Jacques-Cartier	V	67,060	1981
Joffre Lakes	V	1,460	1988
Kabitotikwia River	I	1,965	1985
Kakwa	V	127,690	1987
Kashabowie	IV	2,055	1985
Kawartha Highlands	IV	1,800	1989
Kesagami Wilderness	II	55,977	1983
Kettle Lakes	V	1,261	1957
Killarney Wilderness	II	48,500	1964
Killbear	IV	1,756	1971
Kinaskan Lake	V	1,800	1987
Kokanee Glacier	V	25,900	1922
Kopka River	V	16,200	1989
Kwadacha Wilderness	II	167,540	1973
La Cloche	IV	7,448	1985
La Manche	V	1,394	1966
La Verendrye River	V	18,335	1989
Lady Evelyn-Smoothwater Wilderness	II	72,400	1983
Lake Lovely Water	V	1,300	1988
Lake Nipigon	IV	1,458	1960
Lake Superior	IV	155,659	1950
Lake of the Woods	IV	12,900	1967
Larder River	V	2,500	1985
Lesser Slave Lake	II	7,557	1966
Little Abitibi	IV	20,000	1985
Little Current River	V	9,930	1989

Livingstone Point	I	1,800	1985
Lola Lake	I	6,572	1985
Lower Madawaska River	V	1,200	1989
MacGregor Point	IV	1,204	1975
Makobe-Grays River	V	1,427	1985
Manitou Islands	I	1,925	1989
Manning	V	65,863	1941
Matawin River	I	2,615	1985
Mattawa River	V	3,258	1970
Michipicoten Island	IV	36,740	1985
Minnitaki Kames	I	4,422	1989
Missinaibi	V	99,152	1970
Mississagi	IV	4,900	1973
Mississagi River	V	19,814	1974
Missississagi Delta	I	2,395	1985
Mitlewatch Island	II	155	1961
Monashee	V	7,513	1962
Monkman	II	3,200	1981
Mont Orford	V	3,885	1938
Mont Sainte-Anne	II	6,400	1968
Mont Tremblant	II	124,800	1894
Mount Assiniboine	II	39,052	1922
Mount Carleton	V	17,427	1970
Mount Edziza	II	131,928	1972
Mount Judge Howay	V	6,180	1967
Mount Robson	II	219,829	1913
Mount Seymour	V	3,508	1936
Mount Terry Fox	V	1,930	1982
Muncho Lake	II	88,416	1957
Murphy's Point	IV	1,240	1967
Nagagami Lake	I	1,650	1985
Nagagamisis	IV	8,131	1957
Naikoon	II	72,641	1973
Nancy Greene	V	8,086	1969
Neys	IV	3,445	1965
Nipawin	V	53,613	1931
Nopiming	V	143,750	1976
Notokewin	V	9,667	1979
Obabika River	V	17,000	1989
Obatanga	IV	9,409	1967
Ojibway	V	2,630	1963
Oka	V	2,370	1981
Okanagan Mountain	V	10,462	1973
Opasquia Wilderness	II	473,000	1983
Otoskwin-Attawapiskat River	V	82,569	1989
Paint Lake	V	22,660	1969
Pakwash	IV	3,993	1967
Pantagruel Creek	I	2,685	1989
Peter Lougheed	II	50,142	1977
Petroglyphs	V	1,555	1976

Pipestone River	V	97,375	1989
Pointe Taillon	V	9,220	1985
Polar Bear Wilderness	II	2,408,700	1970
Purcell	V	131,523	1974
Quetico Wilderness	II	475,819	1950
Rene Brunelle	V	2,964	1957
Restoule	IV	1,200	1963
Roderick Haig-Brown Area	II	1,000	1977
Rondeau	IV	3,254	1894
Round Lake	I	2,585	1989
Sable Islands	V	1,980	1985
Saguenay	II	28,360	1983
Samuel de Champlain	IV	2,550	1967
Sandbanks	IV	1,509	1970
Sandbar Lake	V	5,083	1970
Saskatchewan Landing	V	5,597	1973
Sasquatch	V	1,220	1968
Schoen Lake	II	8,170	1977
Sedgman Lake	I	5,710	1985
Severn River	V	82,960	1989
Sibley (Sleeping Giant)	IV	24,435	1950
Silent Lake	IV	1,450	1977
Silver Falls	IV	3,261	1985
Silver Star	V	8,714	1940
Skagit Valley	V	32,508	1973
Slate Islands	IV	6,570	1985
Solace	V	5,943	1989
South Bay	V	1,525	1985
Spatsizi Plateau Widerness Area	II	675,024	1975
Spruce Woods	V	24,860	1964
Squires Memorial	V	1,574	1959
St Mary's Alpine	V	9,146	1973
Stag Lake	V	41,278	1978
Stagleap	V	1,133	1964
Steel River	V	11,240	1989
Stikine River	V	217,000	1987
Stone Mountain	II	25,691	1957
Strathcona	II	201,003	1987
Sturgeon River	V	3,350	1989
Tatlatui	V	105,826	1973
The Pinery	IV	2,533	1957
The Shoals	IV	10,644	1970
Top of the World	IV	8,791	1973
Trout Lake	I	7,150	1989
Turtle River	V	40,052	1989
Tweedsmuir	II	981,120	1938
Upper Madawaska River	V	1,085	1989
Valhalla	V	49,600	1983
Wabakimi Wilderness	V	155,000	1983
Wakami Lake	V	8,806	1973

Wanapitei	IV	2,700	1985
Wasaga Beach	V	1,545	
Waskwei River Protected Area	II	1,028	1964
Wellesley Gray	V	13,963	1987
Wells Gray	II	527,305	1901
West Bay	I	1,120	1985
White Lake	IV	1,726	1963
White Pelican	V	1,247	1971
Whiteswan Lake	V	1,994	1978
Whitney Lake	V	1,490	1982
Wildcat Hill	V	16,997	1971
William A. Switzer	II	2,686	1958
Willmore Wild Park	V	459,673	1959
Winagami Lake	V	1,211	1956
Windigo Bay	I	8,378	1989
Winisk River	V	152,500	1969
Winnange Lake	IV	4,745	1985
Wokpash	V	37,800	1986
Woodland Caribou Wilderness	II	450,000	1983
Yamaska	V	1,289	1983
Young's Point	V	1,090	1971

CAPE VERDE/CAP-VERT

No Areas Listed/pas de sites

CENTRAL AFRICAN REPUBLIC/REPUBLIQUE CENTRAFRICAINE

Summary/Sommaire		
Category\Catégorie I	1	86,000
Category\Catégorie II	2	2,810,000
Category\Catégorie IV	4	1,008,000
Total	**7**	**3,904,000**

National Parks/Parcs nationaux			
Bamingui-Bangoran	II	1,070,000	1933
Manovo-Gounda-Saint Floris	II	1,740,000	1933
Strict Nature Reserves/Réserves strictes de nature			
Vassako-Bolo	I	86,000	1960
Faunal Reserves/Réserves fauniques			
Aouk-Aoukale	IV	330,000	1939
Gribingui-Bamingui	IV	438,000	1940
Koukourou-Bamingui	IV	110,000	1940
Ouandjia-Vakaga	IV	130,000	1925

CHAD/TCHAD

Summary/Sommaire		
Category\Catégorie II	1	114,000
Total	**1**	**114,000**

National Parks/Parcs nationaux
    Manda   II   114,000   1969

CHILE/CHILI

Summary/Sommaire		
Category\Catégorie II	30	8,364,689
Category\Catégorie III	2	13,606
Category\Catégorie IV	33	5,271,423
Total	**65**	**13,649,718**

National Parks/Parcs nationaux

Alberto de Agostini	II	1,460,000	1965
Alerce Andino	II	39,255	1982
Bernardo O'Higgins	II	3,525,901	1970
Bosque Fray Jorge	II	9,959	1941
Cabo de Hornos	II	63,093	1945
Chiloe	II	43,057	1982
Conguillio	II	60,832	1950
El Morado	II	3,000	1974
Hornopiren	II	54,420	1988
Huerquehue	II	12,500	1967
Isla Guamblin	II	10,625	1976
Isla Magdalena	II	157,640	1983
La Campana	II	8,000	1967
Laguna San Rafael	II	1,742,000	1967
Laguna del Laja	II	11,600	1958
Las Palmas de Cocalan	II	3,709	1972
Lauca	II	137,883	1970
Nahuelbuta	II	6,832	1939
Pali-Aike	II	3,000	1970
Pan de Azucar	II	43,754	1986
Puyehue	II	107,000	1941
Queulat	II	154,093	1983
Rio Simpson	II	40,790	1967
Tolhuaca	II	6,374	1935
Torres del Paine	II	181,414	1959
Vicente Perez Rosales	II	226,305	1926
Villarrica	II	61,000	1940
Volcan Isluga	II	174,744	1967

National Reserves/Réserves nationales

Alacalufes	IV	2,313,875	1969
Alto Bio-Bio	IV	35,000	1912
Cerro Castillo	IV	179,550	1970
China Muerta	IV	9,887	1968
Coyhaique	IV	2,150	1948
Isla Mocha	IV	2,368	1988
Katalalixar	IV	674,500	1983
La Chimba	IV	2,583	1988
Lago Carlota	IV	27,110	1965

Lago Cochrane	IV	8,361	1967
Lago General Carrera	IV	178,400	1974
Lago Jeinimeni	IV	38,700	1967
Lago Las Torres	IV	16,516	1969
Lago Palena	IV	41,356	1952
Lago Penuelas	IV	9,094	1965
Lago Rosselot	IV	12,725	1968
Laguna Parrillar	IV	18,814	1977
Las Chinchillas	IV	4,229	1983
Las Guaitecas	IV	1,097,975	1938
Las Vicunas	IV	209,131	1983
Llanquihue	IV	33,972	1912
Magallanes	IV	13,500	1932
Malalcahuello	IV	29,530	1931
Malleco	IV	17,371	1907
Nalcas	IV	13,775	1967
Nuble	IV	55,948	1978
Pampa del Tamarugal	IV	100,650	1988
Ralco	IV	12,421	1972
Rio Blanco	IV	10,175	1932
Rio Clarillo	IV	10,185	1982
Rio de Los Cipreses	IV	38,582	1984
Valdivia	IV	9,727	1929
Villarrica	IV	43,263	1912
Nature Monuments/Monuments de la nature			
Alerce Costero	III	2,308	1964
Salar de Surire	III	11,298	1983

Easter Island/Ile de pâques

National Parks/Parcs nationaux

Rapa Nui (Easter Island)	II	6,800	1935

Juan Fernandez

National Parks/Parcs nationaux

Archipielago de Juan Fernandez	II	9,109	1935

CHINA, PEOPLES REPUBLIC OF/REPUBLIQUE POPULAIRE DE CHINE

Summary/Sommaire		
Category\Catégorie I	4	101,025
Category\Catégorie IV	285	21,846,079
Total	**289**	**21,947,104**

Nature Reserves/Réserves de nature

A Er Jin Shan Ye Luo (Arjin)	IV	1,512,000	1986
Ai Mountain	IV	5,333	1984
Ailao Mountain	IV	50,360	1986
Annanba	IV	390,000	1982
Arjin (A Er Jin Shan) Mountains	IV	4,000,000	1983

Ba Yin Bu Lu Ke (Bayanbulak)	IV	100,000	1980
Babao Mountain	IV	3,200	1984
Badagong Mountain	IV	20,000	1982
Baihua Mountain	IV	1,700	1985
Baima Mountain	IV	180,000	1983
Baishanzu	IV	1,333	1985
Baishilazi	IV	6,667	1981
Baishu River	I	95,292	1963
Bamian Mountain	IV	4,300	1982
Baotianman (Neixiang)	IV	4,200	1980
Baotianman (Henan)	IV	3,333	1982
Bawangling	IV	2,000	1980
Bayanaobao	IV	6,737	1980
Bitahai	IV	14,133	1984
Bulgan River	IV	5,000	1980
Buliu River	IV	45,300	1982
Bunge Ash	IV	1,400	1983
Caohai	IV	5,334	1985
Cathay Silver Fir	IV	4,600	1984
Cha Mountain	IV	2,667	1984
Changbai Mountains	IV	190,582	1961
Changhang Bawanglin	I	2,000	1980
Changling Mountain	IV	3,670	1980
Chebaling	IV	7,545	1982
Chengbi River	IV	16,200	1980
Chengjia	IV	7,867	1983
Chinese Walnut	IV	1,180	1983
Chongzuo	IV	35,000	1981
Chuandong River	IV	11,600	1982
Dadong Mountain	IV	8,000	1985
Dagu River	IV	463,100	1984
Daiyun Mountain	IV	9,731	1985
Dalai Lake	IV	400,000	1986
Daming Mountain	IV	58,200	1980
Daping Mountain	IV	20,400	1982
Dapingdong	IV	2,667	1983
Daqinggou	IV	8,183	1980
Datian	IV	2,500	1976
Dawangling	IV	19,200	1980
Dawei Mountain	IV	15,367	1986
Dawie Mountain	IV	6,300	1982
Daxin	IV	29,900	1980
Daxue Mountain	IV	15,787	1986
Dayao Mountain	IV	13,500	1982
Dayuanyuankou	IV	11,000	1982
Dehou	IV	12,200	1980
Dinghu Mountain	IV	1,140	1956
Dong-tin Lake	IV	184,300	
Dongda Mountain	IV	4,921	1980
Dongzhai	IV	9,333	1982

Dongzhaigang	IV	2,534	1980
Dujia Mountain	IV	6,667	1984
Fenglin	IV	18,400	1958
Fengtongzai	IV	40,000	1978
Fengyang Mountain	IV	4,667	1975
Fenshuiling	IV	10,760	1986
Five Joined Lakes	IV	70,000	1980
Foping	IV	35,000	1978
Fu Mountain	IV	60,700	1984
Fuhai Jengsetas	IV	9,767	1986
Fusui	IV	10,000	1981
Gahai	IV	3,500	1982
Gang	IV	4,600	1985
Ganjia Lake	IV	1,042,000	1983
Ganshiling	IV	2,000	1985
Gaoligong Mountain	IV	123,333	1983
Gar Qu	IV	20,000	1963
Great Suhai Lake	IV	3,500	1982
Guan Mountain	IV	6,467	1976
Guanyin Mountain	IV	3,000	1985
Guniuxiang	IV	6,433	1982
Guozhagou	IV	2,509	1982
Gutian Mountain	IV	1,333	1962
Haba Mountain	IV	21,907	1984
Haiziping	IV	2,780	1984
Hanas	IV	250,000	1980
Heaven Lake	IV	6,667	1983
Hei River	IV	4,200	1982
Heilonggong	IV	3,600	1982
Heishiding	IV	4,000	1979
Helan Mountains	IV	61,000	1982
Hong River	IV	16,333	1984
Hongfeng Lake	IV	11,000	1981
Huagong	IV	15,700	1982
Huakun-Sunjiagou	IV	3,333	1981
Huangfu Mountain	IV	3,587	1982
Huanglei River	IV	65,200	1984
Huanglian Mountain	IV	13,835	1983
Huanglongsi	IV	40,000	1983
Huangsang	IV	25,350	1982
Huangshui River	IV	98,300	1984
Huangzangyu	IV	2,333	1980
Huaping	IV	17,400	1961
Huashuichong	IV	12,000	1982
Huma River	IV	30,000	1982
Huocheng	IV	35,000	1983
Huping Mountain	IV	13,333	1982
Huzhong	IV	194,000	1983
Immortal's Cave	IV	1,733	1981
Jia River	IV	200,000	1984

Jiache	IV	8,287	1984
Jianfengling	IV	1,600	1960
Jiangcun	IV	34,060	1985
Jiangshi	IV	1,187	1986
Jigong Mountain	IV	3,000	1982
Jingangtai	IV	4,200	1982
Jinggang Mountains	IV	15,873	1981
Jingpo Lake	IV	120,000	1980
Jinyun Mountain	IV	1,400	1979
Jiugong	IV	3,995	1983
Jiulian Mountain	IV	4,067	1976
Jou-li Mountain	IV	5,000	1982
Jun Mountain	IV	84,000	1982
Kalamaili Mountain	IV	1,700,000	1982
Kontong Mountain	IV	1,089	1982
Laba River	IV	12,000	1963
Laiyang River	IV	7,000	1986
Lake of Heaven	IV	38,069	1980
Laojieling	IV	15,333	1982
Laojun Mountain (Henan)	IV	2,000	1982
Laojun Mountain (Yunnan)	IV	4,507	1986
Laotie Mountain	IV	17,000	1963
Leigong Mountain	IV	50,000	1982
Lesser Qinling Mountain	IV	4,000	1982
Lesser Wutai Mountain	IV	22,000	1983
Li Mountain	IV	24,800	1983
Liangshui	IV	6,394	1980
Liangucheng	IV	14,000	1982
Lianhua Mountain	IV	6,855	1982
Liankang Mountain	IV	2,000	1982
Liulianling	IV	2,200	1981
Liupan Mountain	IV	7,000	1982
Liupaoshougou	IV	2,000	1981
Longbao	IV	10,000	1984
Longchiman	IV	7,502	1982
Longgang	IV	8,000	1979
Longrui	IV	2,100	1980
Longwang Mountain	IV	1,200	1985
Lu Mountain	IV	30,493	1981
Lugu Lake	IV	8,127	1986
Luo Mountain	IV	8,900	1982
Luofu Mountain	IV	2,400	1985
Luya Mountain	IV	21,453	1980
Mabian Dafengding	IV	30,000	1978
Maicaogou	IV	3,567	1982
Mandarin Duck/Macaque	IV	1,039	1984
Mang Mountain	IV	6,500	1982
Mang River	IV	5,600	1983
Mangrove Forest	IV	3,733	1982
Mazongling	IV	3,490	1980

Medog	IV	62,620	1985
Meigudafengding	IV	16,000	1978
Meihua Mountain	IV	22,133	1985
Melmeg	IV	144,000	1981
Mengda	IV	9,544	1980
Miao'er Mountain	IV	45,100	1976
Mongolian Scotch Pine Seed Stand	IV	1,314	1981
Mount Fanjing	IV	41,902	1978
Mount Tomur	IV	100,000	1980
Muzhu River	IV	127,800	1984
Nangun River	IV	7,000	1980
Nankun Mountain	IV	2,000	1984
Nanliuzhangzi	IV	1,333	1984
Nansi Hu	IV	126,400	1982
Nanyue	IV	8,000	1982
Napahai	IV	2,067	1984
Naz-Quelute	IV	16,400	1986
Nianzigou	IV	1,133	1984
Niao Dao	IV	53,550	1975
Nongxin	IV	10,500	1980
Nu River	IV	375,433	1986
Nudeng	IV	28,040	1983
Old Baldy Summit	IV	5,930	1981
Pangquangou	IV	10,446	1980
Peony Peak	IV	40,000	1980
Phoenix Mountain	IV	3,900	1981
Pi Mountain	IV	3,333	1981
Poyang Lake	IV	22,400	1984
Qiangshan Dongzhaigang	I	2,600	1980
Qianjiadong	IV	5,300	1982
Qingdao Bird	IV	1,065,400	1982
Qinglangang	IV	2,000	1982
Qingliangfeng (1)	IV	1,038	1979
Qingliangfeng (2)	IV	3,000	1986
Qingpilin	IV	1,066	1980
Qingtongxia	IV	3,333	1984
Qingxidong	IV	3,133	1976
Qitai	IV	12,333	1986
Qixinglazi	IV	33,000	1980
Rhesus Macaque	IV	10,667	1982
River Mussel	IV	22,833	1980
Rizhao	IV	40,000	198
Rushan River	IV	95,400	1984
Sanpihu	IV	4,200	1982
Savin Juniper	IV	7,666	1976
Schrenk Spruce	IV	28,000	1983
Shaguogou	IV	1,200	1984
Shapotou	IV	12,000	1983
Shengjin Lake	IV	33,333	1986
Shennongja	IV	77,333	1978

Shibalianshan	IV	1,213	
Shiren Mountain	IV	1,333	1982
Shiwandashan	IV	26,700	1980
Shoulu Mountain	IV	11,060	1980
Shuangtaizi Estuary	IV	7,000	1985
Shunhuang Mountain (Dong'an)	IV	10,400	1982
Shunhuang Mountain (Xinling)	IV	12,500	1982
Song Mountain	IV	6,667	1985
Songfeng Mountain	IV	1,465	1984
Songhua Lake	IV	354,098	1982
Stellate-Hair Vatica Forest	IV	1,666	1980
Stiff-leaf Juniper	IV	6,354	1961
Suoxiyu	IV	5,000	1982
Tacheng	IV	1,500	1980
Taibai Mountains	IV	54,103	1965
Taibaiding	IV	3,533	1982
Taihang	IV	2,000	1982
Tangjia	IV	28,000	1978
Tanyang	IV	10,000	1984
Taohongling	IV	4,500	1981
Taoyuandong	IV	7,000	1982
Tarim	IV	387,900	1980
Taxkorgan	IV	1,500,000	1984
Tianzi Mountain	IV	5,000	1982
Tiebu	IV	23,000	1965
Tongbiguan	IV	34,160	1986
Tou'ersantan	IV	31,937	1982
Urumqi Geological	IV	200,000	1986
Wang River	IV	7,600	1984
Wanglang	IV	27,700	1965
Weide Mountain	IV	6,667	1984
Weihai	IV	39,800	1984
Weiyuan River	IV	7,780	1983
West Tianmu Mountain	IV	1,000	1962
Wolong	IV	200,000	1975
Wuliang Mountain	IV	23,353	1986
Wuling Mountain	IV	14,580	1983
Wulong River	IV	265,200	1984
Wuyi Mountains	IV	56,527	1977
Wuzhi Mountain	IV	18,664	1985
Xiang Hai	IV	105,467	1981
Xiao River	IV	60,000	1981
Xiaoqiaogou	IV	1,894	1986
Xiaoxi	IV	11,000	1982
Xiaozhaizigou	IV	6,700	1979
Xiazhuang	IV	2,000	1984
Xilin Gol Prairie	IV	1,078,600	1985
Xingdou	IV	2,880	1981
Xingkai Lake	IV	16,537	1986
Xinglong Mountain	IV	2,219	1982

Xinkou	IV	1,126	1964
Xipin	IV	1,466	1984
Xisha	IV	330	1980
Xishuangbanna	IV	200,000	1958
Xunbiela River	IV	14,000	1982
Ya Mountain	IV	6,667	1984
Yan Mountain	IV	5,333	1977
Yancheng	IV	40,600	1983
Yanchiwan	IV	424,800	1982
Yangming Mountain	IV	2,600	1982
Yaoshan	IV	10,213	1984
Yi Mountain	IV	3,200	1982
Yiwulu Mountain	IV	14,000	1981
Yuan Mountain	IV	1,000	1985
Yulong Mountain	IV	26,000	1984
Yun Mountain	IV	1,330	1982
Yunwu Mountain	IV	1,300	1982
Zayu	IV	101,400	1985
Zhalong	IV	210,000	1979
Zham	IV	6,852	1985
Zhang-jia-jic State Forest	IV	5,000	
Zhaoging Dinghushan	I	1,133	1956
Zhaohu Mountain	IV	6,667	1984
Zhifu	IV	22,750	1984
Ziyunwanfeng Mountain	IV	11,000	1982
Zuojia	IV	6,008	1982

Wildlife Sanctuaries/Sanctuaires de ressources sauvages

Yuoriqai Tiebu	IV	23,000	1965

Reserves/Réserves

Dafengding Panda	IV	30,000	1978

Sanctuaries/Sanctuaires

Qinghaihu Waterfowl Island	IV	7,850	1975
Qiqihari Zhalong Crane	IV	42,000	1976

Natural Scenery Protection Areas/Aires de protection
du panorama naturel

Fukang Tianchi	IV	6,000	1980

Protected Areas/Aires protégées

Hongze Hu	IV	196,000	1986

Forest Reserves/Réserves forestières

Guilin Miaroshan	IV	13,666	1976
Qianshan Wuyishan	IV	1,400	1977

CHINA, REPUBLIC OF/REPUBLIQUE DE CHINE

Summary/Sommaire		
Category\Catégorie II	2	197,490
Category\Catégorie IV	1	47,000
Category\Catégorie V	2	44,087
Total	**5**	**288,577**

National Parks/Parcs nationaux

Kenting	V	32,631	1982
Taroko	II	92,000	1986
Yangmingshan	V	11,456	1985
Yushan	II	105,490	1985

Preserves/

Ta-Wu Mountain	IV	47,000	1987

CHYPRE
Voir paragraphe CYPRUS

COLOMBIA/COLOMBIE

Summary/Sommaire		
Category\Catégorie I	2	1,947,500
Category\Catégorie II	34	7,306,780
Category\Catégorie IV	6	47,410
Total	**42**	**9,301,690**

Natural National Parks/Parcs nationaux naturels

Amacayacu	II	293,000	1975
Cahuinari	II	575,500	1987
Catatumbo-Bari	II	158,125	1989
Chingaza	II	50,374	1978
Chiribiquete	II	1,280,000	1989
Corales del Rosario	II	19,506	1977
Cordillera de los Picachos	II	286,000	1977
Cueva de los Guarcharos	II	9,000	1961
El Cocuy	II	306,000	1977
El Tuparro	II	548,000	1970
Farallones de Cali	II	150,000	1968
Isla de Gorgona	II	49,200	1983
Isla de Salamanca	II	21,000	1977
La Paya	II	422,000	1984
Las Hermosas	II	125,000	1977
Las Orquideas	II	32,000	1977
Los Katios	II	72,000	1973
Los Nevados	II	38,000	1973
Los Picachos	II	439,000	1989
Macuira	II	25,000	1977
Munchique	II	44,000	1977
Nevado del Huila	II	158,000	1977
Paramillo	II	460,000	1977
Pisba	II	45,000	1977
Purace	I	83,000	1968
Sanquianga	II	80,000	1977
Sierra Nevada de Santa Marta	II	383,000	1964
Sierra de la Macarena	II	630,000	1989
Sumapaz	II	154,000	1977
Tama	II	48,000	1977

Tatama	II	51,900	1987
Tayrona	II	15,000	1964
Tinigua	II	201,875	1989
Utria	II	54,300	1987
Natural Reserves/Réserves naturelles			
Laguna de Sonso	IV	2,045	1979
National Reserves/Réserves nationales			
Nukak	I	855,000	1989
Puinaway	I	1,092,500	1989
Fauna and Flora Sanctuaries/Sanctuaires de faune et de flore			
Cienaga Grande de Santa Marta	IV	23,000	1977
Galeras	IV	7,615	1985
Iguaque	IV	6,750	1977
Los Colorados	IV	1,000	1977
Los Flamencos	IV	7,000	1977

COMOROS/COMORES

No Areas Listed/pas de sites

CONGO

Summary\Sommaire		
Category\Catégorie II	1	126,600
Category\Catégorie IV	9	1,206,500
Total	**10**	**1,333,100**

National Parks/Parcs nationaux			
Odzala	II	126,600	1940
Faunal Reserves/Réserves fauniques			
Conkouati	IV	300,000	1980
Lefini	IV	630,000	1951
Lekoli-Pandaka	IV	68,200	1955
Mont Fouari	IV	15,600	1958
Nyanga Nord	IV	7,700	1958
Tsoulou	IV	30,000	1963
Hunting Reserves/Réserves de chasse			
M'boko	IV	90,000	1955
Mont Mavoumbou	IV	42,000	1955
Nyanga Sud	IV	23,000	1958

COOK ISLANDS/ILES COOK

Summary/Sommaire		
Category\Catégorie IV	1	160
Total	**1**	**160**

National Parks/Parcs nationaux			
Suwarrow Atoll	IV	160	1978

COSTA RICA

Summary/Sommaire		
Category\Catégorie I	6	29,356
Category\Catégorie II	11	446,328
Category\Catégorie IV	8	124,646
Category\Catégorie V	3	5,670
Total	**28**	**606,000**

National Parks/Parcs nationaux
Barra Honda	V	2,295	1974
Braulio Carrillo	II	44,099	1978
Cahuita	V	1,067	1970
Chirripo	II	50,150	1975
Corcovado	II	41,788	1975
Cordillera de Talamanca	II	193,929	1982
Guanacaste	II	32,512	1989
Isla del Coco	II	2,400	1978
Palo Verde	II	5,704	1980
Rinco del Viejo Volcan	II	14,083	1973
Santa Rosa	II	37,117	1971
Tortuguero	II	18,946	1975
Volcan Irazu	V	2,308	1955
Volcan Poas	II	5,600	1970

Biological Reserves/Réserves biologiques
Cabo Blanco	I	1,172	1963
Carara	I	4,700	1978
Hitoy-Cerere	I	9,154	1978
Isla del Cano	IV	200	1978
La Selva	I	1,430	1968
Lomas Barbudal	IV	2,279	1986
Monteverde Cloud Forest	I	10,500	1972

National Wildlife Refuges/Refuges nationaux de faune
et de flore sauvages
Rafael Lucas (Palo Verde)	IV	7,524	1979

Wildlife Refuges/Refuges de ressources sauvages
Barra del Colorado	IV	92,000	1985
Cano Negro	IV	9,669	1984
Gandoca y Manzanillo	IV	5,013	1985
Golfito	IV	2,830	1985
Penas Blancas	IV	2,400	1985
Tapanti	IV	5,131	1982

COTE D'IVOIRE

Summary/Sommaire		
Category\Catégorie I	2	128,000
Category\Catégorie II	8	1,789,500
Category\Catégorie IV	2	102,350
Total	**12**	**2,019,850**

National Parks/Parcs nationaux

Azagny	II	19,000	1981
Banco	II	30,000	1953
Comoe	II	1,150,000	1968
Iles Ehotile	II	10,500	1974
Marahoue	II	101,000	1968
Mont Peko	II	34,000	1968
Mont Sangbe	II	95,000	1976
Tai	II	350,000	1973

Strict Nature Reserves/Réserves strictes de nature

Mont Nimba	I	5,000	1944

Fauna and Flora Reserves/Réserves de faune et de flore

Haut Bandama	I	123,000	1973

Botanical Reserves/Réserves botaniques

Divo	IV	7,350	1975

Partial Faunal Reserves/Réserves fauniques partielles

N'Zo	IV	95,000	1972

CUBA

Summary/Sommaire		
Category\Catégorie I	7	45,224
Category\Catégorie II	11	397,420
Category\Catégorie IV	6	145,692
Category\Catégorie V	5	125,888
Total	**29**	**714,224**

National Parks/Parcs nationaux

Baitiquiri-Cajobabo	II	11,000	
Cienaga de Lanier	II	26,000	
Desembarco del Granma	II	25,764	1986
El Faro	II	5,700	
La Cienega de Zapata	II	50,000	1959
La Guira	II	5,500	
Peninsular de Zapata	II	175,000	
Pico Potrerillo	II	11,500	
Sierra de Cubitas	II	26,000	
Sierra del Cristal	II	26,305	1930

Marine National Parks/Parcs nationaux marins

Cayo Sabinal	II	34,651	1986

Natural Reserves/Réserves naturelles

Cabo Corrientes	I	1,578	1963
Cayo Caguanes	I	12,500	1963
Cayo Cantiles	I	6,800	1986
Cayo Romano	IV	82,554	1986
Cayo Rosario	I	5,000	1986
Cupeyal del Norte	I	10,260	1963
Jaguani	I	4,932	1963
Peninsula de Saetia	I	4,154	1986

Faunal Refuges/Refuges fauniques

Cayo Coco	V	27,188	1986
Cayo Fragoso	IV	7,500	
Cayo Gauyaba	IV	10,455	1986
Cayo Saetia	IV	6,800	
Habonica	IV	3,383	1986
Las Salinas	IV	35,000	

Touristic Natural Areas/Aires naturelles touristiques

Baconao	V	19,700	1986
Cayo Largo	V	37,000	1986
Jibacoa Bacunayagua	V	30,000	1986
Punta Pedernales-Cabo Frances	V	12,000	1986

CYPRUS/CHYPRE

No Areas Listed/pas de sites

CZECHOSLOVAKIAT/CHECOSLOVAQUIE

Summary/Sommaire		
Category\Catégorie I	5	14,069
Category\Catégorie II	5	199,724
Category\Catégorie III	1	1,517
Category\Catégorie IV	13	40,181
Category\Catégorie V	37	1,708,198
Total	**61**	**1,963,689**

National Parks/Parcs nationaux

Krkonose	V	38,500	1963
Mala Fatra	II	22,630	1988
Nizke Tatry	II	81,095	1978
Pieninsky	II	2,125	1967
Slovensky raj	II	19,763	1988
Tatransky	II	74,111	1948

National Nature Reserves/Réserves naturelles nationales

Adrspassko Teplicke skaly	IV	1,772	1933
Choc	IV	1,428	1982
Dropie	IV	5,658	1955
Dumbier	IV	2,043	1973
Janska dolina	IV	1,696	1984
Javorina	IV	11,589	1954
Karlstejn	IV	1,547	1955
Kokorinky dul	I	2,097	1953
Modravske slati	I	3,615	1989
Prameny labe	I	2,884	1980
Prameny upy	I	4,280	1980
Salatin	I	1,193	1982
Stara Reka	IV	1,197	1956
Tlsta	IV	3,066	1981

Vltavsky Luh	IV	1,845	1989
Vychodokrkonosska	IV	2,820	1952
Zapadokrkonosska	IV	4,518	1952
Protected Landscape Areas/Aires de paysages protégés			
Beskydy	V	116,000	1973
Biele Karpaty	V	43,519	1979
Bile Karpaty	V	71,500	1980
Blanik	V	4,000	1981
Blansky les	V	21,235	1989
Cerova vrchovina	V	16,280	1989
Ceske stredohori	V	107,000	1976
Cesky kras	V	13,000	1972
Cesky raj	V	12,500	1955
Horna Orava	V	70,333	1979
Jeseniky	V	75,000	1969
Jizerske hory	V	35,000	1967
Kokorinsko	V	27,000	1976
Krivoklatsko	V	62,792	1978
Kysuce	V	65,462	1984
Labske Piskovce	V	30,000	1972
Luzicke Hory	V	35,000	1976
Male Karpaty	V	65,504	1976
Moravsky kras	V	12,000	1956
Muranska planina	V	21,930	1976
Orlicke hory	V	20,000	1969
Palava	V	7,000	1976
Podyji	V	10,300	1978
Polana	V	20,079	1981
Ponitrie	V	37,665	1985
Slavkovsky les	V	64,000	1974
Slovensky kras	V	36,165	1973
Stiavnicke vrchy	V	77,630	1979
Strazovske vrchy	V	30,979	1989
Sumava	V	160,000	1963
Trebonsko	V	70,000	1979
Velka Fatra	V	60,610	1973
Vihorlat	V	4,383	1973
Vychodne Karpaty	V	66,810	1977
Zahorie	V	27,522	1988
Zdarske vrchy	V	71,500	1970
Natural Areas/Aires naturelles			
Demanovske jaskyne	III	1,517	1972
Udoli Oslavy a Chvojnice	IV	1,002	1975

DENMARK/DANEMARK

Summary/Sommaire		
Category\Catégorie I	5	1,058,877
Category\Catégorie II	1	70,000,000
Category\Catégorie III	2	6,290
Category\Catégorie IV	17	78,742
Category\Catégorie V	42	328,609
Total	**67**	**71,472,518**

Scientific Reserves/Réserves scientifiques

Vejlerne	IV	5,000	1960

Nature Reserves/Réserves de nature

Esrum So and Gribskor	IV	7,280	
Flyndersoe and Stubbergard Soe	IV	1,670	
Hansted	IV	6,500	
Skagen	IV	4,300	
Tipperne	I	3,520	1936
Tisvilde, Melby	IV	2,000	

Major Conservation Areas/Aires de conservation importantes

Aalvand Klithede and Foerby Soe	V	1,200	1977
Agger Tange	IV	6,100	1984
Anholt	V	1,856	1939
Bognaes, Kattinge Vig	V	1,200	1969
Borris Hede	V	1,830	1902
Bulbjerg, Lild Klit and Hjardemaal Klit	V	1,500	1947
Egtved and Vejle River Valleys	V	1,025	1980
Esrum Soe and Surrounding Areas	V	1,900	1952
Fanoe	V	1,400	1964
Flyndersoe-Stubbergaard Soe	V	16,700	1934
Hanstholm Reserve	IV	4,800	1972
Harbooere Tange	V	2,400	1984
Hesseloe Sea Area	V	5,000	1982
Hoeje Moen	III	2,090	1980
Hulrig Klit	IV	2,144	1940
Kaergaard Klitplantage-Loevklitterne-Lyngbos	V	1,670	1955
Konenshus Hede	V	1,300	1953
Lakes at Maribo	V	1,195	1957
Ledreborg Gods	V	1,800	1973
Lyngby, Lodbjerg, Flade Soe	V	3,327	1976
Mols Bjerge	V	2,750	1972
Noerre Hvalsoe and Kisserup Area	V	1,132	1980
Nord-Bornholm	V	2,500	1970
North Coast of Vejle Fjord	V	1,004	1949
Raabjerg Mile and Hulsig Hede	III	4,200	1962
Rands Fjord	V	1,047	1968
Roemoe	IV	2,500	1947
Roennerne	V	1,496	1980
Ryegaard Gods, Tempelkrog and Bramsnaes Vig	V	1,515	1940
Salten Langsoe, Vissingkloster, Mossoe	V	3,950	1971

Saltholm	V	1,600	1983
Skagen Klitplantage, Grenen	IV	2,175	1921
Skallingen and Langli	IV	2,400	1939
Soevind, Sondrup, Aakaer and Vorsoe	V	2,200	1974
Stavns Fjord	V	1,525	1984
Stigsnaes Peninsula	V	1,215	1978
Store Vildnore	V	2,100	1973
Sydlige Fanoe	V	1,400	1985
Toendermarsken	V	5,650	1988
Tranum Area	V	2,160	1956
Tystrup-Bavelse Soerne	V	3,750	1957
Ulfborg-Vind Area	V	1,300	1949
Ulvedybet og Nibe Breding	V	20,304	1930
Vaernengene	V	2,600	1977
Valloe	V	1,383	1981
Veststadil Fjord and Husby Klit	V	1,465	1969
Vorupoer-Stenbjerg	V	2,270	1954
Waddensea Naturereserve	V	95,000	1985
Bird Reserves/Réserves ornithologiques			
Ertholm Bird	I	1,257	
Hirsholmene Bird	I	2,000	1948
Ronner Bird (Laeso)	IV	2,923	1980
Stavnsfjord Bird	IV	16,320	1984
Totten Bird	I	2,100	
Vadehavet Bird	V	120,000	1979
Protected Regions/Régions protégées			
Selso-Lindholm-Bognaes	V	1,990	
Nature Parks/Parcs naturels			
Farum	IV	5,000	
Gudenaens	IV	6,500	
Ulvshale and Nyord	IV	1,130	

Faeroes/Féroés

No Areas Listed/pas de sites

Greenland/Groenland

National Parks/Parcs nationaux			
Greenland	II	70,000,000	1974
Nature Reserves/Réserves de nature			
Melville Bay	I	1,050,000	1977

DJIBOUTI

Summary/Sommaire		
Category\Catégorie II	1	10,000
Total	**1**	**10,000**

National Parks/Parcs nationaux			
Foret du Day	II	10,000	1939

DOMINICA/DOMINIQUE

Summary/Sommaire		
Category\Catégorie II	1	6,840
Total	**1**	**6,840**

National Parks/Parcs nationaux

Morne Trois Pitons	II	6,840	1975

DOMINICAN REPUBLIC/REPUBLIQUE DOMINICAINE

Summary/Sommaire		
Category\Catégorie II	9	491,875
Category\Catégorie IV	5	59,634
Total	**14**	**551,509**

National Parks/Parcs nationaux

Del Este	II	43,400	1975
Isla Cabritos	II	2,600	1974
J. Armando Bermudez	II	76,600	1956
J. del Carmen Ramirez	II	76,400	1958
Jaragua	II	137,400	1983
La Caleta Submarine	IV	1,010	1986
Litoral Sur de Santo Domingo	II	1,075	1968
Los Haitises	II	20,800	1976
Monte Cristi	II	53,600	1983
Sierra de Bahoruco	II	80,000	1983

Scientific Reserves/Réserves scientifiques

Isabel de Torres Natural	IV	2,200	1983
Laguna Redonda y Laguna Limon Natural	IV	10,744	1983
Laguna de Rincon y Cabral Natural	IV	4,780	1983
Valle Nuevo Natural	IV	40,900	1983

DOMINIQUE
Voir paragraphe DOMINICA

ECUADOR/EQUATEUR

Summary/Sommaire		
Category\Catégorie I	3	642,565
Category\Catégorie II	6	2,014,795
Category\Catégorie IV	2	7,994,613
Category\Catégorie V	3	33,691
Total	**14**	**10,685,664**

National Parks/Parcs nationaux

Cotopaxi	II	33,393	1975
Machalilla	II	46,683	1979
Podocarpus	II	146,280	1982
Sangay	II	271,925	1975

Yasuni	II	750,000	1979
Ecological Reserves/Réserves écologiques			
Cayambe-Coca	I	403,103	1970
Cotachi-Cayapas	I	204,420	1968
Manglares-Churute	I	35,042	1979
Biological Reserves/Réserves biologiques			
Limoncocha	IV	4,613	1985
Geobotanical Reserves/Réserves géobotaniques			
Pululahua	V	3,806	1978
National Recreation Areas/Aires de loisirs nationales			
Cajas	V	28,808	1977
El Boliche	V	1,077	1979

Galapagos Islands/Iles Galapagos

National Parks/Parcs nationaux			
Galapagos	II	766,514	1936
Marine Reserves/Réserves marines			
Galapagos	IV	7,990,000	1986

EGYPT/EGYPTE

Summary/Sommaire		
Category\Catégorie I	2	21,000
Category\Catégorie II	1	17,100
Category\Catégorie IV	6	647,200
Total	**9**	**685,300**

National Marine Parks/Parcs marins nationaux			
Ras Mohammed	II	17,100	1983
Scientific Reserves/Réserves scientifiques			
Omayed	I	1,000	1986
Natural Areas/Aires naturelles			
Ashtoun el Gamil - Tanee Island	IV	1,200	1988
Bardawil Lake	IV	60,000	1985
St Catherine (Moussa)	IV	45,000	1988
Zaranikh (El Arish)	IV	12,000	1985
Conservation Areas/Aires de conservation			
Gebel Elba	IV	480,000	1986
Protected Areas/Aires protégées			
Qarun Lake (Quaron)	I	20,000	1989
Tiran-Sanafir Islands	IV	49,000	1986

EL SALVADOR

Summary/Sommaire		
Category\Catégorie II	5	18,369
Category\Catégorie III	1	2,170
Category\Catégorie IV	3	5,613
Total	**9**	**26,152**

National Parks/Parcs nationaux
Cerro Verde	II	6,500	1981
El Imposible	II	5,600	1983
Montecristo	II	3,893	1979
Nancuchiname	II	1,175	1983
Volcan de Conchagua	II	1,201	1983

Biological Reserves/Réserves biologiques
San Diego	IV	2,213	1983

Wildlife Refuges/Refuges de ressources sauvages
Barra de Santiago	IV	2,200	1983
El Jocotal	IV	1,200	1978

Natural Monuments/Monuments naturels
Lavas de San Marcelino	III	2,170	1983

EMIRATS ARAB UNIS
Voir paragraphe UNITED ARAB EMIRATES

EQUATEUR
Voir paragraphe ECUADOR

EQUATORIAL GUINEA/GUINEE EQUATORIALE
No Areas Listed/pas de sites

ESPAGNE
Voir paragraphe SPAIN

ETATS FEDERES DE MICRONESIE
Voir paragraphe FEDERATED STATES OF MICRONESIA

ETATS-UNIS D'AMERIQUE
Voir paragraphe UNITED STATES OF AMERICA

ETHIOPIA/ETHIOPIE

Summary/Sommaire		
Category\Catégorie II	13	3,240,200
Category\Catégorie IV	11	2,982,400
Total	**24**	**6,222,600**

National Parks/Parcs nationaux
Abijatta-Shalla Lakes	II	88,700	1970
Awash	II	75,600	1966
Bale Mountains	II	247,100	1969
Gambella	II	506,100	1974
Mago	II	216,200	1978
Nechisar	II	51,400	1973
Omo	II	406,800	
Simen Mountains	II	17,900	1966
Yangudi Rassa	II	473,100	1976

Marine National Parks/Parcs nationaux marins			
Dahlac	II	200,000	1968
Wildlife Reserves/Réserves de ressources sauvages			
Alledeghi	IV	183,200	1973
Awash West	IV	178,100	1973
Bale	IV	176,600	1973
Chew Bahr	IV	421,200	1973
Gash Setit	IV	70,900	1959
Gewane	IV	243,900	1973
Mille Sardo	IV	876,600	1973
Nakfa	IV	163,900	1959
Shire	IV	75,300	1973
Tama	IV	326,900	1973
Yob	IV	265,800	1959
Sanctuaries/Sanctuaires			
Babile (Elephant)	II	698,200	1970
Senkelle (Swayne's Hartebeest)	II	5,400	1972
Yabello	II	253,700	1985

FEDERATED STATES OF MICRONESIA/ETATS FEDERES DE MICRONESIE

No Areas Listed/pas de sites

FIJI/FIDJI

Summary/Sommaire		
Category\Catégorie I	2	5,342
Total	**2**	**5,342**

Nature Reserves/Réserves de nature			
Ravilevu	I	4,020	1959
Tomaniivi	I	1,322	1958

FINLAND/FINLANDE

Summary/Sommaire		
Category\Catégorie I	16	151,170
Category\Catégorie II	17	354,080
Category\Catégorie V	2	302,000
Total	**35**	**807,250**

National Parks/Parcs nationaux			
Helvetinjaervi	II	2,100	1982
Hiidenportti	II	4,000	1982
Isojaervi	II	1,900	1982
Itainen Suomenlahti	II	800	1981
Kauhaneva-Pohjakangas	II	3,150	1982
Lauhanvuori	II	2,650	1982
Lemmenjoki	II	280,000	1956
Linnansaari	II	3,820	1956

Oulanka	II	20,170	1956
Pallas-Ounastunturi	V	50,000	1938
Patvinsuo	II	8,800	1982
Pyhae-Haekki	II	1,350	1956
Pyhaetunturi	II	4,100	1938
Riisitunturi	II	7,600	1982
Salamajaervi	II	5,530	1982
Seitseminen	II	3,060	1982
Skargaardshavet	II	3,000	1983
Tiilikkajaervi	II	2,050	1982
Urho Kekkonen	V	252,000	1983

Strict Nature Reserves/Réserves strictes de nature

Jussaro	I	2,400	1956
Kevo	I	71,000	1956
Koivusuo	I	2,100	1982
Malla	I	2,950	1938
Maltio	I	14,700	1956
Olvassuo	I	6,000	1982
Paljakka	I	2,660	1956
Pelso	I	1,800	1982
Pisavaara	I	5,000	1956
Runkaus	I	7,150	1956
Salamanpera	I	1,270	1956
Sompio	I	17,600	1956
Sukerijaervi	I	1,900	1982
Ulvinsalo	I	2,500	1956
Vaerrioe	I	11,000	1982
Vaskijarvi	I	1,140	1956

FRANCE

Summary/Sommaire		
Category\Catégorie I	6	39,624
Category\Catégorie II	7	279,966
Category\Catégorie IV	57	226,341
Category\Catégorie V	33	4,441,860
Total	**103**	**4,987,791**

National Parks/Parcs nationaux

Cevennes	V	84,800	1970
Ecrins	II	91,800	1973
Mercantour	II	68,500	1979
Port Cros	II	2,494	1963
Pyrenees Occidentales	II	45,700	1967
Vanoise	II	52,839	1963

Pre-parcs/Pré-Parcs

Cevennes pre-parc	V	228,000	1970
Ecrins pre-parc	V	178,600	1973
Mercantour pre-parc	V	200,000	1979

Pyrenees Occidentales pre-parc	V	206,000	1967
Vanoise pre-parc	V	145,000	1963
Nature Reserves/Réserves de nature			
Aiguilles Rouges	IV	3,279	1974
Baie de Bourgneuf	IV	4,200	
Camargue	I	13,117	1975
Casabianda	IV	1,760	1978
Cherine I	I	1,987	
Contamines-Montjoie	IV	5,500	1979
Foret domaniale du Fango	IV	6,410	1977
Foret diominiale de Cerisy	IV	2,124	1976
Gorges de l'Ardeche	IV	1,572	1980
Grande Sassiere	IV	2,230	1973
Haut Plateaux du Vercors	IV	16,661	1985
Ile St Aubin	IV	2,500	
Iles Lavezzi	IV	5,170	1982
Lac de Grandlieu	IV	2,695	1980
Lac de la Foret d'Orient	IV	2,300	
Mantet	IV	3,028	1984
Moeze	IV	6,700	1985
Mont Ventron	IV	1,647	1989
Montjoie et Passy	IV	2,000	1980
Neouvielle	IV	2,313	1968
Nohedes	IV	2,137	1986
Passy	IV	2,000	1980
Prats de Mollo	IV	2,185	1986
Py	IV	3,929	1984
Scandola	I	1,670	1975
Sept-Iles	I	280	1976
Sixt-Passy	IV	9,200	1977
Val d'Isere – Bonneval-sur-Arc	IV	1,491	1963
Ventron Massif	IV	1,647	1989
Marine Reserves/Réserves marines			
Abers du Leon	IV	2,020	
Archipel de Glenon	IV	3,800	
Baie de Seine and marshes	IV	7,800	
Etang de Bages and Sigean	IV	1,700	
Fiers d'Ars and Fosse de Loix	IV	1,300	
CELRL Sites/Acquisitions CELRL			
Etang de Vic	IV	1,338	1975
Ile Sainte Lucie	IV	227	1975
La Cote Bleue	IV	3,070	1975
Les Agriates	IV	3,933	1975
Marine Parks/Parcs marins			
Cote Bleue	V	3,070	1982
Regional Nature Parks/Parcs naturels régionaux			
Armorique	V	65,000	1969
Ballons des Vosges	V	234,000	1989
Briere	V	40,000	1970
Brotonne	V	40,000	1974

Camargue	V	85,000	1970
Corse	V	200,000	1972
Foret d'Orient	V	70,000	1970
Haut Languedoc	V	145,000	1973
Haut-Jura	V	62,088	1986
Haute Vallee de Chevreuse	V	25,600	1985
Landes de Gascogne	V	206,000	1970
Livradois-Forez	V	297,000	1986
Lorraine	V	205,000	1974
Luberon	V	120,000	1977
Marais Poitevin	V	200,000	1979
Montagne de Reims	V	50,000	1976
Morvan	V	173,000	1970
Nord-Pas-de-Calais	V	146,000	1986
Normandie-Maine	V	234,000	1975
Pilat	V	65,000	1974
Queyras	V	60,000	1977
Vercors	V	135,000	1970
Volcans d'Auvergne	V	347,778	1977
Vosges du Nord	V	120,000	1976
Fishing Reserves/Réserves de pêche			
Calvi	IV	1,075	1978
Porto-Vecchio	IV	1,615	1978
Saint Florent	IV	2,440	1977
Tuccia-Sagone-Cargese	IV	1,620	1978
Ventilegne	IV	1,000	1977

Guadeloupe

National Parks/Parcs nationaux			
Guadeloupe	II	17,500	1989
Natural Reserves/Réserves naturelles			
Grand Cul de Sac Marine	IV	3,700	1987

French Guiana/Guyane française

No Areas Listed/pas de sites

Martinique

Regional Nature Parks/Parcs naturels régionaux			
Martinique	V	70,150	1976

Reunion/Réunion

Nature Reserves/Réserves de nature			
Hauts de St Phillipe	IV	3,500	1987
Mazerin	IV	1,869	1984

Other French islands/Autres îles françaises

No Areas Listed/pas de sites

French Southern Territories/Terres australes français

National Parks/Parcs nationaux
Antarctique francaise	IV	36,700	1924

New Caledonia/Nouvelle-Caledonie

Strict Nature Reserves/Réserves strictes de nature
Montagne des Sources	I	5,870	1950

Marine Reserves/Réserves marines
Yves Merlet	I	16,700	1970

Fauna and Flora Reserves/Réserves de faune et de flore
Maitre and Amedee Islets	V	774	1981

Faunal Reserves/Réserves fauniques
Aoupinie	IV	5,400	1975
Haute Yate (Riv. Blanche and Riv. Bleue TP)	IV	15,900	1960
Lepredour Islet	IV	760	1941
Pam Island	IV	460	1966

Botanical Reserves/Réserves botaniques
Foret de Saille	IV	1,100	1983
Mont Humboldt	IV	3,200	1950
Mont Panie	IV	5,000	1950
Southern	IV	4,466	1972

Territorial Parks/Parcs territoriaux
Thy	II	1,133	1980

Forest Reserves/Réserves forestières
Mont Mou	IV	4,363	

French Polynesia/Polynesie Française

Strict Nature Reserves/Réserves strictes de nature
Taiaro Atoll (W.A. Robinson)	IV	2,000	1977

Reserves/Réserves
Eiao Island	IV	5,180	1971
Hatutu Island	IV	1,813	1971

Unclassified/Non classé
Mohotani	IV	1,554	1971

Wallis and Futuna/Wallis et Futuna

No Areas Listed/pas de sites

GABON

Summary/Sommaire		
Category\Catégorie I	1	480,000
Category\Catégorie IV	4	1,310,000
Total	**5**	**1,790,000**

Strict Nature Reserves/Réserves strictes de nature
Ipassa-Makokou	IV	10,000	1970

Wildlife Management Area/Aires d'exploitation
rationnelle de faune

Lope	IV	500,000	1962
Moukalaba-Dougoula	IV	100,000	1962
Sette-Cama	IV	700,000	1966

Presidential Reserves/Réserves présidentielles

Wonga-Wongue	I	480,000	1967

GAMBIA/GAMBIE

Summary/Sommaire		
Category\Catégorie II	2	12,000
Total	**2**	**12,000**

National Parks/Parcs nationaux

Gambia Saloum/Niumi	II	2,000	1987
Kiang West	II	10,000	1987

GERMAN DEMOCRATIC REPUBLIC/REPUBLIQUE DEMOCRATIQUE ALLEMANDE

Summary/Sommaire		
Category\Catégorie IV	26	36,486
Category\Catégorie V	199	1,961,682
Total	**225**	**1,998,168**

Since this list was compiled, the Federal Republic of Germany and the German Democratic Republic have combined to form an enlarged Federal Republic of Germany.

Depuis de la réalisation de la présente liste, la République fédérale d'Allemagne et la République démocratique allemande ont fusionné pour former la République fédérale d'Allemagne.

Nature Reserves/Réserves de nature

Alter Stolberg	V	4,520	1970
Anklamer Stadtbruch	IV	1,200	1967
Bucher Brack - Bolsdorfer Haken	IV	1,008	1978
Der Bock und Hohe Duene Pramort	IV	1,832	1957
Fischteiche in der Lewitz	IV	1,732	1967
Galenbecker See	IV	1,015	1967
Grosser Winterberg und Zschand	IV	1,069	1961
Hinrichshagen	IV	1,124	1967
Insel Hiddesec	V	1,860	1955
Insel Oie und Kirr	IV	418	1967
Insel Pulitz	IV	149	1937
Insel Usedom	V	37,500	1966
Inseln Bohmke und Werder	IV	118	1971
Inseln Oie und Kirr	IV	450	1967
Inseln im Senftenberger See	IV	899	1981
Jasmund	IV	1,500	1935
Oberharz	IV	1,980	1967
Ostufer der Muritz	IV	4,832	1967

Peenemunder Haken, Struck und Ruden	IV	1,870	1925
Peenetal-Moor	IV	1,478	1981
Seegrund Ahlbeck	IV	1,166	
Serrahn	IV	1,708	1961
Stechlin	IV	2,140	1938
Steckby-Loedderitzer Forst	IV	3,550	1961
Uhlstaedter Heide	IV	1,082	1981
Untere Mulde	IV	1,137	1961
Vessertal	IV	1,649	1939
Vogelinsel Heuwiese und Freesenort	IV	250	1961
Westdarsz und Darszer Ort mit Bernsteininsel	IV	1,130	1957
Landscape Protected Areas/Aires de paysages protégés			
Aga-und Elstertal	V	2,796	1968
Augustusburg-Sternmuhlental	V	1,487	1968
Bad Freienwalde	V	4,340	1965
Barlebener-Jerslebener See mit Elbniederung	V	3,548	1964
Bleicheroder Berge	V	4,103	1970
Blumberger Forst	V	1,960	1965
Bodeniederung	V	7,200	1975
Boxberg-Reichwalder Wald-und Wiesengebiet	V	1,157	1968
Brandenburger Wald-und Seengebiet	V	16,270	1966
Briesetal und Muhlenbecker See	V	3,175	1966
Burgsteinlandschaft	V	2,808	1968
Calau-Altdobern-Reddern	V	4,800	1968
Choriner Endmoranenbogen	V	16,500	1957
Colditzer Forest	V	4,600	1963
Dahlener Heide	V	16,700	1963
Dammuhlenteich	V	1,036	1974
Dippoldiswalder Heide und Wilisch	V	2,420	1974
Dobbertiner Seen u.s.w.	V	12,100	1964
Dobbin-Zietlitzer Feldmark	V	2,000	1938
Dolgener und Hohensprenzer See	V	1,500	1961
Dreigleichen	V	1,698	1960
Dresdener Heide	V	5,876	1971
Dubener Heide	V	11,380	1961
Duen-Helbetal	V	5,600	1963
Eisenberger Holzland	V	1,828	1983
Elbaue Martinskirchen-Muhlberg	V	1,490	1968
Elbhange Dresden-Pirna und Schonfelder Hoch.	V	3,540	1974
Elbtal nordlich von Meissen	V	2,320	1960
Elsteraue	V	10,000	1937
Elsteraue und Teichlandschaft u.s.w.	V	1,860	1968
Elsteraue zwischen Herzberg und Ubigau	V	2,160	1968
Elsterniederung u.s.w.	V	19,650	1968
Endmoranenzug Brohmer u.s.w.	V	5,000	1962
Fahner Hohe	V	4,950	1970
Feldberger Seenlandschaft	V	7,000	1962
Fischland-Darss-Zingst	V	15,000	1966
Flaming	V	38,670	1961
Flemsdorf	V	1,720	1965

Freiberger Mulde-Zschopau	V	7,000	1963
Friedewald und Moritzburger Teichgebiet	V	5,565	1977
Gamengrund	V	2,390	1965
Gebiet um Bad Wilsnack	V	2,700	1964
Geraer Stadtwald	V	1,575	1972
Gotzer Berge	V	2,325	1966
Grabentour	V	2,864	1968
Grosser See bei Furstenwerder	V	1,200	1962
Grosser und Kleiner Gleichberg	V	1,988	1939
Grosssteinberg-Ammelshain	V	2,440	1963
Grunau-Grunheider Wald-und Seengebiet	V	21,700	1965
Gubener Fliesstaler	V	3,200	1968
Gulitzer Endmorane und Kummerower See	V	9,000	1962
Haffkuste	V	12,500	1962
Hainleite	V	5,976	1970
Hakel	V	1,425	1939
Harbke-Allertal	V	22,770	1975
Harz	V	154,700	1960
Havelquellseen Kratzeburg	V	2,600	1962
Heiligenstadter Stadtwald	V	3,025	1960
Helmestausee	V	1,717	1970
Hiddensee	V	1,860	1955
Hildburghauser Wald	V	5,250	1978
Hohburger Berge	V	2,000	1963
Hohes Holz-Saures Holz mit ostlicem Vorland	V	7,240	1964
Ilmtal	V	19,850	1960
Insel Usedom	V	37,500	1966
Inselsee und Heidberg	V	1,300	1964
Jessener Berge	V	1,025	1968
Kleinseenplatte Neustrelitz	V	12,000	1962
Klocksiner Seenkette	V	20,000	1962
Knappensee	V	1,100	1968
Kohrener Land	V	17,000	1959
Konigshainer Berge	V	4,855	1974
Korbaer Teich und Lebusaer Waldgebiet	V	2,258	1968
Kothener See	V	1,790	1966
Krakower Seenlandschaft	V	2,350	1955
Kuhberg-Steinicht	V	1,377	1968
Kuhlung	V	14,000	1966
Kyffhauser	V	7,722	1941
Kyritzer Seenkette	V	1,600	1958
Lausitzer Grenzwall zwischen u.s.w.	V	14,235	1968
Lauta-Hoyerswerda-Wittichenau	V	2,920	1968
Lehniner Wald- und Seengebiet	V	2,525	1966
Leipziger Auewald	V	5,700	1959
Lewitz	V	12,000	1959
Lindenthaler Forst	V	4,070	1975
Lindhorst-Ramstedter Forst	V	5,996	1964
Linkselbische Taler zwiscen u.s.w.	V	2,355	1974
Ludwigsluster Schlosspark u.s.w.	V	1,500	1955

Lychen-Boitzenburg	V	7,500	1962
Madlitz-Falenhagener Seengebiet	V	1,030	1965
Malchiner Becken	V	6,000	1962
Markische Schweiz	V	3,800	1957
Merzdorf-Hirschfelder Waldhohen	V	2,060	1968
Mittelelbe	V	48,200	1957
Mittelheide	V	2,500	1969
Mittlere Mulde	V	9,700	1963
Mittlerer Strelasund	V	2,300	1966
Mittleres Saaletal	V	19,150	1972
Mittleres Warnowtal	V	8,500	1964
Mittleres Zschopautal	V	1,487	1968
Mockern-Magdeburgerforth	V	29,140	1975
Muhlhauser Stadtwald	V	3,496	1970
Muldental-Chemnitzal	V	11,471	1968
Muritz-Seen-Park	V	30,000	1962
Nauen-Brieselang	V	3,225	1966
Naunhof-Brandiser Forst	V	2,750	1963
Neisseaue im Kreis Forst	V	1,330	1968
Neuendorfer See	V	1,600	1968
Neuruppin-Rheinsberg u.s.w.	V	80,200	1966
Noitzscher-und Prellheide	V	1,500	1963
Nordliches Harzvorland	V	13,506	1961
Ober-Uecker-See	V	5,400	1962
Obere Saale	V	21,240	1965
Oberes Vogtland	V	17,100	1968
Oberes Westerzgebirge	V	17,015	1981
Oberes Zschopautal	V	8,207	1968
Oberlausitzer Bergland	V	30,730	1963
Osterzgebirge	V	55,025	1968
Ostrand der Arendseer Hochflache	V	7,210	1964
Ostrugen	V	47,500	1966
Parthenaue-Machern	V	1,300	1963
Peitzer Teichlandschaft mit Hammergraben	V	2,040	1968
Petersberg	V	1,730	1961
Plauer See	V	3,500	1957
Plothener Teichgebiet	V	1,896	1961
Potsdamer Havelseengebiet	V	16,250	1966
Pressnitztal	V	2,300	1984
Rabensteiner Wald-Pfaffenberg	V	1,280	1962
Rambower und Rudower See	V	1,500	1960
Rathenower Wald-und Seengebiet	V	17,325	1966
Rennsteigstreifen	V	3,900	1940
Rinne-Rotenbachtal	V	6,976	1970
Rippachtal	V	2,880	1968
Rodderaue	V	1,720	1960
Rotehofbachtal	V	2,444	1964
Saale	V	28,550	1961
Sachsische Schweiz	V	36,810	1956
Saidenbachtalsperre	V	4,490	1962

Salzwedel-Diesdorf	V	13,310	1975
Schaalsee und Heckenlandschaft Techin	V	2,500	1958
Scharmutzelsee-Storkower u.s.w.	V	10,600	1965
Schlaubetal	V	6,490	1965
Schweriner Seenlandschaft	V	4,300	1938
Schwielochsee	V	4,440	1965
Seendreieck bei Furstensee	V	3,200	1962
Seengebiet Warin-Neukloster	V	7,500	1938
Seenkette bei Comthurey	V	1,200	1962
Sewekow	V	2,850	1966
Spree-und Teichgebiet sudlich Uhyst	V	1,210	1968
Spreeniederung	V	1,850	1974
Spreewald	V	28,700	1968
Sprottetal	V	1,100	1984
Stadtwald Berlin	V	7,548	1972
Staubeckenlandschaft Brasinchen-Spremberg	V	2,925	1968
Steigerwald	V	1,188	1970
Stepenitztal	V	1,600	1958
Strausberger und Blumenthaler	V	6,120	1965
Striegistaler	V	4,233	1968
Sudlich von Zwickau	V	6,200	1968
Sudlicher Dromling	V	2,556	1967
Susser See	V	3,820	1954
Tal der Wilden Weisseritz	V	1,415	1960
Talsperre Kriebstein	V	1,162	1968
Talsperre Pirk	V	1,432	1940
Talsperre Pohl	V	2,300	1962
Talsperre Quitzdorf und Kollmer Hohen	V	4,417	1974
Templiner Seenkreuz	V	11,500	1962
Teupitz-Koriser Seengebiet	V	23,317	1966
Tharandter Wald	V	5,440	1974
Thummlitzwald	V	11,500	1984
Thuringer Wald	V	151,613	1963
Thuringische Rhon	V	61,500	1989
Tollense-Becken	V	10,000	1962
Torgelower See	V	3,000	1962
Triebischtaler	V	1,940	1974
Uchte-Tangerquellen	V	6,681	1975
Untere Havel	V	21,940	1967
Wald- und Restseengebiet Dobern	V	1,850	1968
Wald-u.Seengeb.z.Schwielochsee,Libe.u.Spree.	V	3,850	1968
Walder um Greiz und Werdau	V	5,525	1961
Waldgebiet Huy	V	1,561	1939
Waldgebiet bei Crivitz u. Barniner See	V	1,000	1964
Waldgebiet des Fallstein	V	1,375	1939
Wallensteingraben	V	2,000	1966
Wandlitz-Biesenthal-Prendener Seegebiet	V	5,600	1965
Webellinsee--Grimnitzsee	V	3,790	1965
Weidatalsperre	V	1,680	1961
Wermsdorfer Forst	V	13,000	1963

Westlausitz	V	29,070	1974
Wiesen-und Teichgebiet Eulo und Jamno	V	1,440	1968
Wiesen-und Teichlandschaft Kolkwitz-Hanchen	V	2,020	1968
Wolletzseengebiet	V	7,000	1965
Zeitzgrund	V	1,291	1958
Zichtauer Berge und Klotzer Forst	V	10,800	1964
Zittauer Gebirge	V	6,270	1958
Zuwachs-Kulzauer Forst	V	5,040	1975

GERMANY, FEDERAL REPUBLIC OF/ALLEMAGNE, REPUBLIQUE FEDERALE D'

Summary/Sommaire		
Category\Catégorie II	1	13,100
Category\Catégorie IV	28	132,988
Category\Catégorie V	25	2,809,792
Total	**54**	**2,955,880**

Since this list was compiled, the Federal Republic of Germany and the German Democratic Republic have combined to form an enlarged Federal Republic of Germany.

Depuis de la réalisation de la présente liste, la République fédérale d'Allemagne et la République démocratique allemande ont fusionné pour former la République fédérale d'Allemagne.

National Parks/Parcs nationaux

Bayerischer Wald	II	13,100	1969
Berchtesgaden	V	20,800	1978
Niedersachsisches Wattenmeer	V	240,000	1986
Wattenmeer (Hamburg)	V	11,000	1990
Wattenmeer (Schleswig-Holstein)	V	285,000	1985

Nature Reserves/Réserves de nature

Ammergebirge	IV	28,850	1963
Baerguendle Oytal and Hoefats	IV	3,850	
Die Lucie	IV	1,800	
Dollart	IV	2,140	
Eggstatt-Hemhofer Seenplatte	IV	1,000	
Federsee	IV	1,400	1939
Feldberg	IV	3,231	
Hahnheide	IV	1,450	
Hoher Ifen	IV	2,430	
Isarauen zwischen schaefrlorn und Bad Toelz	IV	1,663	
Karwendel und Karwendelvorgebirge	IV	19,100	1959
Krickenbecker Seen	IV	1,240	
Kuehkopf-knoblochsaue	IV	2,369	
Laacher See	IV	2,100	
Lange Rhoen	IV	2,657	
Langeeog	IV	600	
Luneburger Heide	IV	19,720	1920
Nord-Sylt	IV	1,796	1969
Oberharz	IV	7,030	1954
Oestliche Chiemgauer Alpen	IV	9,500	

Retterschwanger Tal mit Daumen	IV	2,100	
Saupark	IV	2,480	
Schachen und Reintal	IV	4,000	
Schliffkopf	IV	1,380	
Siebengebirge	IV	4,200	
Spiekeroog Ostplate	IV	885	
Wahner Heide	IV	2,630	
Wurzacher Reid	IV	1,387	
Nature Parks/Parcs naturels			
Altmuhltal	V	290,800	1969
Augburg-Westliche Walder	V	117,500	1974
Bayerische Rhon	V	124,000	1967
Bayerischer Spessart	V	171,000	1963
Bergstrase Odenwald	V	162,850	1960
Dummer	V	47,210	1972
Fichtelgebirge	V	100,400	1971
Franken Wald	V	97,170	1973
Frankenhohe	V	110,450	1974
Frankische Schweiz-Veldensteiner Forst	V	234,600	1988
Hasberge	V	80,400	1974
Hessenreuther und Manteler Wald	V	27,000	1975
Hoher Vogelsberg	V	38,447	1958
Nordeifel	V	175,116	1960
Oberpfelzer Wald	V	72,385	1971
Pfalzerwald	V	179,850	1959
Schonbuch	V	15,564	1974
Siebengebirge	V	4,200	1959
Solling-Vogler	V	52,750	1966
Steigerwald	V	128,000	1971
Steinwald	V	23,300	1970

GHANA

Summary/Sommaire		
Category\Catégorie I	1	32,400
Category\Catégorie II	5	1,029,795
Category\Catégorie IV	2	12,442
Total	**8**	**1,074,637**

National Parks/Parcs nationaux			
Bia	II	7,770	1974
Bui	II	207,360	1971
Digya	II	312,595	1971
Mole	II	491,440	1971
Nini-Suhien	II	10,630	1976
Strict Nature Reserves/Réserves strictes de nature			
Kogyae	I	32,400	1976
Wildlife Sanctuaries/Sanctuaires de ressources sauvages			
Bomfobiri	IV	5,184	1975
Owabi	IV	7,258	1971

GREECE/GRECE

Summary/Sommaire		
Category\Catégorie II	8	52,642
Category\Catégorie III	2	18,000
Category\Catégorie IV	5	10,633
Category\Catégorie V	5	22,428
Total	**20**	**103,703**

National Parks/Parcs nationaux

Ainos	II	2,862	1962
Mount Oita	II	7,210	1966
Mount Olympos	II	3,998	1938
Parnassos	II	3,513	1938
Parnitha	II	3,812	1961
Pindos	II	6,927	1966
Prespes	II	19,470	1974
Samaria	II	4,850	1962
Sounion	V	3,500	1974
Vikos-Aoos	V	12,600	1973

Game Refuges/Refuges de faune

Dadia-Lefkimi and Soufli Forest	IV	7,200	1986

Breeding Stations/Stations d'élevage

Antimilos Island	IV	745	1963

Natural Monuments/Monuments naturels

Petrified Forest of Lesbos Island	III	15,000	1985
Piperi Island	IV	438	1980

Aesthetic Forests/Forêts esthétiques

Kalavrita	V	1,750	1977
Kavala	V	2,816	1979
Skiathos Island	III	3,000	1977
Tembi Valley	V	1,762	1974

Controlled Hunting Areas/Zones de chasse surveillées

Dias Island	IV	1,250	1977
Gioura Island	IV	1,000	1979

GRENADA/GRENADE
No Areas Listed/pas de sites

GUATEMALA

Summary/Sommaire		
Category\Catégorie II	2	67,400
Category\Catégorie III	1	2,000
Category\Catégorie IV	4	14,706
Category\Catégorie V	2	4,166
Total	**9**	**88,272**

National Parks/Parcs nationaux

Laguna Lachua	II	10,000	1978

Santa Rosalia	V	1,000	1956
Tikal	II	57,400	1957
Volcan de Pacaya	III	2,000	1963
Biotopes/Biotopes			
Chocon-Machacas	IV	6,400	1981
Mario Dary Rivera (Quetzal)	IV	1,153	1976
Monterrico	IV	6,000	1977
University Biotope for Conservation of Quetzal	IV	1,153	1977
Protected Areas/Aires protégées			
Dos Pilas Cultural Monument	V	3,166	

GUINEA/GUINEE

Summary/Sommaire		
Category\Catégorie I	2	129,170
Total	**2**	**129,170**

Strict Nature Reserves/Réserves strictes de nature
Massif du Ziama	I	116,170	1932
Mount Nimba	I	13,000	1944

GUINEA-BISSAU/GUINEE-BISSAU
No Areas Listed/pas de sites

GUINEE
Voir paragraphe GUINEA

GUINEE-BISSAU
Voir paragraphe GUINEA-BISSAU

GUINEE EQUATORIALE
Voir paragraphe EQUATORIAL GUINEA

GUYANA

Summary/Sommaire		
Category\Catégorie II	1	11,655
Total	**1**	**11,655**

National Parks/Parcs nationaux
Kaieteur	II	11,655	1929

HAITI

Summary/Sommaire		
Category\Catégorie II	2	7,700
Total	**2**	**7,700**

National Parks/Parcs nationaux

La Visite	II	2,200	1983
Macaya	II	5,500	1983

HOLY SEE/SAINT SIEGE
No Areas Listed/pas de sites

HONDURAS

Summary/Sommaire		
Category\Catégorie II	14	588,616
Category\Catégorie IV	20	120,753
Total	**34**	**709,369**

National Parks/Parcs nationaux

Agalta	II	53,000	1987
Azul Meambar	II	20,000	1987
Celaque	II	27,000	1987
Cerro Azul	II	15,000	1987
Islas de la Bahia	II	29,416	
La Tigra	II	7,500	1980
Montana de Comayagua	II	18,000	1987
Montana de Cusuco	II	18,000	
Montana de Yoro	II	15,500	1987
Pico Bonito	II	5,400	1987
Pico de Pijol	II	11,400	1987
Rio Platano	II	350,000	1980
Santa Barbara	II	13,000	1987
Trifinio	II	5,400	1987

Biological Reserves/Réserves biologiques

El Chile	IV	6,000	
El Pital	IV	3,800	
Guajiquiro	IV	7,000	
Guisayote	IV	7,000	
Misaco	IV	4,600	
Montecillos	IV	12,500	
Opalaca	IV	14,500	
Uyuca	IV	1,100	1986
Volcan Pacayita	IV	9,700	
Yerba Buena	IV	3,600	
Yuscaran	IV	2,300	

Wildlife Refuges/Refuges de ressources sauvages

Corralitos	IV	5,500	
El Armado	IV	3,500	
Erapuca	IV	5,600	
La Muralla-Los Higuerales	IV	1,600	
Mixcure	IV	8,000	
Montana Verde	IV	8,300	
Puca	IV	4,900	

Rios de Cuero y Salado	IV	8,500	1988
Texiguat	IV	10,000	
Protected Areas/Aires protégées			
Lancetilla Botanic Garden	IV	1,253	1978

HUNGARY/HONGRIE

Summary/Sommaire		
Category\Catégorie IV	5	12,552
Category\Catégorie V	41	498,597
Total	**46**	**511,149**

National Parks/Parcs nationaux			
Aggtelek	V	19,708	1985
Bukk	V	38,815	1976
Hortobagy	V	52,000	1973
Kiskunsag	V	30,628	1975
Nature Conservation Areas/Aires de conservation de la nature			
Agota-puszta	IV	4,700	1973
Nagybereki Feher-viz	IV	1,537	1977
Pusztakocsi mocsarak (Egyek)	IV	2,815	1973
Tiszadobi arter	IV	1,000	1977
Tiszafuredi madarrezervatum	IV	2,500	1973
Landscape Protected Areas/Aires de paysages protégés			
Badacsonyi	V	7,028	1965
Barcsi osborokas	V	3,417	1974
Beda-Kora-Pancrai	V	6,497	1989
Borzsonyi	V	17,897	1978
Budai	V	10,234	1978
Devavanyai	V	3,433	1975
Ferto-tavi	V	12,542	1977
Gemenci	V	17,779	1977
Gerecsei	V	8,617	1977
Hajdirsagi	V	5,680	1988
Hansagi	V	6,243	1976
Kali-medence	V	9,110	1984
Kelet-Mecseki	V	9,248	1977
Keszthelyi-TK	V	2,711	1984
Kis-Balaton	V	14,745	1986
Koszegi	V	3,987	1980
Kozep-Tiszai	V	7,670	1978
Lazberci	V	3,634	1986
Martelyi	V	2,232	1971
Matrai	V	11,862	1985
Ocsai	V	3,575	1975
Orgovanyi	V	2,953	1976
Orsegi	V	37,911	1978
Pilisi	V	23,323	1978
Pitvarai parztak	V	3,156	1989
Pusztaszeri	V	22,151	1976

Sarreti	V	2,210	1985
Soproni	V	4,905	1977
Szabadkigyosi	V	4,773	1987
Szatmar-Beregi	V	22,246	1982
Szentgyorgyvolgyi	V	1,916	1976
Szigetkozi	V	9,158	1987
Tihanyi	V	1,100	1952
Tokaj-Bodrogzugi	V	4,242	1985
Vertesi	V	13,723	1976
Zempleni	V	26,496	1984
Zselicsegi	V	9,042	1976

ICELAND/ISLANDE

Summary/Sommaire		
Category\Catégorie I	1	270
Category\Catégorie II	3	180,100
Category\Catégorie III	5	38,604
Category\Catégorie IV	5	51,950
Category\Catégorie V	8	645,000
Total	**22**	**915,924**

National Parks/Parcs nationaux			
Jokulsargljufur	II	15,100	1973
Skaftafell	II	160,000	1967
Thingvellir	II	5,000	1928
Nature Reserves/Réserves de nature			
Fjallabak	V	47,000	1979
Flatey	IV	100	1975
Geitland	III	11,750	1988
Herdisarvik	V	4,000	1988
Kringilsarrani	IV	8,500	1975
Miklavatn	IV	1,550	1977
Surtsey	I	270	1965
Thjosarver	IV	37,500	1981
Natural Monuments/Monuments naturels			
Alftaversgigar	III	3,650	1975
Askja i Dyngjufjollum	III	5,000	1978
Lakagigar	III	16,000	1971
Skogafoss	III	2,204	1987
Nature Reserves (Landscape)/Réserves de nature (Paysages)			
Esjufjoll	V	27,000	1978
Herdubreidarfridland	V	17,000	1974
Hornstrandir	V	58,000	1975
Hvannalindir i Krepputungu	IV	4,300	1973
Lonsoraefi	V	32,000	1977
Vatnsfjorour	V	20,000	1975
Conservation Areas/Aires de conservation			
Myvatn Laxa	V	440,000	1974

ILES COOK
Voir paragraphe COOK ISLANDS

ILES MARSHALL
Voir paragraphe MARSHALL ISLANDS

ILES SALOMON
Voir paragraphe SOLOMON ISLANDS

INDIA/INDE

Summary/Sommaire		
Category\Catégorie I	2	196,043
Category\Catégorie II	57	3,329,300
Category\Catégorie IV	299	9,937,205
Category\Catégorie V	1	18,600
Total	**359**	**13,481,148**

National Parks/Parcs nationaux

Anshi	II	25,000	1987
Balphakram	II	22,000	1986
Bandhavgarh	II	44,884	1968
Bandipur	II	87,420	1974
Bannerghatta	II	10,427	1974
Bansda	II	2,399	1976
Bhagwan Mahavir	II	10,700	1978
Corbett	II	52,082	1936
Dachigam	II	14,100	1981
Desert	II	316,200	1981
Dudwa	II	49,029	1977
Eravikulam	II	9,700	1978
Gir	II	25,871	1975
Great Himalayan	II	60,561	1984
Gugamal	II	36,180	1987
Hemis High Altitude	II	410,000	1981
Indira Gandhi	II	11,808	1989
Indravati	II	125,837	1978
Kanger Ghati	II	20,000	1982
Kanha	II	94,000	1955
Kaziranga	II	42,996	1974
Keibul Lamjao	II	4,000	1977
Keoladeo	II	2,873	1981
Khangchendzonga	II	84,950	1977
Kishtwar	II	31,000	1981
Kudremukh	II	60,032	1987
Madhav	II	15,615	1959
Marine (Gulf of Kutch)	II	16,289	1982
Mouling	II	48,300	1986
Nagarahole	II	64,339	1975

Namdapha	II	198,524	1983
Nanda Devi	I	63,033	1982
Nawegaon	II	13,388	1975
Neora Valley	II	8,689	1986
Nokrek	II	6,801	1985
North Simlipal	II	84,570	1978
Palamau	II	21,300	1986
Panna	II	542,666	1981
Pench (Maharashtra)	II	25,726	1975
Pench (Madhaya Pradesh)	II	29,286	1977
Periyar	II	30,500	1982
Pin Valley	II	80,736	1987
Rajaji	II	83,153	1988
Ranthambore	II	39,200	1980
Sanjay Gandhi	II	8,696	1983
Sanjay	II	193,801	1981
Sariska	II	27,380	1982
Satpura	II	52,437	1981
Silent Valley	II	8,952	1980
Singalila	II	7,860	1986
Sirohi	II	4,130	1982
Sundarbans	I	133,010	1984
Tadoba	II	11,655	1955
Valley of Flowers	II	8,950	1982
Velavadar	II	3,408	1976
Sanctuaries/Sanctuaires			
Abohar	IV	18,824	1975
Achanakmar	IV	55,155	1975
Anamalai	IV	84,935	1976
Andhari	IV	50,900	1986
Aner Dam	IV	8,294	1986
Arabithittu	IV	1,350	
Aralam	IV	5,500	1984
Badalkhol	IV	10,435	1975
Bagdara	IV	47,890	1978
Balimela	IV	16,000	
Baltal	IV	20,300	1987
Balukhand	IV	7,200	1984
Bandh Baretha	IV	19,276	1985
Bandli	IV	3,947	1962
Barda	IV	19,931	1979
Barnadi	IV	2,622	1980
Barnawapara	IV	24,466	1976
Bassi	IV	15,290	
Bhadra	IV	49,246	1974
Bhagwan Mahavir	IV	14,852	1967
Bhairamgarh	IV	13,895	1983
Bhensrodgarh	IV	22,914	1983
Bhimashankar	IV	13,100	1985
Bhimbandh	IV	68,190	1976

Bhitar Kanika	IV	17,000	1975
Biligiri Ranga Swamy Temple	IV	32,440	1974
Binsar	IV	4,559	1988
Bir Shikargah	IV	1,093	1975
Bor	IV	6,110	1970
Bori	IV	51,825	1977
Brahmagiri	IV	18,129	1974
Buxa	IV	31,452	1986
Cauvery	IV	51,051	1987
Chail	IV	11,004	1976
Chandaka Dampada	IV	22,000	1982
Chandoli	IV	30,900	1985
Chandra Prabha	IV	7,800	1957
Changthang	IV	400,000	1987
Chaprala	IV	13,500	1986
Chautala	IV	11,396	1987
Chilka	IV	1,553	1987
Chimony	IV	10,500	1984
Chinnar	IV	9,044	1984
Churdhar	IV	5,659	1985
Coringa	IV	23,570	1978
Cotigao	IV	10,500	1968
D'Ering Memorial	IV	19,000	1978
Dalma	IV	19,322	1976
Dampa	IV	68,100	1985
Dandeli	IV	572,907	1975
Daranghati	IV	2,701	1962
Darlaghat	IV	9,871	1962
Darrah	IV	26,583	1955
Debrigarh	IV	34,690	1985
Dipor Beel	IV	4,000	1989
Dumkhal	IV	44,818	1982
Eturnagaram	IV	81,259	1953
Fambong Lho	IV	5,160	1984
Gamgul Siya-Behi	IV	10,546	1949
Gandhi Sagar	IV	36,862	1974
Gautala Autram	IV	26,100	1986
Gautam Budha	IV	25,948	1976
Ghataprabha	IV	2,979	1974
Ghatigaon Great Indian Bustard	IV	51,200	1981
Gir	IV	115,342	1965
Gobind Sagar	IV	12,067	1962
Gomarda	IV	27,782	1972
Govind Pashu Vihar	IV	95,312	1954
Great Indian Bustard	IV	849,644	1979
Gulmarg	V	18,600	1987
Gumti	IV	38,954	1988
Hadgarh	IV	19,160	1978
Halliday Island	IV	583	1976
Harike Lake	IV	4,300	1982

Hastinapur	IV	2,073	1986
Hazaribagh	IV	18,625	1976
Hirapora	IV	11,000	1987
Hokarsar	IV	1,000	
Idukki	IV	7,700	1976
Indira Priyadarshini	IV	1,320	
Intanki	IV	20,202	1975
Itanagar	IV	14,030	1978
Jaikwadi	IV	34,105	1986
Jaisamand	IV	5,200	1956
Jaldapara	IV	11,563	1941
Jamwa Ramgarh	IV	30,000	1982
Jawahar Sagar	IV	10,000	1980
Jessore	IV	18,066	1978
Kabar	IV	20,400	1986
Kachchh Desert	IV	750,622	1986
Kaimur (Uttar Pradesh)	IV	50,075	1982
Kaimur (Bihar)	IV	134,222	1978
Kalakad	IV	22,358	1976
Kalatop and Khajjiar	IV	3,069	1949
Kalsubai Harishchandragad	IV	36,200	1986
Kanawar	IV	6,157	1954
Kapilasa	IV	12,600	1970
Karakoram	IV	180,000	
Karera Great Indian Bustard	IV	20,221	1981
Karlapat	IV	25,500	1969
Katarniaghat	IV	40,009	1976
Katepurna	IV	1,500	
Kawal	IV	89,228	1965
Kedarnath	IV	97,524	1972
Keladevi	IV	67,600	1983
Ken Gharial	IV	4,500	1981
Khalasuni	IV	11,600	1982
Kheoni	IV	12,270	1982
Khokhan	IV	1,760	1954
Kias	IV	1,220	1954
Kinnersani	IV	63,540	1977
Kishanpur	IV	22,712	1972
Koderma	IV	17,795	1985
Kolleru	IV	90,100	1963
Kondakameru	IV	43,000	
Kotgarh	IV	39,950	1981
Koyna	IV	42,400	1985
Kugti	IV	33,000	1962
Kuldiha	IV	27,275	1984
Kumbhalgarh	IV	57,826	1971
Lachipora	IV	8,000	1987
Lakhari	IV	11,835	1985
Lanjamadugu	IV	3,620	1978
Laokhowa	IV	7,014	1979

Lawalang	IV	21,103	1978
Limber	IV	2,600	1987
Lippa Asrang	IV	2,953	1962
Lothian Island	IV	3,885	1976
Maenam	IV	3,534	1987
Mahanadi Baisipalli	IV	16,835	1981
Mahananda	IV	12,722	1976
Mahuadaur	IV	6,325	1976
Majathal	IV	3,164	1962
Malvan	IV	2,912	1987
Manali	IV	3,127	1954
Manas	IV	39,100	1928
Manjira	IV	2,000	1978
Marine (Gulf of Kutch)	IV	29,303	1986
Mehao	IV	28,150	1980
Melghat	IV	159,733	1985
Melkote Temple	IV	4,982	1974
Mookambika	IV	24,700	1974
Mount Abu	IV	28,884	1960
Mudumalai	IV	32,155	1940
Mukurthi	IV	7,846	1982
Mundanthurai	IV	56,738	1962
Nagarjunasagar Srisailam	IV	35,689	1978
Nagzira	IV	15,281	1969
Nahargarh	IV	5,000	1980
Naina Devi	IV	3,719	1962
Nakti Dam	IV	20,640	1985
Nal Sarovar	IV	12,082	1969
Nameri	IV	13,707	1985
Nandini	IV	3,372	1981
Nandur Madmeshwar	IV	10,010	1986
Narayan Sarovar	IV	76,579	1981
Nargu	IV	24,313	1962
Narsingarh	IV	5,719	1974
National Chambal (Rajasthan)	IV	28,000	1983
National Chambal (Madhaya Pradesh)	IV	42,300	1978
National Chambal (Uttar Pradesh)	IV	63,500	1979
Neyyar	IV	12,800	1958
Nongkhyllem	IV	2,900	1981
Noradehi	IV	118,696	1975
Nugu	IV	3,032	1974
Orang	IV	7,260	1985
Overa	IV	3,237	1981
Overa-Aru	IV	42,500	1987
Pabha	IV	4,900	
Pachmarhi	IV	46,086	1977
Painganga	IV	32,462	1986
Pakhal	IV	86,205	1952
Pakhui	IV	86,195	1977
Palamau	IV	76,700	1976

Palpur (Kuno)	IV	34,468	1981
Pamed	IV	26,212	1983
Panpatha	IV	24,584	1983
Papikonda	IV	59,068	1978
Parambikulam	IV	28,500	1973
Parasnath	IV	4,923	1984
Peechi Vazhani	IV	12,500	1958
Pench	IV	11,847	1977
Peppara	IV	5,300	1983
Periyar	IV	47,200	1950
Phansad	IV	7,000	1986
Phen	IV	11,024	1983
Phulwari	IV	51,141	1983
Pobitora	IV	3,883	1987
Pocharam	IV	12,964	1952
Point Calimere	IV	1,726	1967
Pong Dam	IV	32,270	1983
Pranhita	IV	13,603	1980
Pulicat (Andhra Pradesh)	IV	58,000	1976
Pulicat (Tamil Nadu)	IV	46,102	1980
Pushpagiri	IV	10,292	1987
Radhanagari	IV	37,200	1958
Rajgir	IV	3,584	1978
Raksham Chitkul	IV	3,827	1962
Ramgarh Bundi	IV	30,700	1982
Ramnagar	IV	1,290	1981
Rampura	IV	1,501	1988
Ranebennur	IV	11,900	1974
Ranipur	IV	23,031	1977
Ratanmahal	IV	5,565	1982
Ratapani	IV	68,879	1976
Rupi Bhabha	IV	85,414	1982
Sagareshwar	IV	1,100	1985
Sailana	IV	1,296	1983
Sajnakhali	IV	36,234	1976
Sanjay (Dubri)	IV	36,459	1975
Saptasajya	IV	2,000	1970
Sardarpur	IV	34,812	1983
Sariska	IV	49,200	1958
Satkosia Gorge	IV	79,552	1976
Sawai Mansingh	IV	10,325	1984
Sechu Tuan Nala	IV	65,532	1962
Semarsot	IV	43,036	1978
Senchal	IV	3,860	1976
Sepahijala	IV	1,853	1987
Sharavathi Valley	IV	43,123	1974
Shenduruny	IV	10,032	1984
Shergarh	IV	9,871	1983
Shettihally	IV	39,560	1974
Shikari Devi	IV	7,119	1962

Simbalbara	IV	1,720	1958
Simlipal	IV	135,500	1978
Singba	IV	3,250	1984
Singhori (Sindhari)	IV	28,791	1976
Sita Mata	IV	42,294	1979
Sitanadi	IV	55,336	1974
Siwaram	IV	2,992	1978
Sohagabarwa	IV	42,820	1987
Someshwara	IV	8,840	1974
Son Gharial	IV	4,180	1981
Sonai Rupai	IV	17,500	1934
Sonanadi	IV	30,118	1987
Srivenkateswara	IV	50,700	
Srivilliputhur	IV	48,520	1988
Sukhna	IV	2,542	
Sunabeda	IV	44,213	1983
Sunda Mata	IV	10,700	
Surinsar-Mansar	IV	3,958	1981
Talkaveri	IV	10,500	1987
Talra	IV	3,616	1962
Tamor Pingla	IV	60,852	1978
Tansa	IV	30,481	1970
Thattekkad Bird	IV	2,500	1983
Tirthan	IV	6,825	1976
Todgarh Raoli	IV	49,527	1983
Tongri	IV	2,000	
Trishna	IV	17,056	1987
Tundah	IV	41,948	1962
Tungabadra	IV	22,422	
Udanti	IV	24,759	1983
Ushakothi	IV	30,403	1987
Valmikinagar	IV	46,160	1978
Van Vihar	IV	5,993	1955
Wild Ass	IV	495,370	1973
Wynad	IV	34,444	1973
Yagoupokpi Lokchao	IV	18,480	1989
Yawal	IV	17,752	1969

Andaman and Nicobar Islands/Iles Andaman et Nicobar

National Parks/Parcs nationaux

Marine (Wandur)	II	28,150	1983
Mount Harriet Island	II	4,622	1979
Saddle Peak	II	3,255	1979

Sanctuaries/Sanctuaires

Barren Island	IV	810	1977
Battimalve Island	IV	223	1985
Benett Island	IV	346	1987
Bluff Island	IV	114	1987
Bondoville Island	IV	255	1987

Buchanan Island	IV	933	1987
Cinque Island	IV	951	1987
Crocodile (Lohabarrack)	IV	10,600	1983
Defence Island	IV	1,049	1987
East (Inglis) Island	IV	355	1987
East Island	IV	611	1987
Flat Island	IV	936	1987
Interview Island	IV	13,300	1985
James Island	IV	210	1987
Kyd Island	IV	800	1987
Landfall Island	IV	2,948	1987
Narcondum Island	IV	681	1977
North Reef Island	IV	348	1977
Paget Island	IV	736	1987
Pitman Island	IV	137	1987
Point Island	IV	307	1987
Ranger Island	IV	426	1987
Reef Island	IV	174	1987
Roper Island	IV	146	1987
Ross Island	IV	101	1987
Sandy Island	IV	158	1987
Shearme Island	IV	785	1987
Sir Hugh Rose Island	IV	106	1987
South Brother Island	IV	124	1987
South Reef Island	IV	117	1987
South Sentinel Island	IV	161	1977
Spike Island	IV	1,170	1987
Swamp Island	IV	409	1987
Table (Delgarno) Island	IV	229	1987
Table (Excelsior) Island	IV	169	1987
Talabaicha Island	IV	321	1987
Temple Island	IV	104	1987
Tillanchong Island	IV	1,683	1985
West Island	IV	640	1987

Lakshadweep

No Areas Listed/pas de sites

INDONESIA/INDONESIE

Summary/Sommaire		
Category\Catégorie I	79	7,173,667
Category\Catégorie II	19	5,959,006
Category\Catégorie IV	59	4,456,538
Category\Catégorie V	12	210,576
Total	**169**	**17,799,787**

Irian Jaya/Irian Jaya

Marine National Parks/Parcs nationaux marins

Teluk Cenderawasih	II	1,453,500	1990

Nature Reserves/Réserves de nature

Enarotali	I	300,000	1980
Lorentz	I	2,150,000	1978
Pegunungan Cyclops	I	22,520	1978
Pulau Batanta Barat	I	10,000	1981
Pulau Biak Utara	I	11,000	1982
Pulau Misool	I	84,000	1982
Pulau Salawati Utara	I	57,000	1982
Pulau Superiori	I	42,000	1982
Pulau Waigeo Barat	I	153,000	1981
Pulau Yapen Tengah	I	59,000	1982
Rawa Biru	I	4,000	1978
Teluk Bintuni	I	450,000	1982

Game Reserves/Réserves de faune

Pegunungan Jayawijaya	IV	800,000	1981
Pulau Angrameos	IV	2,500	1980
Pulau Dolok	IV	600,000	1978
Wasur	IV	304,000	1982

Recreation Parks/Parcs de loisirs

Teluk Yotefa	V	1,650	1978

Java/Java

National Parks/Parcs nationaux

Baluran "proposed"	II	25,000	1980
Bromo-Tengger-Semeru "proposed"	II	57,606	1982
Gunung Gede Pangrango "proposed"	II	15,000	1980
Meru Betiri "proposed"	II	58,000	1972
Ujung Kulon "proposed"	II	76,119	1980

Marine National Parks/Parcs nationaux marins

Kepulauan Seribu	II	108,000	1982

Nature Reserves/Réserves de nature

Arjuno Lalijiwo	I	4,960	1972
Cibodas-Gunung Gede	I	1,040	1925
Gunung Burangrang	I	2,700	1979
Gunung Celering	I	1,279	1973
Gunung Halimun	I	40,000	1979
Gunung Honje	I	19,499	1979
Gunung Simpang	I	15,000	1979
Gunung Tilu	I	8,000	1978
Gunung Tukung Gede	I	1,700	1979
Kawah Ijen Ungup-Ungup	I	2,468	1920
Kawah Kamojang	I	7,500	1979
Krakatau	I	2,500	1919
Laut Pasir Tengger-Gunung Bromo	I	5,287	1919
Leuweung Sancang	I	2,157	1978
Nusa Barung	I	6,100	1920

Nusa Kambangan	I	4,983	1937
Pulau Panaitan-Pulau Peucang	I	17,500	1937
Pulau Saobi (Kangean Islands)	I	430	1926
Pulau Sempu	I	877	1928
Ranu Kumbolo	I	1,340	1921
Rawa Danau	I	2,500	1921
Tangkuban Perahu	I	1,290	1974
Game Reserves/Réserves de faune			
Banyuwangi Selatan (Blambangan)	IV	62,000	1939
Cikepuh	IV	8,128	1973
Gunung Sawal	IV	5,400	1979
Pulau Bawean	IV	3,832	1979
Yang Plateau	IV	14,145	1962
Recreation Parks/Parcs de loisirs			
Gunung Gamping	V	1,102	1982
Gunung Tampomas	V	1,250	1979
Gunung Tangkuban Perahu	V	1,290	1974

Kalimantan/Kalimantan

National Parks/Parcs nationaux

Gunung Palung "proposed"	II	90,000	1990
Kutai "proposed"	II	200,000	1982
Tanjung Puting "proposed"	II	355,000	1982
Nature Reserves/Réserves de nature			
Bukit Baka (Sumatera)	I	70,500	1987
Bukit Raya	I	110,000	1979
Bukit Tangkiling	I	2,061	1977
Gunung Raya Pasi	I	3,742	1978
Mandor	I	2,000	1937
Muara Kaman Sedulang	I	62,500	1976
Padang Luwai	I	5,000	1982
Pararawan I,II	I	6,200	1979
Sungai Kayan Sungai Mentarang	I	1,600,000	1980
Game Reserves/Réserves de faune			
Gunung Penrisen/Gunung Nyiut	IV	180,000	1982
Kelumpang-Selat Laut-Selat Sebuku	IV	66,650	1981
Pleihari Martapura	IV	36,400	1980
Pleihari Tanah Laut	IV	35,000	1975
Tanjung Puting	IV	300,040	1978
Marine Parks/Parcs marins			
Gunung Asuansang	IV	28,000	
Pulau Sangalaki	IV	280	1982
Recreation Parks/Parcs de loisirs			
Bukit Suharto	V	27,000	
Tanjung Keluang	V	2,000	1984

Lesser Sunda Islands/Les petites Sunda

National Parks/Parcs nationaux

Bali Barat "proposed"	II	77,727	1982

Komodo Island "proposed"	II	40,729	1980
Rinjani "proposed"	II	40,000	1990

Nature Reserves/Réserves de nature

Batukahu I/II/III	I	1,762	1974
Maubesi	I	1,830	1981
May Mull Imburak	I	3,000	1985
Ruteng	I	30,000	
Tanah Pedauh	I	543	1975

Game Reserves/Réserves de faune

Gunung Wanggameti	IV	6,000	
Kateri	IV	4,560	1981
Manupau	IV	12,000	
Pulau Menipo	IV	3,000	1977
Pulau Moyo	IV	18,765	1975
Pulau Padar	IV	1,533	1969
Rinca Island	IV	8,196	1969
Wae Wuul Mburak	IV	3,000	1960

Marine Parks/Parcs marins

Gugus Pulau Teluk Maumer	IV	59,450	1987
Pulau Moyo	IV	6,000	

Recreation Parks/Parcs de loisirs

Danau Kalimutu	V	4,984	1984
Tuti Adagae	V	5,000	1981

Moluccas/Les Moluques

National Parks/Parcs nationaux

Manusela (Wai Nua/Wai Mual) "proposed"	II	189,000	1982

Nature Reserves/Réserves de nature

Pulau Angwarmase	I	800	1978
Pulau Nustarem (Yamdena Is.)	I	3,200	1978
Pulau Nuswatar	I	7,500	1978
Pulau Seho	I	1,250	1972

Game Reserves/Réserves de faune

Pulau Baun	IV	13,000	1974
Pulau Manuk	IV	100	1981

Unclassified/Non classé

Pulau Banda	IV	2,500	1977
Pulau Kasa	IV	2,000	1978
Pulau Pombo	IV	1,000	1973

Sulawesi/Sulawesi

National Parks/Parcs nationaux

Dumoga-Bone "proposed"	II	300,000	1982
Lore Lindu "proposed"	II	231,000	1982

Nature Reserves/Réserves de nature

Bantimurung	I	1,018,000	1980
Bulusaraung	I	5,690	1980
Dua saudara	I	4,299	1978
Gunung Ambang	I	8,638	1978

Gunung Kelabat	I	5,300	1932
Karaenta	I	1,000	1976
Morowali	I	225,000	1986
Paboya	I	1,000	1973
Panua	I	1,500	1938
Pegunungan Peruhumpenai	I	90,000	1979
Pulau Mas Popaya Raja	I	160	1919
Tangkoko Batuangus	I	4,446	
Tangkoko-Dua Saudara	I	4,299	1978
Tanjung Api	I	4,246	1977
Game Reserves/Réserves de faune			
Bontobahari	IV	4,000	1980
Buton Utara	IV	82,000	1979
Gunung Manembo-Nembo	IV	6,500	1978
Lampoko Mampie	IV	2,000	1978
Lombuyan I/II	IV	3,665	1974
Pinjan/Tanjung Matop	IV	1,613	1981
Tanjung Batikolo	IV	5,500	1980
Tanjung Peropa	IV	38,937	1986
Research Forests/Forêts dédiées à la recherche			
Sungai Camba Res	IV	1,300	
Recreation Parks/Parcs de loisirs			
Danau Matado/Mahalano	V	30,000	1979
Danau Towuti	V	65,000	1979

Sumatra/Sumatra

National Parks/Parcs nationaux			
Barisan Selatan "proposed"	II	365,000	1982
Gunung Leuser "proposed"	II	792,675	1980
Kerinci Seblat "proposed"	II	1,484,650	1982
Nature Reserves/Réserves de nature			
Bukit Tapan	I	66,500	1978
Dolok Sibual Bual	I	5,000	1982
Dolok Sipirok	I	6,970	1982
Gunung Indrapura	I	70,000	
Gunung Tujuh	I	6,200	
Indrapura	I	221,136	1929
Janthoi	I	8,000	1984
Kelompok Hutan Bakau Pantai Timur Jambi	I	6,500	1981
Manua	I	1,500	
Pulau Berkeh	I	500	1968
Pulau Burung	I	200	1968
Rimbo Panti	I	2,830	1934
Toba Pananjung	I	1,235	1932
Game Reserves/Réserves de faune			
Bentayan	IV	19,300	1981
Berbak	IV	190,000	1935
Bukit Gedang Seblat	IV	48,750	1981
Bukit Kayu Embun	IV	106,000	1980

Danau Pulau Besar/Danau Bawah	IV	25,000	1980
Dangku	IV	29,080	1981
Dolok Surungan	IV	23,800	1974
Gumai Pasemah	IV	45,883	1976
Gunung Raya	IV	39,500	1978
Isau-Isau Pasemah	IV	12,144	1978
Karang Gading and Langkat Timur Laut	IV	15,765	1980
Kerumutan	IV	120,000	1979
Padang Sugihan	IV	75,000	1983
Rawas Ulu Lakitan	IV	213,437	1979
Sekundur and Langkat (South and West)	IV	213,985	1939
Sumatera Selatan	IV	356,800	1935
Tai-tai Batti	IV	56,500	1976
Way Kambas	IV	130,000	1937
Marine Parks/Parcs marins			
Pulau Weh	IV	2,600	1982
Forest Parks/Parcs forestiers			
Dr. Moch. Hatta Grand	V	70,000	1986
Recreation Parks/Parcs de loisirs			
Pulau Weh	V	1,300	1982

IRAN (ISLAMIC REPUBLIC OF)/IRAN (REPUBLIQUE ISLAMIQUE D')

Summary/Sommaire		
Category\Catégorie I	18	1,904,503
Category\Catégorie II	7	1,075,300
Category\Catégorie III	2	6,150
Category\Catégorie IV	4	1,144,918
Category\Catégorie V	29	3,398,105
Total	**60**	**7,528,976**

National Parks/Parcs nationaux			
Bamou	II	48,075	1962
Golestan	II	91,895	1957
Kavir	II	420,000	1964
Khogir	II	11,570	1982
Sorkheh Hesar	II	9,380	1982
Tandoureh	II	30,780	1968
Uromiyeh Lake	II	463,600	1967
National Nature Monuments/Monuments naturels nationaux			
Alborz-e-Markazi (Central Alborz)	III	4,750	1977
Dehloran	III	1,400	1976
Wildlife Refuges/Refuges de ressources sauvages			
Amirkelayeh	I	1,230	1971
Angoran	I	28,600	1971
Bakhtegan	I	327,820	1968
Bisiton (Varmangeh)	I	31,250	
Dez	I	5,240	1960
Dodangeh	I	6,700	1974
Gamishlo	I	49,250	1971

Karkheh	I	3,600	1960
Khaber-o-Rouchon	I	173,750	1971
Kharko	I	312	1960
Khoshyeylag	I	154,400	1963
Kiamaky	I	84,400	1974
Kolahghazi	I	48,683	1964
Mehroyeh	I	7,468	1971
Miandasht	I	52,000	1974
Miyinkaleh	I	68,800	1970
Shadegan	I	296,000	1972
Touran	I	565,000	1973
Protected Areas/Aires protégées			
Abasbaran	V	7,240	1971
Alborz-e-Markazi	V	399,000	1961
Angoran	V	96,130	1971
Argan	IV	52,800	1972
Bahokalat (Gando)	IV	382,430	1971
Bahramgor	IV	385,000	1973
Bazman	IV	324,688	1968
Bigar	V	25,000	1971
Biseton	V	50,850	1968
Dez	V	10,633	1960
Geno	V	27,500	1972
Ghorkhod	V	34,000	1971
Haftadgoleh	V	82,000	1970
Hamoun	V	193,500	1967
Hara	V	85,686	1972
Hormoud	V	151,284	1976
Jahannoma	V	30,600	1974
Karkheh	V	9,427	1960
Kavir	V	250,000	
Lar River	V	28,000	1976
Lisar	V	33,050	1970
Marakan	V	92,715	1966
Mond	V	46,700	1976
Moteh	V	200,000	1964
Oshtrankoh	V	93,950	1970
Parvar	V	59,840	1962
Salouk	V	16,000	1973
Serany	V	17,800	1971
Siahkesheim	V	4,500	1967
Tandoureh	V	2,300	
Tang Sayyad	V	27,000	1971
Touran	V	1,295,400	1973
Vargin	V	28,000	

IRAQ
No Areas Listed/pas de sites

IRELAND/IRLANDE

Summary/Sommaire		
Category\Catégorie II	3	22,495
Category\Catégorie IV	3	4,315
Total	**6**	**26,810**

National Parks/Parcs nationaux			
Connemara	II	2,699	1980
Glenveagh	II	9,667	1984
Killarney	II	10,129	1932
Nature Reserves/Réserves de nature			
Glenealo Valley	IV	1,958	1988
Knockadoon Head and Capel Island	IV	127	1985
Slieve Bloom Mountains	IV	2,230	1986

ISLANDE
Voir paragraphe ICELAND

ISRAEL

Summary/Sommaire		
Category\Catégorie II	1	30,900
Category\Catégorie IV	16	186,586
Category\Catégorie V	1	8,400
Total	**18**	**225,886**

National Parks/Parcs nationaux			
Mount Carmel	V	8,400	
Nature Reserves/Réserves de nature			
Amasa Mont	IV	1,145	1981
Bashanit Ridge	IV	1,037	1972
Beth-Saida	IV	1,050	
Dead Sea cliffs	IV	6,475	1979
Ein Gedi	IV	2,780	1972
Einot Tzukim (Ein Fesh'ha)	IV	1,640	1980
Hai Bar Yotvata	IV	3,000	1970
Judean desert	IV	45,000	1980
Mount Carmel	II	30,900	1971
Mount Meron	IV	10,000	1956
Odem Forest	IV	1,100	1972
Ramon (Negev Makheteshim)	IV	100,000	
Susita	IV	1,017	1973
Wadi Meitzr	IV	1,054	1972
Wadi Yeetar	IV	1,468	1980
Yahudia Forest	IV	6,620	1973
Yatrata	IV	3,200	1970

ITALY/ITALIE

Summary/Sommaire		
Category\Catégorie II	3	125,892
Category\Catégorie IV	54	277,451
Category\Catégorie V	51	897,222
Total	**108**	**1,300,565**

While compiling the *UN List*, we were advised by the *Ministero dell'Ambiente* that the protected area system in Italy was under review, and that an official list of protected areas was currently unavailable. The list presented here is derived from unofficial sources.

Tandis que la liste était en cours de réalisation, nous avons été informés par le *Ministero dell'Ambiente* que le réseau italien d'aires protégées était en révision et qu'il n'y avait pas, pour l'instant, de liste officielle disponible. La liste que nous proposons ici est tirée de sources non officielles.

National Parks/Parcs nationaux

Abruzzo	II	40,000	1923
Calabria	II	15,892	1968
Circeo	V	8,400	1934
Gran Paradiso	II	70,000	1922
Stelvio	V	134,620	1935

Biogenetic Reserves/Réserves biogénétiques

Badia Prataglia	IV	1,408	1977
Camaldoli	IV	1,168	1977
Campigna	IV	1,191	1977
Marchesale	IV	1,257	1977
Poverella nel Villaggio	IV	1,086	1977
Stornara	IV	1,456	1977
Vallombrosa	IV	1,270	1977

Nature Reserves/Réserves de nature

Abbadia di Fiatra	IV	1,800	1985
Caprera Managed	IV	1,575	1980
Faro S. Martino-Palombaro	IV	4,202	1983
Feudo Ugni	IV	1,563	1981
Foresta de Circeo	IV	3,260	1977
Foresta di Sabaudia	IV	3,070	1978
Foresta di Tarvisio	IV	23,294	1980
Gole del Raganello	IV	1,600	1987
Isola di Caprera	IV	1,575	1980
Isola di Montecristo	IV	1,039	1971
Lago di Campotosto	IV	1,600	1984
Lago di Mezzola - Pian di Spagna	IV	1,586	1983
Larna Branca di S. Eufemia a Maiella	IV	1,300	1987
Monte Mottac	IV	2,410	1971
Monte Rotondo	IV	1,452	1982
Monte Velino	IV	3,550	1987
Monti del Sole	IV	3,032	1975
Pian di Spagna-Lago di Mezzola	IV	1,586	1983
Piani Eterni - Errera - Val Falcina	IV	5,463	1975

Salina di Margherita di Savoia	IV	3,871	1977
Schiara Occidentale	IV	3,172	1975
Somadida	IV	1,676	1972
Tirone-Alto Vesuvio	IV	1,005	1972
Torrente Prescudin	IV	1,670	
Toscane	IV	1,039	
Val Tovanella	IV	1,040	1971
Val di Farme FoR/	IV	4,500	
Valle del Fiume Argentina	IV	3,980	1987
Valle del Fiume Lao	IV	5,200	1987
Valle dell'Orfento	IV	2,057	1971
Valli del Mincio	IV	1,081	1983
Vette Feltrine	IV	2,764	1975
Marine Reserves/Réserves marines			
Ustica	IV	16,000	1986
Marine Nature Reserves/Réserves naturelles marines			
Secche della Meloria	IV	120,000	1982
Marine Sanctuaries/Sanctuaires marins			
Monte Cristo Island	IV	1,035	1979
Forest Reserves/Réserves forestières			
Umbra	IV	10,000	
Regional Urban Parks/Parcs urbains régionaux			
Castelli Romani	V	9,500	1984
Marturanum	V	1,450	1984
Pineta di Castelfusano	V	1,000	1980
Regional Nature Parks/Parcs naturels régionaux			
Adamello	V	48,100	1983
Adda Nord	V	5,580	1983
Adda Sud	V	23,600	1983
Alpe Veglia	V	4,135	1978
Alpi Apuane	V	60,000	1985
Alta Valle Pesio	V	3,955	1978
Alta Valsesia	V	6,435	1979
Argentera	V	25,883	1980
Boschi di Carrega	V	1,000	1982
Bracco-Mesco-Cinque Terre-Montemarcello	V	15,390	1985
Campo dei Fiori	V	5,400	1984
Capanne di Marcarolo	V	11,800	1979
Colli di Bergamo	V	4,979	1977
Dolomiti di Sesto	V	11,635	1981
Fanes-Sennes-Braies	V	25,680	1980
Gran Bosco di Salbertrand	V	2,005	1980
Groane	V	3,445	1976
Gruppo di Tessa	V	33,430	1976
La Mandria	V	6,470	1978
Magra	V	2,040	1982
Maremma	V	9,800	1975
Migliarino-San Rossore-Massaciuccoli	V	22,000	1979
Mincio	V	13,708	1984
Monte Beigua	V	20,160	1985

Monte Corno	V	6,660	1980
Monte di Portofino	V	4,650	1986
Montevecchia e Valle del Curone	V	1,598	1983
Monti Simbruini	V	38,000	1983
Orsiera-Rocciavre	V	10,928	1980
Paneveggio-Pale di San Martino	V	15,800	1967
Pineta di Appiano Gentile e Tradate	V	4,597	1983
Po Delta	V	30,000	1982
Pollino	V	77,000	1986
Prescudin	V	1,647	1974
Puez-Odle	V	9,210	1977
Rieserferner	V	15,000	
Sarntaler Alpen	V	29,800	
Schlern	V	6,400	1974
Sciliar	V	5,850	1974
Serio	V	7,570	1985
Val Troncea	V	3,280	1980
Valle del Lambro	V	6,452	1983
Valle del Ticino (Lombardia)	V	90,640	1974
Valle del Ticino (Piemonte)	V	6,250	1978

Regional Nature Reserves/Réserves régionales de nature

Bosco e Laghi di Palanfre	V	1,050	1979
Cavagrande del Cassibile	IV	2,800	1984
Faggeta Madonia	IV	3,050	1984
Isole dello Stagnone di Marsala	IV	3,380	1984
La Montagne delle Felci e Dei Porri	IV	1,600	1984
Laghi Lungo e Ripasottile	IV	1,948	1985
Lago di Vico	V	3,240	1982
Montagne delle Felci e dei Porri	IV	1,600	1984
Monte Quacella	IV	1,900	1984
Monte Rufeno	IV	2,840	1983
Oasi Faunistica di Vendicari	IV	1,500	1984
Oasi del Simeto	IV	1,350	1984
Zingaro	IV	1,600	1981

JAMAHIRIYA ARABE LIBYENNE
Voir paragraphe LIBYAN ARAB JAMAHIRIYA

JAMAICA/JAMAIQUE
No Areas Listed/pas de sites

JAPAN/JAPON

Summary/Sommaire		
Category\Catégorie I	6	9,033
Category\Catégorie II	15	1,299,114
Category\Catégorie IV	31	344,568
Category\Catégorie V	13	749,703
Total	**65**	**2,402,418**

National Parks/Parcs nationaux

Akan	II	90,481	1934
Ashizuri-Uwakai	V	10,967	1972
Aso-Kuju	V	72,680	1934
Bandai-Asahi	II	187,041	1950
Chichibu-Tama	V	121,600	1950
Chubu-Sangaku	II	174,323	1934
Daisen-Oki	V	31,927	1936
Daisetsuzan	II	230,894	1934
Fuji-Hakone-Izu	V	122,686	1936
Hakusan	II	47,700	1962
Iriomote	II	12,506	1972
Ise-Shima	V	55,549	1946
Joshinetsu Kogen	II	189,028	1949
Kirishima-Yaku	II	54,833	1934
Kushiro Shitsugen	II	26,861	1987
Minami Arupusu	II	35,752	1964
Nikko	V	140,164	1934
Ogasawara	II	6,099	1972
Rikuchu-Kaigan	V	12,348	1955
Rishiri-Rebun-Sarobetsu	II	21,222	1974
Saikai	V	24,653	1955
Sanin-Kaigan	V	8,996	1963
Seto-Naikai	V	62,839	1934
Shikotsu-Toya	II	98,332	1949
Shiretoko	II	38,633	1964
Towada-Hachimantai	II	85,409	1936
Unzen-Amakusa	V	25,496	1934
Yoshino-Kumano	V	59,798	1936

National Wildlife Protection Areas/Aires nationales
de protection de la flore et de la faune sauvages

Gamo	IV	7,790	
Izunuma	IV	1,450	1982
Kushiro Marsh	IV	29,084	1935
Lake Kuccaro	IV	2,803	1983

Wilderness Areas/Aires de nature sauvage

Oigawa-Genryubu	I	1,115	1976
Onnebetsudake	I	1,895	1980
Tokachigawa-genryubu	I	1,035	1977
Tonegawa-genryubu	I	2,318	1977
Wagadake	I	1,451	1981
Yakushima	I	1,219	1975

Protected Areas/Aires protégées

Asama	IV	38,777	1951
Daikoku-jima	IV	107	1972
Danjo-gunto	IV	415	1973
Ishizuchi-yama	IV	9,502	1977
Kakui-jima	IV	662	1952
Kii-Nagashima	IV	7,452	1969
Kita-Alps	IV	63,403	1974

Kominato	IV	4,515	1952
Kutcharo-futo	IV	5,012	1958
Moriyoshi-yama	IV	4,941	1977
Odaisankei	IV	15,971	1972
Seinan	IV	2,182	1979
Tori-shima	IV	453	1954
Wakinosawa	IV	1,166	1964
Yagaji	IV	3,680	1976

Prefecture Wildlife Protection Areas/Aires préfectorales de protection de la faune et de la flore sauvages

Ampal	IV	1,058	1985
Biwa	IV	69,546	1981
Inawashiro	IV	10,933	1984
Kasumigaura	IV	5,290	
Mogami	IV	1,732	1983
Nakaumi	IV	8,800	1984
Shinji	IV	8,800	1982
Tama River Estuary	IV	5,310	1986
Tofutsu	IV	2,051	1982
Ushibori	IV	1,120	
Yudo	IV	3,855	1972
Zuibaiji Estuary	IV	26,708	1986

JORDAN/JORDANIE

Summary/Sommaire		
Category\Catégorie I	1	1,200
Category\Catégorie IV	5	71,700
Category\Catégorie V	1	20,000
Total	**7**	**92,900**

National Parks/Parcs nationaux

Petra	V	20,000

Wildlife Reserves/Réserves de ressources sauvages

Dana	IV	15,000	1989
Shaumari	IV	2,200	1975
Wadi Mujib	IV	21,200	1985
Zubiya	IV	1,300	1987

Reserves/Réserves

Azraq Desert	IV	32,000	1987
Azraq Wetland	I	1,200	1965

KENYA

Summary/Sommaire		
Category\Catégorie II	30	3,277,134
Category\Catégorie IV	6	70,313
Total	**36**	**3,347,447**

National Parks/Parcs nationaux

Aberdare	II	76,619	1950
Amboseli	II	39,206	1974
Chyulu	II	47,100	1983
Hell's Gate	II	6,800	1984
Kora	II	178,780	1989
Lake Nakuru	II	18,800	1967
Longonot	II	5,200	1983
Malka Mari	II	87,600	1989
Meru	II	87,044	1966
Mount Elgon	II	16,923	1968
Mount Kenya	II	71,500	1949
Nairobi	II	11,721	1946
Ol Donyo Sabuk	II	1,842	1967
Ruma	II	12,000	1983
Sibiloi	II	157,085	1973
South Island	II	3,880	1983
Tsavo East	II	1,174,700	1948
Tsavo West	II	906,500	1948

Marine National Parks/Parcs nationaux marins

Kisite/Mpunguti	II	2,800	1978
Mombasa	II	1,000	1986
Watamu	II	1,000	1968

Nature Reserves/Réserves de nature

Arabuko Sokoke	IV	4,332	1979
Mau South West	IV	43,032	1960
Nandi North	IV	3,434	1978
Uaso Narok	IV	1,575	1981

National Reserves/Réserves nationales

Buffalo Springs	II	13,100	1985
Kakamega	II	4,468	1985
Kerio Valley	IV	6,600	1983
Lake Bogoria	II	10,705	1970
Marsabit	II	113,200	1949
Masai Mara	II	151,000	1974
Samburu	II	16,500	1985
Shaba	II	23,910	1974
Shimba Hills	II	19,251	1968
Tana River Primate	II	16,900	1976

Game Sanctuaries/Sanctuaires de faune

Taita Hills	IV	11,340	1973

KIRIBATI

Summary/Sommaire		
Category\Catégorie I	2	20,130
Category\Catégorie IV	1	6,500
Total	**3**	**26,630**

Wildlife Sanctuaries/Sanctuaires de ressources sauvages

Malden Island	I	3,930	1975
Phoenix Island (Rawaki)	IV	6,500	1975
Starbuck	I	16,200	1975

KOREA, DEMOCRATIC PEOPLE'S REPUBLIC OF/REPUBLIQUE POPULAIRE DEMOCRATIQUE DE COREE

Summary/Sommaire		
Category\Catégorie II	1	43,890
Category\Catégorie IV	1	14,000
Total	**2**	**57,890**

National Parks/Parcs nationaux

Kumgang-san	II	43,890	

Nature Protection Areas/Zones de protection de la nature

Paekdu	IV	14,000	1976

KOREA, REPUBLIC OF/REPUBLIQUE DE COREE

Summary/Sommaire		
Category\Catégorie V	17	577,766
Total	**17**	**577,766**

National Parks/Parcs nationaux

Bukhan	V	7,845	1983
Chiak	V	18,209	1984
Chiri	V	44,045	1967
Chuwang	V	10,558	1976
Dogyu	V	21,900	1975
Halla	V	13,300	1970
Kaya	V	5,781	1972
Kyeryong	V	6,098	1968
Kyong Ju	V	13,816	1968
Naejang	V	7,603	1972
Odae	V	29,850	1975
Songni	V	28,340	1970
Sorak	V	37,300	1970
Worak	V	28,450	1984

Marine National Parks/Parcs nationaux marins

Hallyo	V	47,862	1968
Sosan	V	32,899	1978
Tadohae	V	203,910	1981

KUWAIT/KOWEIT

No Areas Listed/pas de sites

LAO PEOPLE'S DEMOCRATIC REPUBLIC/REPUBLIQUE DEMOCRATIQUE POPULAIRE LAO
No Areas Listed/pas de sites

LEBANON/LIBAN

Summary/Sommaire		
Category\Catégorie II	1	3,500
Total	**1**	**3,500**

National Parks/Parcs nationaux
  Mashgara (Machgharah)   II   3,500   1988

LESOTHO

Summary/Sommaire		
Category\Catégorie IV	1	6,805
Total	**1**	**6,805**

National Parks/Parcs nationaux
  Sehlabathebe   IV   6,805   1970

LIBAN
Voir paragraphe LEBANON

LIBERIA

Summary/Sommaire		
Category\Catégorie II	1	130,747
Total	**1**	**130,747**

National Parks/Parcs nationaux
  Sapo   II   130,747   1983

LIBYAN ARAB JAMAHIRIYA/JAMAHIRIYA ARABE LIBYENNE

Summary/Sommaire		
Category\Catégorie II	1	35,000
Category\Catégorie IV	2	120,000
Total	**3**	**155,000**

National Parks/Parcs nationaux
  Kouf   II   35,000   1979
Nature Reserves/Réserves de nature
  Zellaf   IV   100,000   1978
Protected Areas/Aires protégées
  Nefhusa   IV   20,000   1978

LIECHTENSTEIN
No Areas Listed/pas de sites

LUXEMBOURG
No Areas Listed/pas de sites

MADAGASCAR

Summary/Sommaire		
Category\Catégorie I	10	568,802
Category\Catégorie II	5	133,740
Category\Catégorie IV	21	375,190
Total	**36**	**1,077,732**

National Parks/Parcs nationaux

Isalo	II	81,540	1962
Mantadia	II	10,000	1989
Mananara (Terrestrial)	II	23,000	1989
Mananara (Marine)	II	1,000	1989
Montagne d'Ambre	II	18,200	1958

Integral Nature Reserves/Réserves naturelles intégrales

Andohahela	I	76,020	1939
Andringitra	I	31,160	1927
Ankarafantsika	I	60,520	1927
Betampona	I	2,228	1927
Marojejy	I	60,150	1952
Tsaratanana	I	48,622	1927
Tsimanampetsotsa	I	43,200	1927
Tsingy de Bemaraha	I	152,000	1927
Tsingy de Namoroka	I	21,742	1927
Zahamena	I	73,160	1927

Special Reserves/Réserves spéciales

Ambatovaky	IV	60,050	1958
Ambohijanahary	IV	24,750	1958
Ambohitantely	IV	5,600	1982
Analamerana	IV	34,700	1956
Andranomena	IV	6,420	1958
Anjanaharibe-Sud	IV	32,100	1958
Ankarana	IV	18,220	1956
Bemarivo	IV	11,570	1956
Bora	IV	4,780	1956
Cap Sainte Marie	IV	1,750	1962
Foret d'Ambre	IV	4,810	1958
Kalambatritra	IV	28,250	1959
Kasijy	IV	18,800	1956
Mangerivola	IV	11,900	1958
Maningozo	IV	7,900	1956
Manombo	IV	5,020	1962
Manongarivo	IV	35,250	1956
Marotandrano	IV	42,200	1956
Nosy Mangabe	IV	520	1965
Pic d'Ivohibe	IV	3,450	1964
Tampoketsa d'Analamaitso	IV	17,150	1958

MALAWI

Summary/Sommaire		
Category\Catégorie II	5	697,900
Category\Catégorie IV	4	369,000
Total	**9**	**1,066,900**

National Parks/Parcs nationaux

Kasungu	II	231,600	1970
Lake Malawi	II	9,400	1980
Lengwe	II	88,700	1970
Liwonde	II	54,800	1973
Nyika	II	313,400	1966

Game Reserves/Réserves de faune

Majete	IV	78,400	1955
Mwabvi	IV	10,400	1951
Nkohota-Kota	IV	180,200	1930
Vwaza Marsh	IV	100,000	1977

MALAYSIA/MALAISIE

Summary/Sommaire		
Category\Catégorie I	25	84,732
Category\Catégorie II	14	779,233
Category\Catégorie IV	5	297,228
Category\Catégorie V	1	1,011
Total	**45**	**1,162,204**

Peninsular Malaysia/Peninsule Malaisie

National Parks/Parcs nationaux

Taman Negara	II	434,351	1939

Wildlife Reserves/Réserves de ressources sauvages

Krau	IV	53,095	1923
Sungai Dusun	IV	4,330	1964

Wildlife Sanctuaries/Sanctuaires de ressources sauvages

Cameron Highlands	IV	64,953	1962

Parks/Parcs

Templer	V	1,011	1956

Virgin Jungle Reserves/Réserves de forêt vierge

Berembun	I	1,595	1959
Bukit Larut	I	2,747	1962
Gunung Jerai	I	1,579	1960
Gunung Ledang	I	1,134	1969

Sabah

National Parks/Parcs nationaux

Crocker Range	II	139,919	1984

Parks/Parcs

Bukit Tawau	II	27,972	1979

Kinabalu	II	75,370	1964
Pulau Penyu (Turtle Islands)	II	1,740	1977
Pulau Tiga	II	15,864	1978
Tunku Abdul Rahman	II	4,929	1974

Virgin Jungle Reserves/Réserves de forêt vierge

Brantian-Tatulit	I	4,140	1984
Crocker Range	I	3,279	1984
Gomantong,Materis,Bod Tai,Keruak,Pangi	I	1,816	1984
Kabili Sepilok	I	4,294	1931
Kalumpang	I	3,768	1984
Lungmanis	I	6,735	1984
Madai Baturong	I	5,867	1984
Maligan	I	9,240	1984
Mengalong	I	1,008	1984
Milian-Labau	I	2,812	1984
Pin-Supi	I	4,696	1984
Pulau Batik	I	353	1984
Pulau Berhala	I	173	1984
Pulau Sukar	I	760	1984
Sepagaya	I	4,128	1984
Sepilok (Mangrove)	I	1,235	1931
Sungai Imbak	I	18,113	1984
Sungai Kapur	I	1,250	1984
Sungai Lokan	I	1,852	1984
Sungai Simpang	I	1,149	1984
Tabawan, Bohayan, Maganting, Silumpat Islands	I	1,009	1984

Sarawak

National Parks/Parcs nationaux

Bako	II	2,728	1957
Gunung Gading	II	4,106	1983
Gunung Mulu	II	52,865	1974
Kubah	II	2,230	1989
Lambir Hills	II	6,952	1975
Niah	II	3,140	1974
Similajau	II	7,067	1979

Wildlife Sanctuaries/Sanctuaires de ressources sauvages

Lanjak-Entimau	IV	168,758	1983
Samunsam	IV	6,092	1979

MALDIVES

No Areas Listed/pas de sites

MALI

Summary/Sommaire		
Category\Catégorie II	1	350,000
Category\Catégorie IV	6	539,100
Total	**7**	**889,100**

National Parks/Parcs nationaux

Boucle du Baoule	II	350,000	1954

Faunal Reserves/Réserves fauniques

Badinko	IV	193,000	1951
Baring Makana	IV	13,000	1954
Fina	IV	136,000	1954
Kenie-Baoule	IV	67,500	1952
Kongossambougou	IV	92,000	1955
Sounsan	IV	37,600	1954

MALTA/MALTE
No Areas Listed/pas de sites

MARIANNES DU NORD
Voir paragraphe NORTHERN MARIANAS

MAROC
Voir paragraphe MOROCCO

MARSHALL ISLANDS/ILES MARSHALL
No Areas Listed/pas de sites

MAURITANIA/MAURITANIE

Summary/Sommaire		
Category\Catégorie I	1	310,000
Category\Catégorie II	1	1,173,000
Category\Catégorie IV	1	250,000
Total	**3**	**1,733,000**

National Parks/Parcs nationaux

Banc d'Arguin	II	1,173,000	1976

Integral Reserves/Réserves intégrales

Baie du Levrier (Cap Blanc)	I	310,000	1986

Partial Faunal Reserves/Réserves fauniques partielles

El Agher	IV	250,000	1937

MAURITIUS/MAURICE

Summary/Sommaire		
Category\Catégorie IV	3	4,023
Total	**3**	**4,023**

Nature Reserves/Réserves de nature

Ile Plate	IV	253	1972
Macchabee/Bel Ombre	IV	3,611	1951
Round Island	IV	159	1957

MEXICO/MEXIQUE

Summary/Sommaire		
Category\Catégorie I	13	603,303
Category\Catégorie II	33	1,618,173
Category\Catégorie III	1	1,600
Category\Catégorie IV	8	3,730,269
Category\Catégorie V	6	3,466,324
Total	**61**	**9,419,669**

National Parks/Parcs nationaux

Benito Juarez	II	2,737	1937
Bosencheve	II	15,000	1940
Canon de Rio Blanco	II	55,600	1938
Canon del Sumidero	II	21,789	1980
Cascada de Bassaseachic	II	6,263	1981
Cerro de la Estrella	II	1,100	1938
Cofre de Perote	II	11,700	1937
Constitucion de 1857	II	5,009	1962
Cumbres de Majalca	II	4,772	1939
Cumbres de Monterrey	II	246,500	1939
El Chico	II	2,739	1982
El Gogorron	II	25,000	1936
El Potosi	II	2,000	1936
El Tepozteco	II	24,000	1937
El Veladero	II	3,159	1980
Grutas de Cacahuamilpa	III	1,600	1936
Insurgente Jose Maria Morelos y Pavon	II	1,813	1939
Insurgente Miguel Hidalgo y Costilla	II	1,760	1936
Isla Isabel	II	194	1980
Iztaccihuatl-Popocatepetl	II	25,679	1948
La Malinche	II	45,700	1938
Lagunas de Chacahua	II	14,187	1937
Lagunas de Montebello	II	6,022	1959
Lagunas de Zempoala	II	4,669	1936
Los Marmoles	II	23,150	1936
Nevado de Colima	II	22,200	1940
Nevado de Toluca	II	51,000	1936
Pico de Orizaba	II	19,750	1937
Pico de Tancitaro	II	29,316	1940
Sierra de San Pedro Martir	II	63,000	1947
Zoquiapan y Anexas	II	19,418	1937

Biosphere Reserves (National)/Réserves de la biosphère (nationales)

Calakmul	V	723,185	1989
El Triunfo	I	119,177	1972
El Vizcaino	V	2,546,790	1988
Mapimi	V	20,000	1979
Michilia	V	35,000	1979
Montes Azules	II	331,200	1978

Sian Ka'an	II	528,147	1986
Sierra de Manantlan	V	139,577	1987
Marine Reserves/Réserves marines			
La Blanquilla	IV	66,868	1975
Faunal Reserves/Réserves fauniques			
Isla Cedros	I	1,000	1978
Cetacean Sanctuaries/Sanctuaires de Cétacés			
Isla de Guerrero Negro	I	40,000	1979
Refuges/Refuges			
La Mojonera	IV	9,201	1981
La Primavera	IV	30,500	1980
Sierra de Alvarez	IV	16,900	1981
Sierra del Pinacate	IV	28,660	1979
Valle de los Cirios	IV	3,500,000	1980
Natural and Typical Biotopes/Biotopes naturels et typiques			
La Encrucijada	IV	30,000	1972
Special Biosphere Reserves/Réserves spéciales de la biosphère			
Cascadas de Agua Azul	I	2,580	1980
Isla Contoy	I	176	1961
Isla Guadalupe	I	25,000	1922
Isla Tiburon	I	120,800	1963
Islas del Golfo de California	I	150,000	1978
Mariposa Monarca	I	16,100	1980
Ria Celestun	I	59,130	1979
Ria Lagartos	I	47,840	1979
Selva del Ocote	IV	48,140	1982
Sierra de Santa Martha	I	20,000	1980
Volcan de San Martin	I	1,500	1979
Parks/Parcs			
Omiltemi	II	3,600	
National Historic Parks/Parcs historiques nationaux			
Palenque	V	1,772	1981

MONACO
No Areas Listed/pas de sites

MONGOLIA/MONGOLIE

Summary/Sommaire		
Category\Catégorie I	12	224,280
Category\Catégorie II	2	5,393,560
Total	**14**	**5,617,840**

National Parks/Parcs nationaux			
Ar-Toul	II	93,560	1984
Great Gobi Desert	II	5,300,000	1975
Reserves/Réserves			
Batkhan	I	2,000	1957
Bogdkhan	I	4,080	1978

Bogdo-ula	I	54,100	1778
Bulgan-gol	I	2,700	1965
Bulgan-ula	I	4,800	1965
Khasagt-Khayrkhan	I	33,600	1965
Khorgo	I	20,000	1965
Lkhachinvandan-ula	I	75,000	1965
Nagalkhan	I	2,000	1957
Tulga-togo-Zhallavch-ula	I	3,000	1965
Uran-ula	I	3,000	1965
Yolyn-am	I	20,000	1965

MOROCCO/MAROC

Summary/Sommaire		
Category\Catégorie I	6	87,934
Category\Catégorie IV	4	244,425
Category\Catégorie V	1	36,000
Total	**11**	**368,359**

National Parks/Parcs nationaux			
Toubkal	V	36,000	1934
Biological Reserves/Réserves biologiques			
Bokkoyas	I	70,000	1986
Khnifiss/Puerto Cansado	I	6,500	1962
Merja Zerga	IV	7,425	1978
Faunal Reserves/Réserves fauniques			
Iriki	IV	10,000	1967
Takherkhort	I	1,230	1967
Botanical Reserves/Réserves botaniques			
Talassantane	I	2,617	1972
Reserves/Réserves			
Sidi Boughaba	I	5,600	1946
Sidi Chiker	I	1,987	1956
Hunting Reserves/Réserves de chasse			
Bouarfa	IV	220,000	1967
Mouley Bousalham	IV	7,000	1978

MOZAMBIQUE

Summary/Sommaire		
Category\Catégorie IV	1	2,000
Total	**1**	**2,000**

Faunal Reserves/Réserves fauniques			
Ilhas da Inhaca e dos Portugeses	IV	2,000	1965

MYANMAR

Summary/Sommaire		
Category\Catégorie II	1	160,580
Category\Catégorie V	1	12,691
Total	**2**	**173,271**

National Parks/Parcs nationaux			
Alaungdaw Kathapa	II	160,580	1984
Parks/Parcs			
Popa Mountain	V	12,691	1985

NAMIBIA/NAMIBIE

Summary/Sommaire		
Category\Catégorie II	4	8,926,349
Category\Catégorie IV	4	639,953
Category\Catégorie V	1	780,000
Total	**9**	**10,346,302**

National Parks/Parcs nationaux			
Etosha	II	2,270,000	1958
Nature Reserves/Réserves de nature			
Omaruru	IV	1,000	1971
Tsaobis-Leopard	IV	35,000	1969
Game Reserves/Réserves de faune			
Western Caprivi	IV	600,000	1963
Game Parks/Parcs de gibier			
Daan Viljoen	IV	3,953	1967
Namib/Naukluft	II	4,976,800	1979
Skeleton Coast	II	1,639,000	1971
Waterberg Plateau	II	40,549	1972
Recreation Areas/Aires de loisirs			
National West Coast	V	780,000	

NAURU

No Areas Listed/pas de sites

NEPAL

Summary/Sommaire		
Category\Catégorie II	7	864,400
Category\Catégorie IV	4	94,100
Total	11	**958,500**

National Parks/Parcs nationaux			
Khaptad	II	22,500	1986
Langtang	II	171,000	1976
Rara	II	10,600	1977
Royal Bardia	II	96,800	1988

Royal Chitwan	II	93,200	1973
Sagarmatha	II	114,800	1976
Shey-Phoksundo	II	355,500	1984
Wildlife Reserves/Réserves de ressources sauvages			
Koshi Tappu	IV	17,500	1976
Parsa	IV	49,900	1984
Royal Sukla Phanta	IV	15,500	1976
Shivapuri Watershed Reserve	IV	11,200	1985

NETHERLANDS/PAYS-BAS

Summary/Sommaire		
Category\Catégorie I	3	4,211
Category\Catégorie II	5	20,196
Category\Catégorie III	22	220,595
Category\Catégorie IV	42	124,825
Total	**72**	**369,827**

National Parks/Parcs nationaux			
De Biesbosch	IV	7,100	1987
De Groote Peel	IV	1,320	1985
De Hamert	IV	1,460	1989
De Meijnweg	IV	1,600	1990
De Weerribben	IV	3,450	1986
Dwingelderveld	IV	3,600	1986
Hoge Veluwe	IV	5,450	1935
Schiermonnikoog	II	5,400	1989
Veluwezoom	IV	4,720	1930
Zuid-Kennemerland	IV	2,090	1990
Nature Reserves/Réserves de nature			
Alde Feanen	IV	1,850	
Ameland	IV	4,500	
Amsterdamse Waterleidingpuinen	IV	3,370	
Ankeveense-Kortenhoefre-Loosdrechtre Plassen	IV	1,450	1969
Bargerveen	IV	2,100	
Berkenheuvel	IV	1,000	1956
Boswachterij Schoorl	IV	2,000	1894
De Geul en Westerduinen	I	1,681	1926
De Strabrechtse Heide	IV	2,675	1951
Diependal	IV	1,310	
Duinen Terschelling	IV	9,500	
Duinen Texel	IV	2,300	
Duinen Vlieland	IV	5,000	
Eierlands Gat Zeehondenreservaat	IV	20,000	1947
Fochteloerveen	IV	1,715	1972
Goois	III	1,500	1987
Haarler- and Holterberg	IV	1,600	
Hardenberg	IV	1,190	
Haringvliet Forelands	IV	3,600	
Ilperveld	IV	1,516	1961

Kootwijkerzand/Garderen	IV	1,500	
Lauwersmeer	IV	2,500	
Leuvenhorst and Leuvenumse Bos	IV	1,855	
Loonse and Drunense Duinen	IV	1,730	
Mayendel	IV	1,400	
Meijnweg	IV	1,015	
Nieuwkoopse Plassen	IV	1,500	1968
North Veluwe	IV	2,850	1954
Oerd en Steile Bank	I	1,200	
Oostvaardersplassen	III	5,600	
Planken Wambuis	IV	1,965	
Schouwen Duinen	IV	3,064	1980
Slikken van Flakkee	IV	3,700	
Strabrechtse Heide	IV	1,020	
Stroomdallandschap Drenthe Aa	IV	1,250	1965
Tlonger- and Lindevallei	IV	1,000	
Varkensland and Waterland	IV	1,010	
Wassenaarse Duinen	I	1,330	

Natural Monuments/Monuments naturels

Berkheide	III	1,000	1990
Boschplaat Natural Monument	III	4,400	1974
Deurnse Peel	III	1,500	1980
Dollard	III	5,000	1977
Eemmeer	III	1,200	1976
Engbertsdjiksvenen	III	1,000	1985
Gras- and Rietgorzen Haringvliet	III	1,030	1971
Kop van Schouwen	III	2,200	1978
Krammer-Volkerak	III	3,430	1988
Kwelders Friesland	III	1,370	1982
Kwelders Groningen	III	1,230	1982
Mariapeel	III	1,100	1964
Markiezaatsmeer Zuid	III	1,860	1982
Mispeleindse -/Landschotse Heide	III	1,135	1983
Oosterschelde	III	24,000	1990
Schorren van de Eendracht	III	1,000	1982
Ventjagersplaten and Slijkplaat	III	1,090	1980
Verdronken Land van Saeftinghe	III	3,500	1976
Waddenzee	III	154,800	1981
Zwarte Meer	III	1,650	1990

Aruba

No Areas Listed/pas de sites

Netherlands Antilles/Antilles néderlandaise

National Parks/Parcs nationaux

Christoffel (Curacao)	II	1,860	1978
Washington-Slagbaai (Bonaire)	II	5,900	1969

Marine Parks/Parcs marins

Bonaire	II	6,000	1979

Underwater Parks/Parcs sous-marins
Curacao　　　　　　　　　　　　　　II　　1,036　　1983

NEW ZEALAND/NOUVELLE-ZELANDE

Summary/Sommaire		
Category\Catégorie I	36	394,698
Category\Catégorie II	11	2,101,059
Category\Catégorie III	5	20,991
Category\Catégorie IV	100	322,385
Total	**152**	**2,839,133**

National Parks/Parcs nationaux
Abel Tasman　　　　　　II　　22,543　　1942
Arthur's Pass　　　　　II　　94,422　　1929
Egmont　　　　　　　　II　　33,540　　1900
Fiordland　　　　　　　II　1,023,186　1904
Mount Aspiring　　　　II　285,589　　1964
Mount Cook　　　　　　II　69,923　　1953
Nelson Lakes　　　　　II　96,112　　1956
Tongariro　　　　　　　II　76,504　　1894
Urewera　　　　　　　II　207,462　　1954
Westland　　　　　　　II　117,547　　1960
Whanganui　　　　　　II　74,231　　1986
National Park Special Areas/Aires spéciales
de parcs nationaux
Fiordland (Sinbad Gully Stream)　I　2,160　　1974
Fiordland (Takahe)　　I　177,252　　1953
Mount Aspiring　　　　I　1,722　　1973
Secretary Island　　　I　8,980　　1973
Solander Island　　　　I　120　　1973
Scientific Reserves/Réserves scientifiques
Tom Shand　　　　　　I　309　　1974
Waituna Wetlands　　　I　3,557　　1983
Nature Reserves/Réserves de nature
Anglem　　　　　　　I　16,977　　1907
Antipodes Islands　　　I　611　　1961
Auckland Islands　　　I　62,564　　1934
Bench Island　　　　　I　121　　1926
Big Mangere Island　　I　113　　1967
Bounty Islands　　　　I　136　　1961
Campbell Islands　　　I　11,331　　1954
Chetwode Islands　　　I　324　　1962
Curtis Island　　　　　IV　306　　1934
Cuvier Islands　　　　I　171　　1951
Double and Stanley Islands　I　120　　1963
Farewell Spit　　　　　I　11,388　　1938
Hen and Chickens Islands　I　842　　1928
Kapiti Island　　　　　I　1,970　　1975
Kermadec Islands　　　I　3,089　　1934

Little Barrier Island	I	2,817	1895
Mokohinau Islands	I	108	1888
Mount Uwerau	I	1,012	1966
Pegasus	I	67,441	1907
Poor Knights Islands	I	271	1975
Rangatira	I	219	1967
Snares Islands	I	243	1961
Three Kings	I	685	1956
Waitangiroto	I	1,214	1957
Wildlife Sanctuaries/Sanctuaires de ressources sauvages			
Stephens Island	I	150	1966
Wildlife Refuges/Refuges de ressources sauvages			
Lake Alexandrina/McGregor's Lagoon	IV	2,200	1957
Pouto Point	IV	6,789	1957
Wairau River Lagoons	IV	1,040	1959
Whale (Motuhora) Island	IV	140	1953
Marine Reserves/Réserves marines			
Poor Knights Islands	I	2,410	1981
State Forest Ecological Areas/Aires écologiques forestières publiques			
Big River	IV	6,733	1980
Blackwater	IV	9,150	1980
Coal Creek	IV	3,025	1980
Diggers Ridge	IV	4,235	1982
Flatstaff	IV	1,622	1980
Greenstone	IV	1,144	1980
Kapowai	IV	1,400	1982
Lake Christabel	IV	10,648	1981
Lake Hochstetter	IV	1,803	1981
Lillburn	IV	2,670	1982
Manganuiowae	IV	1,760	1981
Mangatutu	IV	2,533	1980
Moehau	IV	3,634	1977
Onekura	IV	2,351	1981
Papakai	IV	3,366	1982
Pororari	IV	6,448	1980
Pukepoto	IV	1,906	1980
Roaring Meg	IV	3,600	1980
Saltwater	IV	1,438	1981
Saxton	IV	4,120	1980
Tiropahi	IV	3,451	1980
Waikoau	IV	2,800	1982
Waipapa	IV	1,830	1979
Waipuna	IV	1,910	1980
Forest Sanctuaries/Sanctuaires forestiers			
Hihitahi	I	2,170	1973
Ngatukituki	I	1,600	1973
Waipoua	I	9,105	1952
Reserves/Réserves			
Lake Whangape	IV	1,450	

Ecological Areas/Zones écologiques

Fletchers Creek	IV	2,586	1980

Scenic Reserves/Réserves panoramiques

Arapawa Island	IV	1,035	1973
Bluemine Island	IV	377	1912
Chance, Penguin and Fairy Bays	IV	1,599	1903
Chaslands	IV	1,334	1937
Codfish Island	I	1,396	1915
Crescent Island	IV	117	1973
D'Urville Island	IV	4,072	1912
Glen Allen	IV	1,000	1914
Glenhope	IV	5,936	1907
Glory Cove	IV	1,297	1903
Gordon Park	IV	1,817	1938
Gouland Downs	IV	6,564	1917
Hakarimata	IV	1,795	1905
Isolated Hill	IV	2,160	1924
Jordan Stream	IV	1,151	1916
Karamea Bluff	IV	1,445	1910
Kenepuru Sound	IV	1,687	1895
Kenny Isle	IV	154	1938
Lake Ianthe	IV	1,308	1905
Lake Kaniere	III	7,252	1906
Lake Okareka	III	1,143	1930
Lake Okataina	III	4,388	1974
Lake Tarawera	III	5,819	1973
Leithen Bush	IV	1,342	1978
Lewis Pass	IV	13,737	1907
Lower Buller Gorge	IV	5,941	1907
Mangamuka Gorge	IV	2,832	1927
Matahuru	IV	1,336	1905
Maungatautari	III	2,389	1927
Maurihoro	IV	1,797	1936
Mercury Island	IV	226	1972
Meremere Hill	IV	1,368	1982
Moeatoa	IV	1,212	1927
Mokau River	IV	2,273	1920
Motukawanui	IV	355	1981
Moturua Island	IV	136	1981
Mount Courtney	IV	1,772	1912
Mount Hercules	IV	8,024	1911
Mount Stokes	IV	4,396	1977
Mount Te Kinga	IV	3,747	1905
Nydia Bay	IV	1,408	1938
Paradise Bay	IV	2,743	1977
Paterson Inlet Islands	IV	126	1907
Pelorus Bridge	IV	1,010	1906
Pokaka	IV	8,068	1982
Port Pegasus Islands	IV	838	1907
Pryse Peak	IV	3,646	1903

Pukeamaru Range	IV	3,265	1907
Punakaiki	IV	2,037	1914
Rahu	IV	2,132	1936
Rakeahua	IV	6,463	1903
Rangitoto Island	IV	2,333	1980
Robertson Range	IV	3,689	1912
Saltwater Lagoon	IV	1,359	1928
Ship Cove	IV	1,093	1896
South Cape	IV	5,077	1903
Tahuakai	IV	1,561	1983
Tangarakau	IV	2,640	1918
Tapuaenuku	IV	2,226	1962
Te Arowhenua	IV	1,705	1981
Te Kopia	IV	1,408	1911
Te Tapui	IV	2,382	1925
Tennyson Inlet	IV	5,596	1896
Toatoa	IV	2,847	1982
Ulva	IV	259	1922
Upper Buller Gorge	IV	5,920	1979
Waioeka Gorge	IV	18,645	1933
Waipapa	IV	2,528	1974
Waipori Falls	IV	1,352	1913
Waituhui Kuratau	IV	1,319	1953
Wanganui River	IV	35,858	1915
Warbeck River	IV	1,283	1931
Whangamumu	IV	2,154	1981

Unclassified/Non classé

Waipoua Kauri Management Area	IV	3,747	1976
White Island	IV	238	1953

NICARAGUA

Summary/Sommaire		
Category\Catégorie II	3	27,300
Category\Catégorie IV	3	16,000
Total	**6**	**43,300**

National Parks/Parcs nationaux

Archipielago Zapatera	II	10,000	1983
Saslaya	II	11,800	1971
Volcan Masaya	II	5,500	1978

Natural Reserves/Réserves naturelles

Volcan Cosiguina	IV	8,000	1976
Volcan Maderas	IV	4,000	1983

Wildlife Refuges/Refuges de ressources sauvages

Rio Escalante-Chacocente	IV	4,000	1983

NIGER

Summary/Sommaire		
Category\Catégorie I	1	1,280,500
Category\Catégorie II	1	220,000
Category\Catégorie IV	2	153,740
Total	**4**	**1,654,240**

National Parks/Parcs nationaux
W du Niger	II	220,000	1954

Integral Nature Reserves/Réserves naturelles intégrales
Addax	I	1,280,500	1988

Total Faunal Reserves/Réserves fauniques intégrales
Gadabedji	IV	76,000	1955
Tamou	IV	77,740	1962

NIGERIA

Summary/Sommaire		
Category\Catégorie II	1	534,082
Category\Catégorie IV	14	1,012,509
Total	**15**	**1,546,591**

National Parks/Parcs nationaux
Kainji Lake	II	534,082	1975

Game Reserves/Réserves de faune
Dagida	IV	29,422	
Falgore (Kogin Kano)	IV	92,000	1969
Gilli-Gilli	IV	36,200	
Hadejia (Baturiya) Wetlands	IV	29,700	1985
Kambari	IV	41,400	1969
Kashimbila	IV	189,600	1977
Kwale	IV	1,340	1981
Lame/Burra	IV	205,967	1972
Ologbo	IV	19,440	1981
Orle	IV	5,440	1981
Udi/Nsukka	IV	5,600	1981
Upper Ogun/Old Oyo	IV	110,000	1973
Yankari	IV	224,000	1956

Wildlife Parks/Parcs de ressources sauvages
Pandam	IV	22,400	1972

NIUE

No Areas Listed/pas de sites

NORTHERN MARIANAS/MARIANNES DU NORD

Summary/Sommaire		
Category\Catégorie I	3	1,129
Total	**3**	**1,129**

Preserves/Réserves
Asuncion Island	I	722	1985
Uracas Island (Farallon de Parjaros)	I	202	1985

Unclassified/Non classé
Maug Island	I	205	1958

NORWAY/NORVEGE

Summary/Sommaire		
Category\Catégorie I	24	2,637,285
Category\Catégorie II	17	1,910,200
Category\Catégorie IV	5	18,705
Category\Catégorie V	21	196,248
Total	**67**	**4,762,438**

National Parks/Parcs nationaux
Anderdalen	II	6,800	1970
Borgefjell	II	108,700	1963
Dovrefjell	II	26,500	1974
Femundsmarka	II	38,600	1971
Gressamoen	II	18,000	1970
Gutulia	II	1,900	1968
Hardangervidda	II	342,800	1981
Jotunheimen	II	114,000	1980
Ovre Anarjakka	II	139,000	1975
Ovre Dividal	II	74,100	1971
Ovre Pasvik	II	6,300	1970
Rago	II	16,700	1971
Rondane	II	57,200	1962
Stabbursdalen	II	9,600	1970

Nature Reserves/Réserves de nature
Blodskyttodden/Barvikmyran	I	2,650	1983
Faerdesmyra	I	1,210	1972
Fokstumyra	IV	7,500	1923
Froan	I	40,000	1979
Grandefjaera	I	2,100	1983
Grytdalen	IV	1,600	1978
Havmyran	I	4,000	1982
Hukkelvatna	I	1,050	1983
Javreoaivit	I	3,000	1981
Karlsoeyaer	I	1,000	1977
Kraakvaagsvaet	IV	1,190	1983
Kvisleflaa	I	3,350	1981
Lille Soclensjoe	I	1,630	1981
Makkaurhalvoeya	I	11,350	1983
Nekmyrene	I	1,880	1981
Nord-Fugloy	I	2,130	1975
Nordre Oeyeren	IV	6,900	1975
Oera	I	1,560	1979
Osdalen	I	4,800	1969

Ovdaldasvarri	I	1,430	1983
Reinoey	I	1,300	1981
Semska-Stoedi	I	1,300	1976
Skogvoll	I	5,500	1983
Smoldalen	I	1,325	1974
Stabbursneset	I	1,620	1983
Vignesholmane	IV	1,515	1982
Vikna	I	2,100	1973

Landscape Protected Areas/Aires de paysages protégés

Brannsletta	V	1,880	1983
Dovre	V	5,700	1974
Favnvassdalen	V	1,390	1983
Femundsmarka	V	7,000	1971
Froan	V	4,000	1979
Gardsjoen	V	2,000	1983
Grytdalen	V	1,600	1978
Indre Vassfaret	V	4,200	1985
Innerdalen	V	7,300	1977
Jaerstrendene	V	1,608	1977
Mosvatn/Austfjellet	V	30,600	1981
Osterdalen	V	2,700	1983
Reisa	V	8,000	1986
Skaupsjoen/Hardangerjokulen	V	55,900	1981
Skipsfjorddalen	V	4,200	1978
Strandaa/Os	V	1,670	1983
Utladalen	V	30,000	1980
Vaeret	V	500	1982
Vassfaret and Vidalen	V	20,000	1985
Veoy	V	100	1970
Vidmyr-Hovden	V	5,900	1986

Svalbard and Jan Mayan Islands/Svalbard et des îles de Jan Mayan)

National Parks/Parcs nationaux

Northwest Spitzbergen	II	356,000	1973
Prins Karl's Forland	II	64,000	1973
South Spitzbergen	II	530,000	1973

Nature Reserves/Réserves de nature

Northeast Svalbard	I	1,903,000	1973
Southeast Svalbard	I	638,000	1973

Bouvet Island/Ile Bouvet

Nature Reserves/Réserves de nature

Bouvet Island	I	5,000	1971

NOUVELLE-ZELANDE
Voir paragraphe NEW ZEALAND

OMAN

Summary/Sommaire		
Category\Catégorie IV	2	54,000
Total	**2**	**54,000**

National Nature Reserves/Réserves naturelles nationales
Qurm	IV	1,000	1986

Reserves/Réserves
Wadi Serin/Jabal Aswad Arabian Tahr	IV	53,000

OUGANDA
Voir paragraphe UGANDA

PAKISTAN

Summary/Sommaire		
Category\Catégorie II	6	882,195
Category\Catégorie IV	43	2,700,723
Category\Catégorie V	4	72,051
Total	**53**	**3,654,969**

National Parks/Parcs nationaux
Ayubia	V	1,684	1984
Chinji	II	6,095	1987
Chitral Gol	II	7,750	1984
Dhrun	II	167,700	1988
Hazar Ganji-Chiltan	V	15,555	1980
Hingol	II	165,004	1988
Khunjerab	II	226,913	1975
Kirthar	II	308,733	1974
Lal Suhanra	V	37,426	1972
Margalla Hills	V	17,386	1980

Wildlife Sanctuaries/Sanctuaires de ressources sauvages
Agram Basti	IV	29,866	1983
Astore	IV	41,472	1975
Bajwat	IV	5,464	1964
Baltistan	IV	41,457	1975
Borraka	IV	2,025	1976
Buzi Makola	IV	145,101	1972
Chashma Lake	IV	33,084	1974
Cholistan	IV	660,949	1981
Chorani	IV	19,433	1972
Chumbi Surla	IV	55,945	1978
Daphar	IV	2,286	1978
Dhoung Block	IV	2,098	1977
Dureji	IV	178,259	1972
Gut	IV	165,992	1983
Hab Dam	IV	27,219	1972
Hadero Lake	IV	1,321	1977

Haleji Lake	IV	1,704	1977
Islamabad	IV	7,000	1980
Kachau	IV	21,660	1972
Kargah	IV	44,308	1975
Keti Bunder North	IV	8,948	1977
Keti Bunder South	IV	23,046	1977
Khurkhera	IV	18,345	1972
Kinjhar (Kalri) Lake	IV	13,468	1977
Koh-e-Geish	IV	24,356	1969
Kolwah Kap	IV	33,198	1972
Mahal Kohistan	IV	70,577	1972
Manshi	IV	2,321	1977
Maslakh	IV	46,559	1968
Naltar	IV	27,206	1975
Nara Desert	IV	223,590	1980
Raghai Rakhshan	IV	125,425	1971
Ras Koh	IV	99,498	1962
Rasool Barrage	IV	1,138	1974
Runn of Kutch	IV	320,463	1980
Sasnamana	IV	6,607	1971
Satpara	IV	31,093	1975
Shashan	IV	29,555	1972
Sheikh Buddin	IV	15,540	1977
Sodhi	IV	5,820	1983
Takkar	IV	43,513	1968
Taunsa Barrage	IV	6,567	1972
Ziarat Juniper	IV	37,247	1971

PALAU

Summary/Sommaire		
Category\Catégorie III	1	1,200
Total	**1**	**1,200**

Wildlife Reserves/Réserves de ressources sauvages
Ngerukewid Islands	III	1,200	1956

PANAMA

Summary/Sommaire		
Category\Catégorie I	2	6,833
Category\Catégorie II	11	1,188,049
Category\Catégorie IV	2	2,258
Category\Catégorie V	1	129,000
Total	**16**	**1,326,140**

National Parks/Parcs nationaux
Altos de Campana	II	4,816	1977
Cerro Hoya	II	32,557	1984
Chagres	V	129,000	1984

Darien	II	597,000	1980
General Omar Torrijos	II	240,000	1986
La Amistad	II	207,000	1988
Portobelo	II	34,846	1976
Sarigua	II	8,000	1984
Soberania	II	22,104	1980
Volcan Baru	II	14,000	1976
National Marine Parks/Parcs marins nationaux			
Bastimentos	II	14,500	1989
Isla Bastimentos	II	13,226	1988
Scientific Reserves/Réserves scientifiques			
Isla Maje	I	1,433	1977
Wildlife Refuges/Refuges de ressources sauvages			
Islas Taboga y Uraba	IV	258	1984
Penon de la Onda	IV	2,000	1984
Natural Monuments/Monuments naturels			
Barro Colorado	I	5,400	1977

PAPUA NEW GUINEA/PAPOUASIE-NOUVELLE-GUINEE

Summary/Sommaire		
Category\Catégorie II	3	7,323
Category\Catégorie IV	2	21,693
Total	**5**	**29,016**

National Parks/Parcs nationaux			
Jimi Valley	II	4,180	1986
McAdam	II	2,080	1970
Varirata	II	1,063	1969
Wildlife Management Areas/Aires de gestion			
des ressources sauvages			
Crown Island (III)	IV	5,969	1977
Long Island (III)	IV	15,724	1977

PARAGUAY

Summary/Sommaire		
Category\Catégorie II	8	1,156,538
Category\Catégorie V	4	29,193
Total	**12**	**1,185,731**

National Parks/Parcs nationaux			
Caaguazu	II	6,000	1976
Cerro Cora	II	5,538	1976
Defensores del Chaco	II	780,000	1975
Teniente Encisco	II	40,000	1980
Tinfunque	II	280,000	1966
Ybycui	II	5,000	1973
Ypacarai	II	16,000	1990
Ytyturuzu	II	24,000	1990

Biological Reserves/Réserves biologiques

Itabo	V	11,260	1982
Limo'y	V	14,332	1982
Mbaracayu	V	1,356	1982
Tatiyupi	V	2,245	1982

PAYS-BAS
Voir paragraphe NETHERLANDS

PERU/PEROU

Summary/Sommaire		
Category\Catégorie II	7	2,381,026
Category\Catégorie III	6	149,531
Category\Catégorie IV	9	2,952,186
Category\Catégorie V	2	35,092
Total	**24**	**5,517,835**

National Parks/Parcs nationaux

Cerros de Amotape	II	91,200	1975
Cuervo	II	2,500	1961
Huascaran	II	340,000	1975
Manu	II	1,532,806	1973
Rio Abiseo	II	274,520	1983
Tingo Maria	II	18,000	1965
Yanachaga-Chemillen	II	122,000	1987

National Reserves/Réserves nationales

Calipuy	IV	64,000	1981
Junin	IV	53,000	1974
Lachay	IV	5,070	1977
Pacaya Samiria	IV	2,080,000	1982
Pampa Galeras	IV	6,500	1967
Paracas	IV	335,000	1975
Salinas y Aguada Blanca	IV	366,936	1979
Titicaca	IV	36,180	1978

National Sanctuaries/Sanctuaires nationaux

Ampay	III	3,635	1987
Calipuy	III	4,500	1981
Huayllay	III	6,815	1974
Manglares de Tumbes	III	2,972	1988
Pampas del Heath	III	102,109	1983
Tabaconas-Namballe	III	29,500	1988

Historical Sanctuaries/Sanctuaires historiques

Chacamarca	V	2,500	1974
Machu Picchu	V	32,592	1981

Nature Reserves/Réserves de nature

Tambopata	IV	5,500	1977

PHILIPPINES

Summary/Sommaire		
Category\Catégorie II	9	215,753
Category\Catégorie III	6	21,050
Category\Catégorie IV	9	324,643
Category\Catégorie V	4	22,553
Total	**28**	**583,999**

National Parks/Parcs nationaux

Basilan	II	3,100	1939
Bataan	IV	23,688	1945
Bulusan Volcano	II	3,673	1935
Calauit Island	IV	3,400	1976
Lake Dapao	IV	1,500	1965
Lake Imelda (Dana Lake)	V	2,193	1972
Mainit Hot Spring	III	1,381	1957
Mayon Volcano	III	5,459	1938
Minalungao	III	2,018	1967
Mount Apo	II	72,814	1936
Mount Arayat	V	3,715	1933
Mount Banahaw-San Cristobal	V	11,133	1941
Mount Canlaon	II	24,558	1934
Mount Data	V	5,512	1940
Mount Isarog	II	10,112	1938
Mount Malindang	II	53,262	1971
Mounts Banahaw-San Cristobal	II	11,133	1941
Mounts Iglit-Baco	IV	75,445	1970
Naujan Lake	IV	21,655	1956
Rajaha Sikatuna	IV	9,023	1987
Rizal (Luneta)	III	1,335	1955
St Paul Subterranean River	II	3,901	1971
Taal Volcano	III	4,537	1967
Tirad Pass	III	6,320	1938

Wildlife Sanctuaries/Sanctuaires de ressources sauvages

F.B. Harrison	IV	140,000	1920
Liguasan Marsh	IV	43,930	1941
Magapit	IV	6,002	1932

Marine Parks/Parcs marins

Tubbataha Reefs	II	33,200	1988

POLAND/POLOGNE

Summary/Sommaire		
Category\Catégorie II	13	134,732
Category\Catégorie IV	19	64,880
Category\Catégorie V	46	2,030,488
Total	**78**	**2,230,100**

National Parks/Parcs nationaux			
Babia Gora	II	1,734	1933
Bialowieza	II	5,317	1932
Bieszczady	II	15,337	1973
Gorce	II	6,750	1981
Kampinos	II	35,486	1959
Karkonosze	II	5,563	1959
Ojcow	V	1,592	1956
Pieniny	II	2,329	1932
Roztocze	II	6,857	1974
Slowinski	II	18,247	1967
Swietokrzyski	II	5,906	1950
Tatra	II	21,164	1955
Wielkopolski	II	5,198	1933
Wigierski	V	14,840	1989
Wolinski	II	4,844	1960
Nature Reserves/Réserves de nature			
Czerwone Bagno	IV	11,630	1957
Jata	IV	1,117	1952
Jezioro Dobskie	IV	1,833	1976
Jezioro Druzno	IV	3,022	1967
Jezioro Kosno	IV	1,232	1982
Jezioro Nidzkie	IV	2,935	1973
Jezioro Siedmiu Wysp	IV	1,000	1956
Kurianskie Bagno	IV	1,714	1985
Las Warminski	IV	1,798	1982
Lasy Janowskie	IV	2,677	1984
Nadgoplanski Park Tysiaclecia	IV	12,684	1967
Paslece	IV	4,116	1970
Puszcza Bialowieska	IV	1,357	1969
Rzeka Drweca	IV	1,287	1961
Slonsk	IV	4,166	1977
Stawy Milickie	IV	5,324	1963
Stawy Przemkowskie	IV	1,046	1984
Wielki Bytyn	IV	1,826	1989
Wielki	IV	4,116	1970
Landscape Parks/Parcs paysagers			
Bolimowski	V	25,900	1986
Brodnicki	V	22,240	1985
Chelmski	V	23,500	1983
Doliny Slupi	V	120,201	1981
Drawski	V	63,642	1979
Gor Opawskich	V	4,830	1988
Gory Sw. Anny	V	5,780	1988
Gostyn sko-Wloclawski	V	51,344	1979
Inski	V	51,843	1982
Kaszubski	V	34,544	1983
Kazimierski	V	38,670	1979
Kozienicki	V	45,535	1983
Krasnabrodzki	V	40,184	1988

Ksiazanski	V	4,500	1981
Lagowski	V	10,070	1985
Lasy Janowskie	V	62,950	1984
Mazowiecki	V	25,510	1986
Mazurski	V	69,219	1977
Mierzeja Wislana	V	22,390	1985
Nadmorski	V	27,610	1978
Narwianski	V	47,915	1985
Poleski	V	27,500	1983
Popradzki	V	78,000	1987
Przedborski	V	31,120	1988
Pszczewski	V	57,587	1986
Puszczy Knyszynskiej	V	125,349	1988
Puszczy Solskiej	V	115,246	1988
Slezanski	V	12,200	1988
Snieznicki	V	28,800	1981
Sobiborski	V	19,000	1983
Stolowogorski	V	13,600	1981
Strzelecki	V	10,300	1983
Suwalski	V	14,901	1976
Szczecinski	V	22,384	1982
Trojmiejski	V	33,107	1979
Tucholski	V	52,928	1985
Wdzydzki	V	17,650	1983
Wigierski	V	21,301	1976
Wzniesienie Elblaskie	V	33,292	1985
Zaleczanski	V	14,278	1979
Zespol Jurajskich	V	246,276	1980
Zespol Parkow Ponidzia	V	82,648	1986
Zespol Swietokrzyskie	V	100,625	1988
Zywiecki	V	57,587	1986

PORTUGAL

Summary/Sommaire		
Category\Catégorie II	2	99,422
Category\Catégorie III	2	3,888
Category\Catégorie IV	9	73,221
Category\Catégorie V	8	277,111
Total	**21**	**453,642**

National Parks/Parcs nationaux
Peneda-Geres	II	71,422	1971

Nature Reserves/Réserves de nature
Berlenga	IV	1,020	1981
Estuario do Sado	IV	24,000	1980
Estuario do Tejo	IV	14,563	1976
Lagoa do Fogo	IV	2,920	1974
Sapal de Castro Marim	IV	2,089	1975
Serra da Malcata	IV	21,759	1981

Natural Monuments/Monuments naturels

Monte de Barca e Agoluda	III	1,158	1980
Penedo do Lexim	III	2,730	1975

Nature Parks/Parcs naturels

Alvao	V	7,365	1983
Arrabida	V	10,821	1976
Montezinho	V	75,000	1979
Ria Formosa	V	16,000	1987
Serra S. Mamede	V	31,750	1989
Serra de Estrela	V	100,000	1976
Serras de Aires e Candeeiros	V	34,000	1979

Azores/Açores

Nature Reserves/Réserves de nature

Caldeira do Faial	IV	1,086	1972
Montanha do Pico	IV	2,384	1972

Protected Landscapes/Paysages protégés

Lagoa das Sete Cidades	V	2,175	1980

Macao

No Areas Listed/pas de sites

Madeira/Madère

Nature Reserves/Réserves de nature

Ilhas Selvagens	IV	3,400	1971

Nature Parks/Parcs naturels

Madeira	II	28,000	1979

QATAR

No Areas Listed/pas de sites

REPUBLIQUE ARAB SYRIENNE
Voir paragraphe SYRIAN ARAB REPUBLIC

REPUBLIQUE CENTRAFRICAINE
Voir paragraphe CENTRAL AFRICAN REPUBLIC

REPUBLIQUE DE CHINE
Voir paragraphe CHINA, REPUBLIC OF

REPUBLIQUE DE COREE
Voir paragraphe KOREA, REPUBLIC OF

REPUBLIQUE DEMOCRATIQUE ALLEMANDE
Voir paragraphe GERMAN DEMOCRATIC REPUBLIC

REPUBLIQUE DEMOCRATIQUE POPULAIRE LAO
Voir paragraphe LAO PEOPLE'S DEMOCRATIC REPUBLIC

REPUBLIQUE DOMINICAINE
Voir paragraphe DOMINICAN REPUBLIC

REPUBLIQUE POPULAIRE DE CHINE
Voir paragraphe CHINA, PEOPLES REPUBLIC OF

REPUBLIQUE POPULAIRE DEMOCRATIQUE DE COREE
Voir paragraphe KOREA, DEMOCRATIC PEOPLE'S REPUBLIC OF

REPUBLIQUE SOCIALISTE SOVIETIQUE BIELORUSSIE
Voir paragraphe BYELORUSSIAN SOVIET SOCIALIST REPUBLIC

REPUBLIQUE SOCIALISTE SOVIETIQUE UKRAINE
Voir paragraphe UKRAINIAN SOVIET SOCIALIST REPUBLIC

REPUBLIQUE-UNIE DU CAMEROUN
Voir paragraphe CAMEROON, UNITED REPUBLIC OF

REPUBLIQUE-UNIE DU TANZANIA
Voir paragraphe TANZANIA, UNITED REPUBLIC OF

ROMANIA/ROUMANIE

Summary/Sommaire		
Category\Catégorie I	1	14,600
Category\Catégorie II	1	54,400
Category\Catégorie IV	20	112,496
Category\Catégorie V	14	380,078
Total	**36**	**561,574**

National Parks/Parcs nationaux

Apuseni	V	57,900	1990
Bucegi	V	35,700	1990
Caliman	V	15,300	1990
Ceahliu	V	17,200	1990
Cheile Bicazului	V	11,600	1990
Cheile Carasului	V	30,400	1990
Cheile Nerei-Beusnita	V	37,100	1990
Cozia	V	17,100	1990
Domogled-Valea Cernei	V	60,100	1990
Piatra Craiului	V	14,800	1990
Retezat	II	54,400	1935
Rodna	V	56,700	1990

Nature Reserves/Réserves de nature

Bicaz and Lacul Rosu	IV	5,369	1955

Bila-Lala	IV	5,135	1973
Bucegi	V	3,748	1943
Caliman	IV	1,625	
Cheile Bicazului	IV	3,241	1955
Cheile Carasului	IV	1,025	1982
Cheile Nerei-Beusnita	IV	11,098	1943
Cozia	IV	7,284	
Padurea-Letea	IV	5,212	1938
Perisor-Zatoane-Sacalin	V	16,400	1961
Periteasca-Gura Portita	IV	3,900	1961
Piatra Craiului	IV	1,459	1958
Pietrile Boghii-Pietroasa	IV	1,737	1971
Pietrosul Mare	IV	5,865	1932
Rosca-Buhaiova-Hrecisca	I	14,600	1961
Rosca-Letea	IV	16,400	1961
Saritoarea Bohodeiului	IV	1,950	1981
Scarisoara-Belioara	IV	6,507	1941
Sesul Craiului-Belicara	IV	6,507	1941
Sfintu Gheorghe-Perisor-Palade	IV	15,000	
Snagov Forest and Snagov Lake	IV	1,767	1952
Nature Parks/Parcs naturels			
Gradistea Muncelului-Cioclovina	V	6,030	1979
Forest Reserves/Réserves forestières			
Ceahlau-Politele cu crini	IV	5,424	1955
Domogled-Tesna-Virful lui Stan	IV	5,991	1932

ROYAUME-UNI DE GRANDE BRETAGNE ET D'IRELANDE DU NORD
Voir paragraphe UNITED KINGDOM OF GREAT BRITAIN AND
NORTHERN IRELAND

RWANDA

Summary/Sommaire		
Category\Catégorie II	2	327,000
Total	**2**	**327,000**

National Parks/Parcs nationaux

Akagera	II	312,000	1934
Volcans	II	15,000	1929

SAHARE OCCIDENTALE
Voir paragraphe WESTERN SAHARA

SAINT KITTS AND NEVIS/SAINTE-KITTS-ET-NEVIS
No Areas Listed/pas de sites

SAINT LUCIA/SAINTE-LUCIE
No Areas Listed/pas de sites

SAINT-MARIN
Voir paragraphe SAN MARINO

SAINT SIEGE
Voir paragraphe HOLY SEE

SAINT VINCENT AND THE GRENADINES/
SAINTE-VINCENT-ET-GRENADINES
No Areas Listed/pas de sites

SAINTE-KITTS-ET-NEVIS
Voir paragraphe SAINT KITTS AND NEVIS

SAINTE-LUCIE
Voir paragraphe SAINT LUCIA

SAINTE-VINCENT-ET-GRENADINES
Voir paragraphe SAINT VINCENT AND THE GRENADINES

SAMOA OCCIDENTALE
Voir paragraphe WESTERN SAMOA

SAN MARINO/SAINT-MARIN
No Areas Listed/pas de sites

SAO TOME AND PRINCIPE/SAO TOME-ET-PRINCIPE
No Areas Listed/pas de sites

SAUDI ARABIA/ARABIE SAOUDITE

Summary/Sommaire		
Category\Catégorie I	2	325,000
Category\Catégorie IV	4	4,879,400
Category\Catégorie V	1	415,000
Total	**7**	**5,619,400**

National Parks/Parcs nationaux

Asir	V	415,000	1981

Protected Areas/Aires protégées

Farasan Islands	I	60,000	1989
Harrat al-Harrah	IV	1,377,500	1987
Hawtah bani Tamin	IV	236,900	1988
Khunfah	IV	2,045,000	1987
Mahazat as Sayed	I	265,000	1988
Tubayq	IV	1,220,000	1989

SENEGAL

Summary/Sommaire		
Category\Catégorie II	6	1,012,450
Category\Catégorie IV	4	1,168,259
Total	**10**	**2,180,709**

National Parks/Parcs nationaux			
Basse-Casamance	II	5,000	1970
Delta du Saloum	II	76,000	1976
Djoudj	II	16,000	1971
Iles de la Madeleine	II	450	1949
Langue de Barbarie	II	2,000	1976
Niokolo-Koba	II	913,000	1954
Faunal Reserves/Réserves fauniques			
Ferlo-Nord	IV	487,000	1971
Ferlo-Sud	IV	633,700	1972
Ndiael	IV	46,550	
Popenguine	IV	1,009	1986

SEYCHELLES

Summary/Sommaire		
Category\Catégorie I	1	35,000
Category\Catégorie II	3	3,568
Total	**4**	**38,568**

National Parks/Parcs nationaux			
Praslin	II	675	1979
Marine National Parks/Parcs nationaux marins			
Curieuse	II	1,470	1976
St Anne	II	1,423	1973
Strict Nature Reserves/Réserves strictes de nature			
Aldabra	I	35,000	1976

SIERRA LEONE

Summary/Sommaire		
Category\Catégorie IV	3	100,700
Total	**3**	**100,700**

National Parks/Parcs nationaux			
Outamba-Kilimi	IV	98,000	1981
Nature Reserves/Réserves de nature			
Mamunta-Mayoso	IV	1,500	1980
Wildlife Sanctuaries/Sanctuaires de ressources sauvages			
Tiwai Island	IV	1,200	1987

SINGAPORE/SINGAPOUR

Summary/Sommaire		
Category\Catégorie IV	1	2,715
Total	**1**	**2,715**

Nature Reserves/Réserves de nature
Central Catchment	IV	2,715	1951

SOLOMON ISLANDS/ILES SALOMON
No Areas Listed/pas de sites

SOMALIA/SOMALIE
No Areas Listed/pas de sites

SOUDAN
Voir paragraphe SUDAN

SOUTH AFRICA/AFRIQUE DU SUD

Summary/Sommaire		
Category\Catégorie I	1	39,000
Category\Catégorie II	13	3,055,361
Category\Catégorie IV	160	3,198,168
Category\Catégorie V	4	17,250
Total	**178**	**6,309,779**

Strict Nature Reserves/Réserves strictes de nature
Prince Edward Islands	I	39,000	1948

Cape Province/Province de Cap

National Parks/Parcs nationaux
Addo Elephant	II	8,879	1931
Addo Elephant (Suurberg extension)	II	20,788	1985
Augrabies Falls	II	9,415	1966
Bontebok	II	2,786	1960
Kalahari Gemsbok	II	959,103	1931
Karoo	II	27,011	1979
Mountain Zebra	II	6,536	1937
Tsitsikamma Forest and Coastal	II	3,318	1964

Nature Reserves/Réserves de nature
Akkerendam	IV	2,301	1962
Andries Vosloo Kudu	IV	6,493	1973
Cape of Good Hope	IV	7,675	1939
Commando Drift	IV	5,983	1978
De Hoop	IV	17,846	1956
De Vasselot	IV	2,560	1974
Doornkloof	IV	8,765	1981
Fernkloof	IV	1,446	1971

Gamka Mountain	IV	9,428	1970
Gamkapoort	IV	8,000	1980
Goukamma	IV	2,230	1960
Greyton	IV	2,220	1977
Hester Malan	IV	6,576	1966
Karoo	IV	14,000	1979
Ladismith-Klein Karoo	IV	2,766	1974
Little Karoo	IV	35,000	1987
Mont Rochelle	IV	1,759	1982
Montagu Mountain	IV	1,200	1972
Nietgenaamd	IV	1,577	1978
Oviston	IV	13,000	1968
Paarl Mountain	IV	1,910	1977
Rolfontein	IV	4,749	1970
Silvermine	IV	2,150	1965
Somerset East-Bosberg	IV	1,650	1967
Spitskop	IV	2,740	1967
Storms River	IV	13,700	1925
Table Mountain	IV	2,904	1963
Thomas Baines	IV	1,003	1963
Vrolijkheid	IV	1,827	1957
Ysternek	IV	1,212	1972
Wilderness Areas/Aires de nature sauvage			
Groendal	IV	25,047	1896
Mountain Catchment Areas/Bassins versants de montagne			
Anysberg/Klein Swartberg	IV	58,785	1912
Cedarberg	IV	126,375	1971
Groot Swartberg/Swartberg East	IV	121,002	1912
Groot Winterhoek	IV	81,188	1913
Hawequas	IV	115,910	1913
Hottentots Holland	IV	84,936	1907
Kammanassie	IV	45,508	1923
Kouga/Baviaanskloof	IV	172,208	1923
Langeberg East	IV	71,300	1896
Langeberg West	IV	77,096	1914
Matroosberg	IV	95,256	1977
Outeniqua	IV	158,515	1936
Riviersonderend	IV	69,453	1900
Rooiberg	IV	25,344	1934
Sederberg	IV	126,375	1897
Tsitsikamma Mountains	IV	80,000	
Indigenous Forests/Forêts indigènes			
Knysna	IV	44,230	1894
Tsitsikamma	IV	15,651	1890
State Forests/Forêts publiques			
Alexandria	IV	23,566	1896
Bathurst	IV	5,315	1897
East London Coast	IV	4,369	1887
Otterford	IV	11,467	1896
Sandveld	IV	3,624	1966

Suurberg	IV	21,121	1896
Walker Bay	IV	7,118	1895

Natal

National Parks/Parcs nationaux

Royal Natal	II	8,856	1916

Nature Reserves/Réserves de nature

Albert Falls Public Resort	V	3,012	1975
Amatikulu	IV	2,928	
Chelmsford Public Resort	V	6,845	1975
Coleford	IV	1,272	1948
False Bay	IV	2,247	1954
Itala	IV	25,896	1973
Kamberg	IV	2,232	1951
Loteni	IV	3,984	1953
Maphelana	IV	1,102	
Midmar Public Resort	V	2,831	1968
Mt Currie	IV	1,541	1984
Mzimkulwana	IV	22,751	1979
Oribi Gorge	IV	1,809	1950
Spioenkop Public Resort	V	4,562	1975
Umtamvuna	IV	3,137	1971
Vergelegen	IV	1,159	1967
Vernon Crookes	IV	2,189	1972
Weenen	IV	2,929	1975

Marine Reserves/Réserves marines

St Lucia	IV	23,700	1979

Game Reserves/Réserves de faune

Giant's Castle	IV	34,638	1903
Hluhluwe	IV	23,067	1897
Mkuzi	IV	30,503	1912
Ndumu	IV	10,117	1924
Richards Bay	IV	1,200	1935
St Lucia	IV	36,826	1897
Umfolozi	IV	47,753	1897

Wilderness Areas/Aires de nature sauvage

Mdedelelo	IV	27,000	1973
Mkhomazi	IV	48,600	1973
Mzimkulu	IV	28,340	1973
Ntendeka	IV	5,230	1905

Parks/Parcs

False Bay	IV	2,247	1954
St Lucia	IV	12,545	1939
Tembe Elephant	IV	29,878	1983

State Forests/Forêts publiques

Drakensberg	IV	190,000	1930
Dukuduku	IV	15,055	1930
Sodwana/Cape Vidal	IV	57,954	1956
Weza (part)	IV	9,000	1904

Orange Free State/Etat libre d'Orange

National Parks/Parcs nationaux

Golden Gate Highlands	II	6,241	1963

Nature Reserves/Réserves de nature

Erfenis Dam	IV	3,808	1977
Hendrik Verwoerd Dam	IV	47,201	1979
Kalkfontein Dam	IV	5,263	1971
Koppies Dam	IV	4,325	1976
Rustfontein	IV	2,170	1974
Sandveld	IV	37,735	1980
Soetdoring	IV	6,173	1978

Game Reserves/Réserves de faune

Willem Pretorius	IV	12,005	1970

Other areas/Autres aires

Tussen-die-Riviere Game Farm	IV	22,000	1972

Transvaal

National Parks/Parcs nationaux

Kruger	II	1,948,528	1926

Nature Reserves/Réserves de nature

AFB Hoedspruit	IV	4,236	
Abe Bailey	IV	1,888	1982
Barberspan	IV	3,086	1954
Bloemhof Dam	IV	22,072	1975
Blouberg East	IV	6,848	1977
Blouberg West	IV	4,450	1982
Blyde River Angling Waters	IV	1,800	1980
Blyde River	IV	22,664	1965
Boskop Dam	IV	3,160	1975
Bronkhorstspruit Dam	IV	1,285	1977
Doorndraai Dam	IV	7,229	1973
FC Erasmus Trust Forest	IV	6,600	1977
Fanie Botha	IV	2,638	1978
Hans Merenskey	IV	5,282	1954
Hans Strijdom	IV	3,618	1978
Happy Rest	IV	1,585	1975
Hartebeespoort Dam	IV	2,500	1969
Jericho Dam	IV	1,453	1977
Langjan	IV	4,774	1954
Lekgalameetse	IV	18,125	1979
Loskop Dam	IV	14,800	1954
Mangombe	IV	3,000	
Messina	IV	3,571	1980
Nooitgedacht Dam	IV	3,420	1980
Nylsvley	IV	3,121	1967
Ohrigstad Dam	IV	2,563	1954
Percy Fyfe	IV	2,986	1954
Pongola	IV	6,222	1979
Potlake	IV	2,928	1977

Roodeplaat Dam	IV	1,667	1977
Rust de Winter Dam	IV	1,358	1954
Rustenburg	IV	4,257	1967
SA Lombard	IV	3,663	1967
Sterkspruit	IV	1,600	1978
Suikerbosrand	IV	13,337	1974
Vaalkop Dam	IV	1,873	1983
Verloren Valei	IV	6,055	1984
Vhembe	IV	2,503	1975
Wolkberg Caves	IV	1,488	1969
Wolwespruit	IV	2,333	1975
Game Reserves/Réserves de faune			
Manyeleti	IV	22,772	1967
Sanctuaries/Sanctuaires			
Melkbos Houtbay (Lobster)	IV	83,400	
Saldanha Bay Rock (Lobster)	IV	83,400	
St Helena Bay Rock (Lobster)	IV	14,000	
State Forests/Forêts publiques			
Ceylon	IV	3,500	1935
Entabeni	IV	1,924	1924
Morgenzon	IV	1,264	1978
Nelshoogte/Berlin	IV	3,500	1923
Serala (including Wolkberg WA)	IV	21,998	1977
Uitsoek	IV	2,270	1953
Woodbush/De Hoek	IV	6,626	1916

Bophuthatswana

National Parks/Parcs nationaux			
Borakalalo	IV	7,380	1970
Pilanesberg	II	50,000	1979

Ciskei

Nature Reserves/Réserves de nature			
Cata Forest	IV	1,592	1913
Dontsa Forest	IV	1,209	1913
Game Parks/Parcs de gibier			
Tsolwana	IV	7,557	1977
Protected Areas/Aires protégées			
Cwengcwe Forest	IV	3,276	1926
Izeleni Forest	IV	1,330	1917
Pirie Forest	IV	5,239	1922
Rabula Forest	IV	3,884	1912
Zingcuka Forest	IV	3,731	1913

Transkei

Nature Reserves/Réserves de nature			
Cwebe	IV	2,140	1975
Dwesa	II	3,900	1975

Venda

National Parks/Parcs nationaux

Nwanedi	IV	3,200	1980

SPAIN/ESPAGNE

Summary/Sommaire		
Category\Catégorie II	9	122,763
Category\Catégorie IV	51	1,571,040
Category\Catégorie V	101	1,817,288
Total	**161**	**3,511,091**

National Parks/Parcs nationaux

Aigues Tortes y Lago de San Mauricio	II	10,230	1955
Caldera de Taburiente	II	4,690	1954
Donana	II	50,720	1969
Montana de Covadonga	II	16,925	1918
Ordesa y Monte Perdido	II	15,608	1918
Tablas de Daimiel	II	1,928	1973

Biological Reserves/Réserves biologiques

Bosque de Muniellos	V	5,542	1982

Natural Reserves/Réserves naturelles

Caidas de la Negra	IV	1,926	1987
Els Aiguamolls de l'Emporda	IV	4,866	1983
Foz de Arbayun	IV	1,164	1987
Laguna de Fuentepiedra	IV	1,364	1984
Larra	IV	2,353	1987
Mas de Melons	IV	1,140	1987

National Game Reserves/Réserves de gibier nationales

Alto Pallars-Aran	IV	94,231	1966
Arroyo de la Rocina	IV	1,005	
Bahia del Santona	IV	2,893	
Benasque	IV	23,750	1966
Cadi	IV	27,202	1966
Cameros	IV	92,918	1973
Cerdana	IV	19,437	1966
Cijara	IV	24,999	1966
Cortes de la Frontera	IV	12,342	1973
Degana	IV	11,914	1966
Fresser y Setcasas	IV	20,200	1966
Fuentes Carrionas	IV	47,755	1966
Islas d'Espalmador, Espardell y Islotes	IV	175	
La Buitrera	IV	1,200	1982
Las Batuecas	IV	20,976	1973
Los Ancares Leoneses	IV	38,300	1973
Los Ancares	IV	7,975	1966
Los Circos	IV	22,844	1966
Los Valles	IV	28,765	1966
Mampodre	IV	30,858	1966
Montes Universales	IV	59,260	1973

Muela de Cortes	IV	36,009	1973
Picos de Europa	IV	7,630	1970
Puertos de Beceite	IV	30,418	1966
Ria de Villaviciosa	IV	1,032	
Ria del Eo	IV	2,000	
Riano	IV	71,538	1966
Saja	IV	180,186	1966
Serrania de Cuenca	IV	25,724	1973
Serrania de Ronda	IV	21,982	1970
Sierra Espuna	IV	13,855	1973
Sierra Nevada	IV	35,430	1966
Sierra de Gredos	IV	22,815	1970
Sierra de Tejeda y Almijara	IV	20,398	1973
Sierra de la Culebra	IV	65,891	1973
Sierra de la Demanda	IV	73,819	1973
Somiedo	IV	89,650	1966
Sonsaz	IV	68,106	1973
Sueve	IV	8,300	1966
Urbion	IV	100,023	1973
Villafafila	IV	42,000	1986
Vinamala	IV	49,230	1966

Natural Landscapes/Paysages naturels

Brazo del Este	V	1,336	1989
Desfiladero de los Gaitanes	V	2,016	1989
Desierto de Tabernas	V	11,625	1989
Embalse de Cordobilla	V	1,460	1989
Karst de Yesos de Sorbas	V	2,375	1989
Ladera de Vallebron	V	2,142	1987
Los Ajaches	V	2,876	1987
Los Reales de Sierra Bermeja	V	1,236	1989
Macizo de Pedraforca	V	1,671	1982
Macizo de Tauro	V	1,179	1987
Marismas de Isla Cristina	V	2,145	1989
Marismas del Odiel	V	7,185	1984
Marismas del Rio Piedras y Flecha del Rompido	V	2,530	1989
Punta Entina-Sabinar	V	1,960	1989
Sierra Alhamilla	V	8,500	1989
Sierra Pelada y Rivera del Asserador	V	12,980	1989
Torcal de Antequera	V	1,171	1978
Valle del Monasterio de Poblet	V	2,477	1984
Vertiente sur del Massis de l'Albera	V	2,413	1986

Natural Sites of National Interest/Sites naturels
d'intérêt national

Cumbre, Circo y Lagunas de Penalara	IV	1,012	1930
Pinar de la Acebeda	IV	1,000	1930

Natural Areas/Aires naturelles

Ses Salines de Ibiza, Formentera e Islotes	IV	1,180	1985

Nature Parks/Parcs naturels

Acantilado y Pinar de Barbate	V	2,017	1989
Albufera de Valencia	V	21,000	1986

Anaga	V	14,119	1987
Ayagaures y Pilancones	V	10,166	1987
Bahia de Cadiz	V	10,000	1989
Bandama	V	1,508	1987
Barranco Quintero, El Rio, La Madera y Dorado	V	1,485	1987
Barranco de la Rajita y Roque de la Fortaleza	V	1,788	1987
Barranco de las Angustias	V	1,508	1987
Barrancos de los Hombres y Fagundo y Acantila	V	1,058	1987
Betancuria	V	15,538	1987
Cabaneros	V	25,615	1988
Cabo de Gata-Nijar	V	26,000	1987
Cadi Moixero	V	41,342	1983
Canon del Rio Lobos	V	9,580	1985
Carrascal de la Font Roja	V	2,450	1987
Cornalvo	V	10,570	1988
Cuenca Alta del Rio Manzanares	V	37,500	1978
Cuenca de Tejeda	V	5,968	1987
Cumbre Vieja y Teneguia	V	8,023	1987
Cumbres	V	8,929	1987
Dehesa del Moncayo	V	1,389	1978
Delta del Ebro	V	7,736	1983
Despenaperros	V	6,000	1989
Dunas de Corralejo e Isla de Lobos	V	2,526	1982
El Hierro	V	11,980	1987
El Montgo	V	2,700	1987
Entorno de Donana	V	54,250	1989
Guayadeque	V	1,203	1987
Hayedo de Tejera Negra	V	1,641	1978
Inagua, Ojeda y Pajonales	V	8,448	1987
Islas Cies	V	433	1980
Jandia	V	11,938	1987
La Geria	V	15,189	1987
La Isleta	V	1,258	1987
Ladera S. Ursula, Los Organos, Altos del Vall	V	12,114	1987
Lago de Sanabria	V	5,027	1978
Lagunas de Ruidera	V	3,772	1979
Los Alcornocales	V	170,025	1989
Macizo de Adeje y Barranco del Infierno	V	2,057	1987
Macizo de Pena Cabarga	V	2,588	1989
Macizo de Suroeste	V	10,538	1987
Majona	V	1,920	1987
Monfrague	V	17,852	1979
Montana de Montserrat	V	3,630	1987
Monte Doramas	V	4,262	1987
Monte Lentiscal	V	2,969	1987
Monte el Valle	V	1,900	1979
Montes de Malaga	V	4,762	1989
Montes de los Sauces y Punta Llana	V	3,173	1987
Montseny	V	17,370	1928
Pozo Negro	V	9,237	1987

S'Albufera de Mallorca	V	1,700	1988
Saja Besaya	V	24,500	1988
Sant Llorenc de Munt i L'Obal	V	9,638	1987
Senorio de Bertiz	V	2,040	1984
Sierra Espuna	V	9,961	1978
Sierra Nevada	V	140,200	1989
Sierra de Aracena y Picos de Aroche	V	184,000	1989
Sierra de Baza	V	52,337	1989
Sierra de Cardena y Montoro	V	41,212	1989
Sierra de Castril	V	12,265	1989
Sierra de Cazorla, Segurla y las Villas	V	214,300	1986
Sierra de Grazalema	V	51,695	1984
Sierra de Hornachuelos	V	67,202	1989
Sierra de Huetor	V	12,428	1989
Sierra de Maria	V	18,962	1987
Sierra de las Nieves	V	16,564	1989
Sierras Magina	V	19,900	1989
Sierras Subbeticas de Cordoba	V	31,568	1988
Sierras de Andujar	V	60,800	1989
Somiedo	V	29,122	1988
Tagaiga	V	1,735	1987
Tamadaba	V	8,010	1987
Teno	V	7,647	1987
Urkiola	V	5,768	1989
Valle Gran Rey	V	1,960	1987
Volcan de la Corona y el Malpais de la Corona	V	2,690	1987
Zona Volcanica de la Garrotxa	V	12,112	1982

Canary Islands/Iles Canaries

National Parks/Parcs nationaux

Garajonay	II	3,984	1981
Teide	II	13,571	1954
Timanfaya	II	5,107	1974

Nature Parks/Parcs naturels

Corona Forestal de Tenerife	V	37,173	1987
Islotes del Norte de Lanzarote y de los Risco	V	8,929	1986

Alhucemas, Ceuta, Chafarinas, Melilla, Penon de Velez/Alhucemas, Ceuta, Chafarinas, Melilla, Penon de Velez)

No Areas Listed/pas de sites

SRI LANKA

Summary/Sommaire		
Category\Catégorie I	3	31,574
Category\Catégorie II	11	460,180
Category\Catégorie IV	29	291,954
Total	**43**	**783,708**

National Parks/Parcs nationaux

Flood Plains	II	17,350	1984
Gal Oya	II	25,900	1954
Horton Plains	II	3,160	1988
Lahugala Kitulana	II	1,554	1980
Maduru Oya	II	58,850	1983
Ruhuna (Yala)	II	97,878	1938
Somawathiya Chaitiya	II	37,762	1986
Uda Walawe	II	30,821	1972
Wasgomuwa	II	37,063	1980
Wilpattu	II	131,693	1938
Yala East	II	18,149	1969

Strict Natural Reserves/Réserves naturelles strictes

Hakgala	I	1,142	1938
Ritigala	I	1,528	1941
Yala	I	28,904	1938

Nature Reserves/Réserves de nature

Minneriya-Giritale	IV	7,529	1988
Tirikonamadu	IV	25,019	1986

Natural Heritage Wilderness Areas/Aires de nature
sauvage du patrimoine naturel

Sinharaja	IV	7,648	1988

Sanctuaries/Sanctuaires

Anuradhapura	IV	3,501	1938
Buddhangala	IV	1,841	1974
Bundala	IV	6,216	1969
Chundikulam	IV	11,150	1938
Gal Oya Valley North-East	IV	12,432	1954
Gal Oya Valley South-West	IV	15,281	1954
Giant's Tank	IV	3,941	1954
Katagamuwa	IV	1,004	1938
Kokilai	IV	2,995	1951
Kudumbigala	IV	4,403	1973
Madhu Road	IV	26,677	1968
Mihintale	IV	1,000	1938
Minneriya-Giritale	IV	6,693	1938
Padaviya Tank	IV	6,475	1963
Pallekele-Kahalla-Balaluwewa	IV	21,690	1989
Peak Wilderness	IV	22,380	1940
Polonnaruwa	IV	1,523	1938
Ravana Ella	IV	1,932	1979
Senanayake Samudra	IV	9,324	1954
Seruwila-Allai	IV	15,540	1970
Sigiriya	IV	5,099	1990
Telwatte	IV	1,424	1938
Trincomalee Naval Headworks	IV	18,130	1963
Vavunikulam	IV	4,856	1963
Victoria-Randenigala-Rantambe	IV	42,087	1987
Wirawila-Tissa	IV	4,164	1938

SUDAN/SOUDAN

Summary/Sommaire		
Category\Catégorie II	7	6,873,000
Category\Catégorie IV	5	742,500
Category\Catégorie V	1	116,000
Total	**13**	**7,731,500**

National Parks/Parcs nationaux

Bandingilo	II	50,000	1985
Boma	II	2,280,000	1981
Dinder	II	890,000	1935
Nimule	II	41,000	1954
Radom	II	1,250,000	1980
Shambe	II	62,000	1985
Southern	II	2,300,000	1939

Wildlife Sanctuaries/Sanctuaires de ressources sauvages

Arkawit	IV	82,000	1939
Arkawit-Sinkat	IV	12,000	1939
Khartoum Sunt Forest	IV	1,500	1939

Game Reserves/Réserves de faune

Bengangai	IV	17,000	1939
Sabaloka	V	116,000	1946
Tokar	IV	630,000	1939

SUEDE
Voir paragraphe SWEDEN

SUISSE
Voir paragraphe SWITZERLAND

SURINAME

Summary/Sommaire		
Category\Catégorie I	4	466,000
Category\Catégorie II	2	86,570
Category\Catégorie IV	8	210,400
Total	**14**	**762,970**

Nature Reserves/Réserves de nature

Boven Coesewijne	IV	27,000	1986
Brinckheuvel	I	6,000	1972
Copi	IV	28,000	1986
Coppename monding	IV	12,000	1966
Eilerts de Haan	I	220,000	1966
Galibi	IV	4,000	1969
Peruvia	IV	31,000	1986
Raleighvallen-Voltzberg	II	78,170	1966
Sipaliwini	I	100,000	1972
Tafelberg	I	140,000	1966

Parcs nationaux et aires protégées

Upper Coesewijne	IV	27,000	1986
Wane kreek	IV	45,400	1986
Wia-wia	IV	36,000	1961
Nature Parks/Parcs naturels			
Brownsberg	II	8,400	1969

SWAZILAND

Summary/Sommaire		
Category\Catégorie IV	3	39,545
Total	**3**	**39,545**

Nature Reserves/Réserves de nature			
Malolotja	IV	18,000	1972
Mlawula/Ndzinda	IV	17,000	1977
Wildlife Sanctuaries/Sanctuaires de ressources sauvages			
Mlilwane	IV	4,545	1960

SWEDEN/SUEDE

Summary/Sommaire		
Category\Catégorie II	15	589,212
Category\Catégorie IV	73	1,061,822
Category\Catégorie V	11	107,374
Total	**99**	**1,758,408**

National Parks/Parcs nationaux			
Abisko	II	6,877	1909
Bla Jungfrun	II	198	1926
Gotska Sandon	II	3,700	1909
Muddus	II	47,880	1942
Padjelanta	II	167,100	1962
Peljekaise	II	14,000	1909
Sanfjallet	II	2,622	1909
Sarek	II	193,100	1909
Skuleskogen	II	2,650	1984
Sonfjallet	II	10,400	1909
Stora Sjofallet	II	127,800	1909
Store Mosse	II	7,500	1982
Tiveden	II	1,215	1983
Tofsingdalen	II	1,588	1930
Vadvetjakka	II	2,582	1920
Nature Reserves/Réserves de nature			
Alajaure	IV	16,400	1980
Archipelago of Djuro	IV	320	1980
Archipelago of Luro	IV	600	1967
Archipelago of Millesvik	IV	243	1980
Archipelago of Varmland	IV	1,200	1980
Bennebol	IV	9,370	1970
Biskopso	IV	275	1983

Bjorko	IV	300	1980
Bjuralvern	IV	2,151	1982
Bjurum, Dagsnas	IV	3,500	1952
Bullero	IV	475	1967
Dundret	IV	5,500	1970
Florarna	IV	4,952	1976
Glaskogen	IV	28,000	1970
Gryt	IV	298	1968
Hall-Hangvar	IV	2,161	1967
Hallands Vadero	IV	310	1958
Haparanda Sandskar	IV	180	1961
Hartso	IV	630	1981
Hastholmen-Ytteron	IV	377	1975
Hermano	IV	610	1967
Hokensas	IV	5,240	1969
Holmoarna	IV	2,800	1980
Hovfjallet	IV	1,400	1969
Innerviskfjardarna	V	1,540	1974
Kallovaratjeh	IV	1,985	1970
Kilsviken	IV	1,000	1971
Klaveron	IV	625	1966
Klingavalsan	IV	2,250	1968
Komosse	IV	1,700	1980
Lacka	IV	130	1978
Laholmsbukten	IV	7,500	1972
Lake Takern	IV	5,420	1975
Lango	IV	690	1980
Langviksskar	IV	276	1983
Licknevarpefjarden	IV	1,720	1970
Lilla Karlso	IV	164	1955
Misterhult	IV	1,500	1967
Njupeskar	IV	1,447	1970
Ostra Kullaberg	IV	1,000	1965
Rago	IV	233	1980
Ringso	IV	810	1980
Rodkullen-Sor-Aspen	IV	579	1970
Rogen	IV	40,300	1976
Rone Ytterholme-Laus Holmar	IV	1,590	
Roro	IV	150	1976
Sandsjobacka	V	5,119	1968
Serri	IV	3,548	1970
Sjalbottna-O Lagno	IV	150	1977
Sjaunja	IV	285,000	1986
Slado-Askeskar	IV	250	1965
Stadsholmen	IV	720	1968
Stora Karlso	IV	240	1970
Stora Nassa	IV	310	1965
Stromsholm	IV	1,228	1979
Sydbillingen	IV	1,750	1981
Tandovala	IV	3,450	1987

Tarnasjon	IV	11,800	
Tinaset	IV	2,500	1983
Tromto	IV	374	1982
Vaggo	IV	136	1975
Verkean	IV	1,430	1975
Vindelfjallen	IV	550,000	1974
Nature Conservation Areas/Aires de conservation de la nature			
Brattforsheden	V	10,000	1984
Fegen	V	3,668	1980
Firth of Gullmarn	V	11,860	1983
Hackeberga	V	4,350	1982
Halle-Hunneberg	V	5,950	1982
Kinnekulle	V	7,000	1982
Malingsbo-Kloten	V	49,800	1981
Nordingra	V	5,307	1983
Stigfjorden	V	2,780	1979
Unclassified/Non classé			
Archipelago of Segerstad	IV	750	1979
Blahammarsmyren	IV	1,200	
Hartso-Enskars skargard	IV	4,500	
Krankesjon	IV	1,825	
Panken-Arnofjorden	IV	1,400	
Pirttimysvuoma	IV	7,500	
Ripakaisenvuoma	IV	10,000	
Skatelovsfjorden	IV	1,500	
Stigsfjorden-Kalvofjorden	IV	4,000	
Svenskundsviken	IV	1,000	
Tamnaren	IV	3,900	
Tisjoomradet	IV	3,000	

SWITZERLAND/SUISSE

Summary/Sommaire		
Category\Catégorie II	1	16,887
Category\Catégorie IV	14	94,272
Total	**15**	**111,159**

National Parks/Parcs nationaux			
Swiss	II	16,887	1914
Nature Reserves/Réserves de nature			
Binntal	IV	4,650	
Combe Grede	IV	1,202	
Creux du Van et Gorges de L'Areuse	IV	1,100	
Engstlen See - Junigbach - Achtelsass	IV	10,500	
Gelten-Iffigen	IV	4,300	
Grimsel	IV	10,000	
Hohgant	IV	1,504	
Holloch Karst	IV	9,240	
La Pierreuse	IV	3,255	

Val de Bagnes	IV	20,000
Vallee de Joux et Haut Jura Vaudois	IV	22,000
Vallee du Doubs	IV	3,400
Valli di Languard, dal Fain, and Minor	IV	1,750
Vallon de Nant	IV	1,371

SYRIAN ARAB REPUBLIC/REPUBLIQUE ARAB SYRIENNE
No Areas Listed/pas de sites

TANZANIA, UNITED REPUBLIC OF/REPUBLIQUE-UNIE DU TANZANIA

Summary/Sommaire		
Category\Catégorie II	11	3,913,075
Category\Catégorie IV	9	8,000,000
Total	**20**	**11,913,075**

National Parks/Parcs nationaux

Arusha	II	13,700	1967
Gombe	II	5,200	1968
Katavi	II	225,300	1974
Kilimanjaro	II	75,575	1973
Lake Manyara	II	32,000	1960
Mahale Mountain	II	161,300	1985
Mikumi	II	323,000	1964
Ruaha	II	1,295,000	1964
Rubondo	II	45,700	1977
Serengeti	II	1,476,300	1951
Tarangire	II	260,000	1970

Game Reserves/Réserves de faune

Biharamulo	IV	130,000	1959
Kizigo	IV	400,000	
Maswa	IV	220,000	1969
Moyowosi	IV	600,000	1982
Rungwa	IV	900,000	1951
Selous	IV	5,000,000	1922
Umba	IV	150,000	1974
Uwanda	IV	500,000	1971

Forest Reserves/Réserves forestières

Uzungwa	IV	100,000	1959

TCHAD
Voir paragraphe CHAD

TCHECOSLOVAQUIE
Voir paragraphe CZECHOSLOVAKIA

TERRITOIRE DU TRAITE DE L'ANTARCTIQUE
Voir paragraphe ANTARCTIC TREATY TERRITORY

THAILAND/THAILANDE

Summary/Sommaire		
Category\Catégorie II	55	2,841,940
Category\Catégorie IV	25	2,220,720
Category\Catégorie V	3	43,086
Total	**83**	**5,105,746**

National Parks/Parcs nationaux

Ao Phangnga	II	40,000	1981
Chae Son	II	59,200	1988
Chaloem Rattanakosin (Tham Than Lot)	II	5,900	1980
Chat Trakan	II	54,300	1987
Doi Inthanon	II	48,240	1972
Doi Khuntan	V	25,529	1975
Doi Suthep-Pui	II	26,106	1981
Erawan	II	55,000	1975
Hat Chao Mai	II	23,088	1981
Hat Nai Yang NP (including Ko Phuket reefs)	II	9,000	1981
Hat Nopharat Thara – Mu Ko Phi Phi	II	38,996	1983
Huai Huat	II	82,856	1988
Kaeng Krachan	IV	291,000	1981
Kaeng Tana	II	8,000	1981
Khao Chamao-Khao Wong	II	8,368	1975
Khao Khitchakut	II	5,870	1977
Khao Laem Ya – Mu Ko Samet	V	13,100	1981
Khao Lam Pi – Hat Thai Muang	II	7,200	1986
Khao Luang	II	57,000	1974
Khao Pu – Khao Ya	II	69,400	1982
Khao Sam Lan	V	4,457	1981
Khao Sam Roi Yot	II	9,808	1966
Khao Sok	II	64,552	1980
Khao Yai	II	216,863	1962
Khlong Lan	II	30,000	1982
Laem Son	II	31,500	1983
Lansang	II	10,400	1979
Mae Ping	II	100,300	1981
Mae Wong	II	89,400	1987
Mae Yom	II	45,475	1986
Mu Ko Chang	II	65,000	1982
Mu Ko Phetra	II	49,438	1984
Mu Ko Similan	II	12,800	1982
Mu Ko Surin	II	13,500	1981
Mukdahan	II	4,550	1988
Nam Nao	II	96,600	1972
Namtok Mae Surin	II	39,660	1981
Namtok Phlui (Khao Sabup)	II	13,450	1975
Pang Sida	II	84,400	1982
Phu Chong – Na Yoi	II	68,600	1987
Phu Hin Rong Kla	II	30,700	1984

Phu Kao – Phu Phan Kham	II	32,200	1985
Phu Kradung	II	34,812	1962
Phu Phan	II	66,470	1972
Phu Rua	II	12,084	1979
Ramkamhaeng	II	34,100	1980
Sai Yok	II	50,000	1980
Si Laana	II	140,600	1989
Si Nakarin	II	153,200	1981
Si Phangnga	II	24,608	1988
Si Satchanalai	II	21,320	1981
Tarutao	II	149,000	1974
Tat Ton	II	21,718	1980
Thaleban	II	10,168	1980
Thap Lan	II	224,000	1981
Thung Salaeng Luang	II	126,240	1972
Ton Krabak Yai	II	14,900	1981
Wiang Kosai	II	41,000	1981

Wildlife Sanctuaries/Sanctuaires de ressources sauvages

Doi Chiang Dao	IV	52,100	1978
Doi Luang	IV	9,700	1984
Doi Pha Chang	IV	57,675	1980
Doi Pha Muang	IV	58,320	1980
Huai Kha Khaeng	IV	257,464	1972
Khao Ang Ru Nai	IV	10,810	1977
Khao Banthat	IV	126,699	1975
Khao Phanom Dong Rak	IV	31,600	1978
Khao Sanam Phriang	II	10,000	1985
Khao Soi Dao	IV	74,502	1972
Khlong Nakha	IV	48,000	1972
Khlong Phraya	IV	9,500	1980
Khlong Saeng	IV	115,615	1974
Mae Tun	IV	117,300	1978
Mae Yuam Fang Khwa	IV	29,200	1986
Maenam Phachi	IV	48,931	1978
Omkoi	IV	122,400	1983
Phu Khieo	IV	156,000	1972
Phu Luang	IV	84,799	1974
Phu Miang-Phu Thong	IV	54,500	1977
Phu Wua	IV	18,650	1975
Salawin	IV	87,500	1978
Thung Yai Naresuan	IV	320,000	1974
Ton Nga Chang	IV	18,200	1978
Yot Dom	IV	20,255	1977

TOGO

Summary/Sommaire		
Category\Catégorie II	3	357,290
Category\Catégorie IV	8	289,616
Total	**11**	**646,906**

Parcs nationaux et aires protégées

National Parks/Parcs nationaux

Fazao-Malfakassa	II	192,000	1950
Fosse aux Lions	II	1,650	
Keran	II	163,640	1950

Faunal Reserves/Réserves fauniques

Aboulaye	IV	30,000	
Akaba	IV	25,626	
Djamde	IV	1,650	
Galangashie	IV	7,500	
Haho-Yoto	IV	18,000	
Kpessi	IV	28,000	
Oti Mandouri	IV	147,840	
Togodo	IV	31,000	1952

TOKELAU
No Areas Listed/pas de sites

TONGA
No Areas Listed/pas de sites

TRINIDAD AND TOBAGO/TRINITE-ET-TOBAGO

Summary/Sommaire		
Category\Catégorie IV	6	15,278
Total	**6**	**15,278**

Wildlife Sanctuaries/Sanctuaires de ressources sauvages

Bush Bush	IV	1,554	1968
Central Range	IV	2,153	1934
Little Tobago	IV	101	1928
Northern Range	IV	1,350	1935
Southern Watershed	IV	1,874	1934
Trinity Hill	IV	8,246	1934

TUNISIA/TUNISIE

Summary/Sommaire		
Category\Catégorie I	1	450
Category\Catégorie II	5	41,780
Category\Catégorie IV	1	3,000
Total	**7**	**45,230**

National Parks/Parcs nationaux

Bou Kornine	II	1,939	1987
Djebel Bou-Hedma	II	16,488	1980
Djebel Chambi	II	6,723	1980
Ichkeul	II	12,600	1980
Zembra and Zembretta	II	4,030	1973

Natural Reserves/Réserves naturelles

Lac de Tunis	IV	3,000	1973

Marine Reserves/Réserves marines
   Galiton   I   450   1980

TURKEY/TURQUIE

Summary/Sommaire		
Category\Catégorie I	1	1,300
Category\Catégorie II	11	194,435
Category\Catégorie IV	3	23,150
Category\Catégorie V	3	50,291
Total	**18**	**269,176**

National Parks/Parcs nationaux

Dilek Yarimadisi	II	10,985	1966
Gelibolu Yarimadisi (Galipoli)	V	33,000	1973
Goreme	V	9,576	1986
Ilgaz Dagi	II	1,088	1976
Karatepe-Aslantas	V	7,715	1958
Koprulu Kanyon	II	36,614	1973
Kovada Golu	II	6,534	1970
Munzur	II	42,800	1971
Olimpos-Beydaglari	II	69,800	1972
Soguksu	II	1,050	1959
Spildag	II	5,505	1968
Termessos	II	6,702	1970
Uludag	II	11,338	1961
Yedigoller	II	2,019	1965

Nature Reserves/Réserves de nature

Sultan Sazligi	IV	9,000	1988
Yukarigokdere	I	1,300	1987

Special Protection Areas/Aires spécialement protégées

Goksu Delta	IV	13,000	1989
Koycegiz-Dalyan	IV	1,150	1988

TUVALU

No Areas Listed/pas de sites

UGANDA/OUGANDA

Summary/Sommaire		
Category\Catégorie II	4	769,800
Category\Catégorie IV	14	980,629
Category\Catégorie V	1	5,200
Total	**19**	**1,755,629**

National Parks/Parcs nationaux

Kidepo Valley	II	134,400	1962
Lake Mburo	II	53,600	1982
Murchison Falls (Kabalega)	II	384,000	1952
Queen Elizabeth (Rwenzori)	II	197,800	1952

Nature Reserves/Réserves de nature			
Budongo	IV	1,041	
Game Reserves/Réserves de faune			
Ajai	IV	15,800	1962
Bokora Corridor	IV	205,600	1964
Bugungu	IV	52,000	1968
Gorilla	IV	2,900	1964
Karuma	IV	82,000	1964
Katonga	IV	20,800	1964
Kibale Forest Corridor	IV	56,000	1964
Kigezi	IV	33,000	1952
Kyambura	IV	15,700	1965
Matheniko	IV	160,000	1964
Pian-Upe	IV	231,400	1964
Toro	IV	55,488	1929
Sanctuaries/Sanctuaires			
Dufile, Otze and Mount Kei	IV	48,900	
Entebbe	V	5,200	

UKRAINIAN SOVIET SOCIALIST REPUBLIC/REPUBLIQUE SOCIALISTE SOVIETIQUE UKRAINE

Summary/Sommaire		
Category\Catégorie I	11	158,737
Category\Catégorie II	2	132,803
Category\Catégorie IV	4	173,367
Total	**17**	**464,907**

National Parks/Parcs nationaux			
Karpatskiy	II	50,303	1980
Shatskiy	II	82,500	1983
Zapovedniki/Zapovednik			
Askaniya Nova	I	11,054	1921
Chernomorskiy	I	71,899	1927
Dunaiskie Plavni	I	14,851	1981
Kanevskiy	I	1,030	1968
Karadagskiy	I	1,370	1979
Karpatskiy	I	18,544	1968
Luganskiy	I	1,580	1968
Polesskiy	I	20,104	1968
Rastoch'e	I	2,080	1984
Ukrainskiy Stepnoy	I	1,634	1961
Yaltinskiy	I	14,591	1973
Hunting Reserves/Réserves de chasse			
Azovo-Sivashskoye	IV	57,430	1957
Dneprovsko-Teterevskoye	IV	37,891	1967
Krymskoye	IV	42,957	1957
Zalesskoye	IV	35,089	1957

UNION OF SOVIET SOCIALIST REPUBLICSU/NION DES REPUBLIQUES SOCIALISTES SOVIETIQUES

Summary/Sommaire		
Category\Catégorie I	139	21,681,556
Category\Catégorie II	16	1,690,316
Total	**155**	**23,371,872**

National Parks/Parcs nationaux

Ala-Archa	II	19,400	1976
Bashkiriya	II	98,134	1986
Bayanaul'sky	II	45,500	1985
Gauya	II	83,750	1973
Lakhemaaskiy	II	64,911	1971
Lithuanian SSR	II	30,000	1974
Losinyy Ostrov	II	10,058	1983
Mariy Chodra	II	36,600	1985
Pribaikalskiy	II	412,750	1986
Priel'brusskiy	II	101,000	1986
Samarskaya Luka	II	128,000	1984
Sevan	II	150,000	1978
Sochinskiy	II	190,000	1983
Tbilisskiy	II	19,410	1973
Uzbekistan People's Park	II	31,503	1978
Zabaikalskiy	II	269,300	1986

Zapovedniki/Zapovednik

Adzhametskiy	I	4,848	1957
Ak-Gel'skiy	I	4,400	1978
Akhmetskiy	I	16,297	1980
Aksu-Dzhabagly	I	75,094	1927
Algetskiy	I	6,000	1965
Alma-Atinskiy	I	73,342	1961
Altaiskiy	I	881,238	1968
Amu-Dar'inskiy	I	50,506	1982
Astrakhanskiy	I	63,400	1919
Azas	I	337,290	1985
Baday-Tugay	I	5,929	1971
Badkhyzskiy	I	87,680	1941
Baikalo-Lenskiy	I	659,919	1986
Barguzinskiy	I	263,200	1916
Barsakel'messkiy	I	18,300	1939
Bashkirskiy	I	79,609	1930
Bassegi	I	19,422	1982
Baykal'skiy	I	165,724	1969
Besh-Aral'skiy	I	116,732	1979
Bol'shekhekhtsizskiy	I	45,123	1963
Borzhomskiy	I	18,048	1959
Bryanskiy Les	I	11,778	1987
Bureinskiy	I	358,444	1987
Chapkyalyay	I	8,477	1975

Chatkal'skiy	I	35,686	1947
Dagestanskiy	I	19,061	1987
Dal'nevostochnyy	I	64,316	1978
Darvinskiy	I	112,630	1945
Dashti-Dzhumskiy	I	19,700	1983
Dauzsky	I	631,300	1986
Dilizhanskiy	I	24,232	1958
Endlaskiy	I	8,162	1985
Geigel'skiy	I	7,131	1926
Girkanskiy	I	2,904	1969
Gissarskiy (Kyzylsuyskiy and Mirakinskiy)	I	87,538	1983
Grini	I	1,477	1957
Il'menskiy	I	30,380	1920
Ilisuinsky	I	9,345	1987
Ismaillinskiy	I	5,778	1981
Issyk-Kul'skiy	I	18,999	1948
Kabardino-Balkarskiy	I	74,099	1976
Kamanos	I	3,650	1979
Kandalakshskiy	I	58,100	1932
Kaplankyrskiy	I	570,000	1979
Karayazskiy	I	4,155	1978
Kavkazskiy	I	263,277	1924
Kazbegskiy	I	8,707	1976
Kedrovaya Pad'	I	17,897	1916
Khinganskiy	I	97,836	1963
Khoperskiy	I	16,178	1935
Khosrovskiy	I	29,680	1958
Kintrishskiy	I	13,893	1959
Kitabskii	I	5,378	1979
Kivach	I	10,460	1931
Kodry	I	5,177	1971
Komsomol'skiy	I	63,866	1963
Kopetdagskiy	I	49,793	1976
Kostomukhskiy	I	47,457	1983
Krasnovodskiy	I	262,037	1928
Kronotskiy	I	1,099,000	1967
Krustkalny	I	2,902	1977
Kugitangskiy	I	27,100	1986
Kurgal'dzhinskiy	I	237,138	1968
Kuril'skiy	I	65,365	1984
Kyzyl-Agachskiy	I	88,360	1929
Kyzylkumskiy	I	10,141	1971
Lagodekhskiy	I	17,818	1912
Laplandskiy	I	278,436	1930
Lazovskiy	I	116,524	1957
Les na Vorskle	I	1,038	1979
Liakhvskiy	I	6,385	1977
Magadanskiy	I	883,805	1982
Malaya Sos'va	I	92,921	1976
Mariamdzhvarskiy	I	1,040	1959

Markakol'skiy	I	75,040	1976
Matsaluskiy	I	39,697	1957
Mordovskiy	I	32,148	1935
Narynskiy	I	18,260	1983
Naurzumskiy	I	87,694	1934
Nigulasskiy	I	2,771	1957
Nizhne-Svirskiy	I	40,972	1980
Nuratinskiy	I	22,537	1975
Okskiy	I	22,911	1935
Olekminskiy	I	847,102	1984
Ozenbuzgskiy	I	21,653	1989
Pechoro-Ilychskiy	I	721,322	1930
Pinezhskiy	I	41,244	1975
Pirkulinskiy	I	1,520	1968
Pitsyundo-Myusserskiy	I	3,761	1966
Pozonaiskiy	I	56,669	1988
Prioksko-Terrasnyy	I	4,945	1948
Pskhu-Gumistinskiy	I	40,819	1976
Putozanskiy	I	1,887,251	1988
Ramit	I	16,168	1959
Redenskiy Les	I	5,664	1976
Repetekskiy	I	34,600	1928
Ritsinskiy	I	16,289	1957
Saguramskiy	I	5,247	1946
Sary-Chelekskiy	I	23,868	1959
Sayano-Shushenskiy	I	390,368	1976
Severo-Osetinskiy	I	28,999	1967
Shikaokhskiy	I	18,000	1975
Shirvanskiy	I	17,745	1969
Shul'gan Tash	I	22,531	1986
Sikhote-Alinskiy	I	347,052	1935
Slitere	I	15,037	1921
Sokhondinskiy	I	211,007	1973
Stolby	I	47,154	1925
Suzkhanskiy	I	28,014	1986
Syunt-Khasardagskiy	I	29,700	1976
Taymyrskiy	I	1,348,708	1979
Teberdinskiy	I	84,996	1936
Teychi	I	19,047	1982
Tigrovaya Balka	I	49,700	1938
Tsentral'nochernozemnyy	I	4,847	1969
Tsentral'novesnoy	I	21,380	1931
Tsentralno-Sibirskiy	I	972,017	1985
Turianchaiskiy	I	12,634	1958
Ussuriyskiy	I	40,432	1932
Ust'Lenskiy	I	1,433,000	1986
Ustiyurtskiy	I	223,300	1984
Vashlovanskiy	I	8,034	1935
Verkhne-Tazovskiy	I	631,308	1986
Vil'sandiyskiy	I	10,689	1910

Visimskiy	I	13,750	1971
Vitimskiy	I	585,021	1982
Viydumyaeskiy	I	1,194	1957
Volzhsko-Kamskiy	I	8,034	1960
Voronezhskiy	I	31,053	1927
Vrangel Island	I	795,650	1976
Yuganskiy	I	648,636	1982
Yuzhno-Uzalskiy	I	254,914	1978
Zaaminskiy	I	15,600	1959
Zakatal'skiy	I	23,843	1930
Zavidovskiy	I	125,442	1972
Zeravshanskiy	I	2,352	1975
Zeyskiy	I	82,567	1963
Zhigulevskiy	I	23,140	1966
Zhuvintas	I	5,457	1946

UNITED ARAB EMIRATES/EMIRATS ARAB UNIS

No Areas Listed/pas de sites

UNITED KINGDOM OF GREAT BRITAIN AND NORTHERN IRELAND/ ROYAUME-UNI DE GRANDE BRETAGNE ET D'IRELANDE DU NORD

Summary/Sommaire		
Category\Catégorie I	3	19,331
Category\Catégorie II	1	4,128
Category\Catégorie IV	45	148,687
Category\Catégorie V	110	4,541,304
Total	**159**	**4,713,450**

National Parks/Parcs nationaux

Brecon Beacons	V	133,400	1957
Dartmoor	V	94,500	1951
Exmoor	V	68,632	1954
Lake District	V	228,000	1951
North York Moors	V	143,221	1952
Northumberland	V	103,079	1956
Peak District	V	142,285	1951
Pembrokeshire Coast	V	57,937	1952
Snowdonia	V	217,100	1951
The Broads	V	28,800	1989
Yorkshire Dales	V	176,113	1954

National Nature Reserves/Réserves naturelles nationales

Abernethy Forest	IV	2,296	1982
Beinn Eighe	IV	4,758	1951
Ben Lawers	IV	3,974	1962
Ben Lui	IV	2,104	1961
Ben Wyvis	IV	5,673	1984
Blackwater Estuary	IV	1,031	1983
Blar Nam Faoileag	IV	2,126	1985

Bridgwater Bay	IV	2,559	1954
Caenlochan	IV	3,639	1961
Caerlaverock	IV	5,585	1957
Cairngorms	IV	25,949	1954
Cairnsmore of Fleet	IV	1,922	1975
Creag Meagaidh	IV	3,948	1986
Dengie	IV	2,011	1984
Dyfi	IV	2,095	1972
Glen Roy	IV	1,168	1970
Glen Tanar	IV	4,185	1979
Gualin	IV	2,522	1971
Holkham	IV	3,925	1967
Inchnadamph	IV	1,295	1956
Inverpolly	IV	10,857	1961
Lindisfarne	IV	3,278	1964
Loch Druidibeg	IV	1,677	1958
Loch Leven	IV	1,597	1964
Loch Maree Islands	IV	200	
Monach Isles	IV	577	1966
Moor House	IV	3,894	1952
Muir of Dinnet	IV	1,415	1977
Newborough Warren/Ynys Llanddwyn	IV	1,405	1955
North Rona and Sula Sgeir	IV	130	1984
North Strangford Lough	IV	1,015	1987
Noss	IV	313	1955
Rannoch Moor	IV	1,499	1958
Rhum	IV	10,794	1957
Ribble Marshes	IV	2,302	1979
Scolt Head Island	IV	737	
Skomer Island	IV	307	1959
St Kilda	IV	853	1957
Stackpole	IV	199	1981
Strathfarrar	IV	2,189	1977
Upper Teesdale	IV	3,497	1963
Y Wyddfa-Snowdon	IV	1,677	1964
National Scenic Areas/Aires scéniques nationales			
Assynt-Coigach	V	90,200	1980
Ben Nevis and Glen Coe	V	101,600	1980
Cuillin Hills	V	21,900	1980
Deeside and Lochnagar	V	40,000	1980
Dornoch Firth	V	7,500	1980
East Stewartry Coast	V	5,200	1980
Eildon and Leaderfoot	V	3,600	1980
Fleet Valley	V	5,300	1980
Glen Affric	V	19,300	1980
Glen Strathfarrar	V	3,800	1980
Hoy and West Mainland	V	14,800	1980
Jura	V	21,800	1980
Kintail	V	16,300	1980
Knapdale	V	19,800	1980

Knoydart	V	39,500	1980
Kyle of Tongue	V	18,500	1980
Kyles of Bute	V	4,400	1980
Loch Lomond	V	27,400	1980
Loch Rannoch and Glenlyon	V	48,400	1980
Loch Sheil	V	13,400	1980
Loch Tummel	V	9,200	1980
Loch na Keal	V	12,700	1980
Lynn of Lorn	V	4,800	1980
Morar, Moidart and Ardnamurchan	V	15,900	1980
Nith Estuary	V	9,300	1980
North Arran	V	23,800	1980
North West Sutherland	V	20,500	1980
River Earn (Comrie and St Fillans)	V	3,000	1980
River Tay (Dunkeld)	V	5,600	1980
Scarba, Lunga and the Garvellachs	V	1,900	1980
Shetland	V	15,600	1980
South Lewis, Harris and North Uist	V	108,600	1980
South Uist Machair	V	6,100	1980
St Kilda	V	900	1980
The Cairngorm Mountains	V	67,200	1980
The Small Isles	V	15,500	1980
The Trossachs	V	4,600	1980
Trotternish	V	5,000	1980
Upper Tweeddale	V	12,300	1980
Wester Ross	V	145,300	1980

Areas of Outstanding Natural Beauty/Aires à la beauté
naturelle exceptionnelle

Anglesey	V	21,500	1967
Antrim Coast and Glens	V	70,600	1988
Arnside and Silverdale	V	7,500	1972
Cannock Chase	V	6,800	1958
Causeway Coast	V	4,050	1989
Chichester Harbour	V	7,500	1964
Chilterns	V	80,000	1965
Clwydian Range	V	15,600	1965
Cornwall	V	93,200	1959
Cornwall Extension	V	2,500	1983
Cotswolds	V	150,700	1966
Cranbourne Chase and West Wiltshire Downs	V	96,000	1983
Dedham Vale	V	5,700	1970
Dedham Vale Extension	V	1,500	1978
Dorset	V	103,600	1959
East Devon	V	26,700	1963
East Hampshire	V	39,100	1962
Forest of Bowland	V	80,300	1964
Gower	V	18,900	1956
High Weald	V	145,000	1983
Howardian Hills	V	20,500	1987
Isle of Wight	V	18,900	1963

Isles of Scilly	V	1,600	1976
Kent Downs	V	84,500	1968
Lincolnshire Wolds	V	56,000	1973
Lleyn	V	15,500	1957
Malvern Hills	V	10,400	1959
Mendip Hills	V	20,600	1972
Mourne	V	57,012	1986
Norfolk Coast	V	45,000	1968
North Devon	V	17,100	1960
North Pennines	V	199,800	1988
North Wessex Downs	V	173,800	1972
Northumberland Coast	V	12,900	1958
Quantock Hills	V	9,900	1957
Shropshire Hills	V	77,700	1959
Solway Coast	V	10,700	1964
South Devon	V	33,200	1960
South Hampshire Coast	V	7,800	1967
Suffolk Coast and Heaths	V	39,100	1966
Surrey Hills	V	41,400	1958
Sussex Downs	V	98,100	1966
Wye Valley	V	32,500	1971

Unclassified/Non classé

New Forest	V	37,500	1079

Anguilla/Anguille

No Areas Listed/pas de sites

Bermuda/Bermudes

Nature Reserves/Réserves de nature

Castle Harbour Islands	IV	200	1979

Preserves/Réserves

North Shore Coral Reef	IV	12,000	1966

British Indian Ocean Territory/Territoire britannique de l'ocean Indien

No Areas Listed/pas de sites

British Virgin Islands/Iles Vierges britannique

No Areas Listed/pas de sites

Cayman Islands/Iles Caïmans

Marine Parks/Parcs marins

Little Sound	I	1,731	1986
North Sound	IV	3,310	1986

Falkland Islands/Iles Malouines

No Areas Listed/pas de sites

Gibraltar
No Areas Listed/pas de sites

Hong Kong/Hong-Kong
Country Parks/Parcs régionaux

Lam Tsuen	V	1,520	1979
Lantau North	V	2,220	1978
Lantau South	V	5,640	1978
Ma On Shan	V	2,880	1979
Pat Sin Leng	V	3,125	1978
Plover Cove	V	5,224	1978
Sai Kung East	V	4,477	1978
Sai Kung West	V	3,000	1978
Shing Mun	V	1,400	1977
Tai Lam	V	5,330	1979
Tai Mo Shan	V	1,440	1979
Tai Tam	V	1,585	1977

Montserrat
No Areas Listed/pas de sites

Pitcairn Islands/Iles Pitcairn
No Areas Listed/pas de sites

Saint Helena, Ascension, Tristan da Cunha/Sainte-Hélène, Ascension, Tristan da Cunha
Wildlife Reserves/Réserves de ressources sauvages

Gough Island	I	6,500	1976
Jews Point	I	11,100	1979

South Georgia/South Sandwich Islands/Géorgie du Sud/Iles Sandwich du Sud
No Areas Listed/pas de sites

Turks and Caicos/Turques-et-Caïques
National Parks/Parcs nationaux

Grand Turk Cays Land and Sea	V	134	1987
Grand Turk West Shore	V	1,000	1987
Leeward Land and Sea	V	500	1987

UNITED STATES OF AMERICA/ETATS-UNIS D'AMERIQUE

Summary/Sommaire		
Category\Catégorie I	14	210,107
Category\Catégorie II	60	20,239,036
Category\Catégorie III	232	18,029,505
Category\Catégorie IV	336	47,159,904
Category\Catégorie V	328	12,710,624
Total	**970**	**98,349,176**

National Parks/Parcs nationaux

Acadia	II	15,590	1919
Arches	II	29,260	1971
Badlands	II	98,463	1978
Big Bend	II	286,572	1944
Biscayne	II	41,967	1980
Bryce Canyon	II	14,405	1924
Canyonlands	II	136,542	1964
Capitol Reef	II	97,870	1971
Carlsbad Caverns	II	18,921	1930
Channel Islands	II	100,987	1980
Crater Lake	II	74,150	1902
Everglades	II	585,867	1947
Glacier	II	410,058	1910
Grand Canyon	II	493,441	1919
Grand Teton	II	124,140	1929
Great Basin	II	31,080	1986
Great Smoky Mountains	II	209,160	1934
Guadalupe Mountains	II	31,364	1972
Hot Springs	II	2,330	1921
Isle Royale	II	215,740	1940
Kings Canyon	II	187,069	1940
Lassen Volcanic	II	43,293	1916
Mammoth Cave	II	20,541	1934
Mesa Verde	II	20,830	1906
Mount Rainier	II	95,268	1899
North Cascades	II	204,284	1968
Olympic	II	371,225	1938
Petrified Forest	II	37,880	1962
Redwood	II	42,400	1968
Rocky Mountain	II	107,519	1915
Sequoia	II	163,115	1890
Shenandoah	II	84,921	1926
Theodore Roosevelt	II	28,150	1978
Voyageurs	II	87,772	1971
Wind Cave	II	11,223	1903
Yellowstone	II	899,139	1872
Yosemite	II	308,273	1890
Zion	II	59,308	1909

National Wildlife Refuges/Refuges nationaux de faune et de flore sauvages

Agassiz	IV	24,726	1937
Alamosa	IV	4,523	1962
Alligator River	IV	56,297	
Anahuac	IV	9,897	1963
Ankeny	IV	1,132	1965
Aransas	IV	42,407	1937
Arapaho	IV	7,393	1967
Ardoch	IV	1,092	
Arrowwood	IV	6,453	1935

Ash Meadows	IV	5,174	
Atchafalaya	IV	6,178	
Attwater's Prairie Chicken	IV	3,234	1972
Audubon	IV	5,969	1956
Back Bay	IV	1,859	1938
Banks Lake	IV	1,639	
Baskett Slough	IV	1,009	1965
Bear Lake	IV	7,269	1968
Bear River	IV	26,337	
Bear Valley	IV	1,378	
Benton Lake	IV	5,015	
Big Boggy	IV	1,770	
Big Lake	IV	4,466	
Big Stone	IV	4,371	
Bitter Lake	III	9,457	
Blackbeard Island	IV	2,275	1940
Blackwater	IV	6,353	
Bogue Chitto (Louisiana)	IV	8,324	
Bogue Chitto (Mississippi)	IV	2,648	
Bombay Hook	IV	6,124	
Bon Secour	IV	1,819	
Bosque del Apache	IV	23,162	1939
Bowdoin	IV	5,094	
Brazoria	IV	4,941	
Breton	IV	3,664	1904
Browns Park	IV	5,449	
Buenos Aires	IV	45,126	
Buffalo Lake (Texas)	IV	3,104	
Butte Sink	IV	3,275	
Cabeza Prieta	IV	348,042	
Cache River	IV	1,898	
Camas	IV	4,284	
Cape Romain	IV	13,861	1932
Carolina Sandhills	IV	18,319	
Catahoula	IV	2,150	
Cedar Island	IV	5,073	
Charles M. Russell	IV	364,808	1936
Chase Lake	IV	1,776	1908
Chassahowitzka	IV	12,317	
Chautauqua	IV	2,510	
Chickasaw	IV	6,266	
Chicot	IV	2,592	
Chincoteague	IV	3,853	
Choctaw	IV	1,708	
Cibola	IV	1,277	
Clarence Cannon	IV	1,513	1964
Clear Lake	IV	13,543	
Coachella Valley	IV	1,049	
Cold Springs	IV	1,262	1909
Columbia	IV	11,985	1944

Colusa	IV	1,636	
Conboy Lake	IV	2,290	1965
Crab Orchard	IV	17,682	
Creedman Coulee	IV	1,105	
Crescent Lake	IV	18,556	
Crocodile Lake	IV	1,619	
Cross Creeks	IV	3,589	
D'Arbonne	IV	7,055	
Dakota Lake	IV	1,116	
De Soto (Iowa)	IV	1,417	
De Soto (Nebraska)	IV	1,751	
Deer Flat	IV	4,562	
Delevan	IV	2,282	
Delta	IV	19,763	1935
Des Lacs	IV	7,915	
Desert	IV	643,471	
Edwin B. Forsythe	IV	14,017	
Erie	IV	3,238	
Eufaula (Georgia)	IV	1,309	
Eufaula (Alabama)	IV	3,211	
Fallon	IV	7,250	
Felsenthal	IV	26,285	1975
Fish Springs	IV	5,758	1959
Fishermen Island	IV	415	1969
Flint Hills	IV	7,478	1966
Fort Niobrara	IV	7,563	1912
Grasslands	IV	10,669	
Grays Lake	IV	6,652	1965
Great Dismal Swamp (Virginia)	IV	33,154	1973
Great Dismal Swamp (North Carolina)	IV	9,945	
Great Meadows	IV	1,168	1944
Great Swamp	IV	2,809	1964
Great White Heron	IV	2,996	
Grulla	III	1,309	1969
Hagerman	IV	4,585	1945
Halfbreed Lake	IV	1,748	
Harris Neck	IV	1,119	1962
Hart Mountain	IV	100,994	
Hatchie	IV	5,285	1965
Havasu	IV	3,138	1941
Hillside	IV	6,239	1975
Holla Bend	IV	2,274	1957
Horicon	IV	8,495	1941
Imperial (Arizona)	IV	7,206	1941
Imperial (California)	IV	3,223	1941
Iroquois	IV	4,381	1958
J. Clark Salyer	IV	23,771	
J.N. Ding Darling	IV	2,037	1945
Kern	IV	4,297	
Kesterson	IV	2,388	

Kirtlands Warbler	IV	2,127	
Kirwin	IV	4,365	
Klamath Forest	IV	6,633	
Kofa	IV	267,102	1939
Kootenai	IV	1,123	
La Creek	IV	6,650	
Lacassine	IV	13,213	
Laguna Atascosa	IV	18,301	
Lake Alice	IV	4,534	
Lake George	IV	1,263	
Lake Ilo	IV	1,637	
Lake Mason	IV	6,773	
Lake Nettie	IV	1,237	
Lake Thibadeau	IV	1,567	
Lake Woodruff	IV	7,494	1964
Lake Zahl	IV	1,548	
Las Vegas	IV	3,499	
Lee Metcalf	IV	1,131	1964
Lewis and Clark	IV	15,390	
Little Pend Oreille	IV	16,200	
Long Lake	IV	9,046	1932
Lostwood	IV	10,048	
Lower Hatchie	IV	1,678	
Lower Klamath (California)	IV	19,027	
Lower Klamath (Oregon)	IV	2,680	
Lower Rio Grande Valley	IV	10,662	
Lower Suwannee	IV	15,856	
Loxahatchee	IV	58,792	1951
Mackay Island	IV	2,526	
Malheur	IV	74,707	
Mark Twain (Illinois)	IV	6,714	1958
Mark Twain (Iowa)	IV	4,241	1958
Martin	IV	1,791	
Mattamuskeet	IV	20,323	
Maxwell	IV	1,498	
McFaddin	IV	17,397	
McNary	IV	1,470	1955
Medicine Lake	IV	9,243	
Merced	IV	1,038	
Merritt Island	IV	56,356	
Mid-Continent	IV	1,999	
Mingo	IV	8,779	
Minidoka	IV	8,386	
Minnesota Valley	IV	2,973	
Missisquoi	IV	2,365	
Mississippi River Caue (Illinois)	V	8,148	1974
Mississippi River Caue (Iowa)	IV	12,278	1974
Mississippi River Caue (Minnesota)	IV	6,246	1974
Mississippi River Caue (Wisconsin)	IV	16,338	1974
Mississippi Sandhill Crane	IV	7,692	1974

Modoc	IV	1,038	
Monomy	IV	1,094	
Monte Vista	IV	5,746	
Montezuma	IV	2,605	
Moody	IV	1,424	
Moosehorn	IV	9,211	1937
Morgan Brake	IV	1,324	
Muleshoe	IV	2,352	
Muscatatuck	IV	3,128	
National Bison Range	IV	7,509	
National Elk	IV	9,989	
National Key Deer	IV	3,068	
Necedah	IV	17,681	
Nisqually	IV	1,145	
North Platte	IV	2,044	
Noxubee	IV	18,786	1940
Okefenokee (Florida)	IV	1,490	1937
Okefenokee (Georgia)	IV	158,518	1937
Optima	IV	1,755	
Oregon Islands	IV	233	
Ottawa	IV	2,346	
Ouray	IV	4,651	
Overflow	IV	2,875	
Oyster Bay	IV	1,298	
Pablo	IV	1,030	
Paharanagat	IV	2,179	
Panther Swamp	IV	10,993	
Parker River	IV	1,888	
Pathfinder	IV	6,807	
Patuxent	IV	1,896	
Pea Island	IV	2,376	
Pee Dee	IV	3,418	
Pelican Island	IV	1,780	
Petit Manan	IV	1,350	
Piedmont	IV	14,044	1939
Pinckney Island	IV	1,641	1975
Pine Island	IV	163	1908
Pinellas	IV	159	1956
Pixley	IV	2,426	
Plum Tree Island	IV	1,327	
Pocasse	IV	1,047	
Prime Hook	IV	3,929	
Pungo	IV	5,002	
Quillayute	IV	121	
Quivira	IV	8,837	
Rachel Carson	IV	1,280	
Red Rock Lakes	IV	14,050	
Rice Lake	IV	6,629	
Ridgefield	IV	1,874	
Rock Lake	IV	2,230	

Ruby Lake	IV	15,230	
Sabine	IV	56,472	
Sacramento	IV	4,367	1937
Saddle Mountain	IV	12,478	1971
Salt Plains	IV	12,958	1930
Salton Sea	IV	15,219	
San Andres	IV	23,172	
San Bernard	IV	9,904	1967
San Francisco Bay	IV	6,978	1972
San Juan Islands	IV	182	1914
San Luis	IV	3,009	
San Pablo Bay	IV	4,737	
Sand Lake	IV	8,039	1935
Santee	IV	17,673	1941
Savannah (Georgia)	IV	4,586	1927
Savannah (South Carolina)	IV	5,785	
Seedskadee	IV	6,011	1965
Seney	IV	38,659	
Sequoyah	IV	8,424	1971
Sevilleta	IV	92,394	1973
Sheldon	IV	231,037	1931
Sherburne	IV	11,981	1965
Shiawassee	IV	3,639	1953
Silver Lake	IV	1,356	
Slade	IV	1,215	1941
Squaw Creek	IV	2,802	
St Johns	IV	2,533	
St Marks	IV	26,399	1931
St Vincent	IV	5,057	1968
Stillwater	IV	9,802	
Sutter	IV	1,049	1945
Swan Lake	IV	4,321	1937
Swanquarter	IV	6,335	
Tamarac	IV	14,252	1938
Tennessee	IV	20,800	
Tensas River	IV	22,259	
Tewaukon	IV	3,327	1935
Texas Point	IV	3,626	
Tishomingo	IV	6,668	1943
Trempealeau	IV	2,275	
Tule Lake	IV	15,646	1928
Turnbull	IV	6,304	1937
Ul Bend	IV	22,700	
Umatilla (Oregon)	IV	3,596	1969
Umatilla (Washington)	IV	5,672	1969
Union Slough	IV	1,152	1938
Upper Klamath	IV	5,045	1928
Upper Mississippi (Iowa)	IV	8,230	1924
Upper Mississippi (Minnesota)	IV	7,189	1924
Upper Mississippi (Wisconsin)	IV	19,425	1924

Upper Ouachita	IV	8,460	1978
Upper Souris	IV	12,997	
Valentine	IV	27,174	1935
Wallops Island	IV	1,366	
Wapanocca	IV	2,219	1961
War Horse	IV	1,293	
Washita	IV	3,274	
Wassaw Island	IV	4,078	1968
Waubay	IV	1,047	
Wheeler	IV	13,839	
White River	IV	45,746	
Wichita Mountains	IV	23,903	
Willapa	IV	5,830	
William L. Finley	IV	2,157	
Willow Creek-Lurline	IV	1,586	
Willow Lake	IV	1,062	
Wolf Island	IV	2,076	1930
Yazoo	IV	5,051	
National Marine Sanctuaries/Sanctuaires marins nationaux			
Bitter Creek	IV	5,482	1973
Channel Islands	V	405,506	1980
Cordell Bank	V	128,777	1989
Gray's Reef	IV	5,441	1981
Gulf of the Farallones	V	307,044	1981
Key Largo Coral Reef	V	32,388	1975
Looe Key	V	1,554	1981
National Estuarine Research Reserves/Réserves nationales de recherche estuarienne			
Chesapeake Bay	IV	2,374	1981
Great Bay	IV	3,002	1989
Hudson River	IV	2,023	1982
Narragonsett Bay	IV	1,286	1980
North Carolina	IV	4,743	1982
Rookery Bay	IV	3,805	1978
Sapelo Island	IV	2,892	1976
South Slough	IV	2,502	1974
Waquoint Bay	IV	1,077	1988
Weeks Bay	IV	1,483	1986
National Scientific Reserves/Réserves scientifiques nationales			
Ice Age	I	13,153	1964
Research Natural Areas/Aires naturelles dédiées à la recherche			
Jordan Craters	I	12,166	1975
Lost Forest	I	3,620	1973
National Reserves/Réserves nationales			
Pinelands	V	438,210	1978
National Preserves/Réserves nationales			
Big Cypress	II	21,198	1974
Big Thicket	V	34,712	1974

National Rivers/Fleuves nationaux
Buffalo	V	38,100	1972
New River Gorge	V	25,101	1978

National Scenic Rivers/Fleuves nationaux pittoresques
Lower St Croix	V	3,512	1972
Middle Delaware	V	1,113	1978
Obed	V	2,125	1976
Ozark	V	32,209	1972
Rio Grande (Texas)	V	3,885	1978
Rio Grande (New Mexico)	V	6,820	1970
Salmon River	V	12,943	1968
St Croix	V	25,373	1969
Wolf River	V	2,228	1968

National Monuments/Monuments nationaux
Agate Fossil Beds	III	1,236	1965
Bandelier	III	14,904	1916
Black Canyon of the Gunnison	III	5,682	1933
Canyon de Chelly	III	33,536	1931
Cedar Breaks	III	2,469	1933
Chaco Canyon	III	8,708	1907
Chiricahua	III	4,853	1924
Colorado	III	8,274	1911
Congaree Swamp	III	6,125	1976
Craters of the Moon	III	21,669	1924
Death Valley	III	837,388	1933
Devil's Tower	V	1,346	1906
Dinosaur	III	82,655	1915
Florissant Fossil Beds	III	1,698	1969
Fort Jefferson	III	19,083	1935
Fort Matanzas	III	120	1924
Fort Pulaski	V	2,229	1924
Fossil Butte	III	3,280	1972
Great Sand Dunes	III	14,596	1932
J.D. Rockefeller, Jr.	III	9,672	1977
John Day Fossil Beds	III	5,671	1974
Joshua Tree	III	226,781	1936
Lava Beds	III	18,856	1925
Lehman Caves	III	3,098	1922
Marble Canyon	III	13,197	1969
Natural Bridges	III	3,040	1908
Organ Pipe Cactus	III	133,925	1937
Pinnacles	III	6,587	1908
Saguaro	III	33,836	1933
Saint Croix Island	III	100	1949
Scotts Bluff	V	1,209	1919
Sunset Crater	III	1,230	1930
White Sands	III	58,614	1933
Wupatki	III	14,267	1924

National Natural Landmarks/Eléments naturels nationaux marquants			
Amboy Crater	III	2,327	
Anza-Borrego Desert State Park	III	211,016	
Attwater's Prairie Chicken	III	3,234	1972
Big Lake	III	4,466	
Canaan Valley	III	6,222	
Cassia Silent City of Rocks	III	7,474	
Cinder Cone	III	10,342	
Como Bluff	III	1,487	
Grants Lava Flow	III	21,719	
Hagerman Fauna sites	III	1,566	
Henderson Sloughs	III	1,737	
Henry Mountains	III	13,187	
Hualapai Valley Joshua Trees	III	1,212	
Kilbourne Hole	III	2,327	
Laguna Atascosa	III	18,301	
Lake Agassiz	IV	8,888	
Lance Creek Fossil Area	III	4,008	
McCurtain County Wilderness Area	III	5,691	
Muleshoe	III	2,352	
Salt Plains	II	12,948	1930
Sand Hills	III	9,696	
Turtle Mountains	III	38,525	
White River	III	45,746	
National Lakeshores/Littoraux lacustres nationaux			
Apostle Island	V	17,084	1970
Indiana Dunes	V	5,073	1966
Pictured Rocks	V	28,661	1966
Sleeping Bear Dunes	V	28,775	1970
National Seashores/Rivages marins nationaux			
Assateague Island	V	16,038	1965
Canaveral	V	23,321	1975
Cape Cod	V	18,018	1961
Cape Hatteras	V	12,270	1937
Cape Lookout	V	11,493	1966
Cumberland Island	V	14,924	1972
Fire Island	V	7,834	1964
Gulf Islands	V	57,084	1971
Padre Island	V	54,196	1968
Point Reyes	V	28,733	1972
Wilderness Areas/Aires de nature sauvage			
McCurtain County	I	5,691	
Porcupine Mountains	I	16,486	1944
Natural Environment Areas/Aires d'environnement naturel			
Zekiah Swamp	IV	2,020	
Natural Areas/Aires naturelles			
Big Lazer Creek	IV	1,122	1974
Lewis Island	IV	2,276	1974

Pigeon Mountain	IV	2,993	1974

Outstanding Natural Areas/Aires naturelles exceptionnelles

Amargosa Canyon-Dumont Dunes	V	9,196	1975
Desert View Natural Environment Area	V	7,531	1970
El Malpais	V	33,936	1970
Escalente Canyons	V	52,116	1970
Goshute Canyon	V	3,042	1967
Guadalupe Canyon	V	1,462	1968
Highland Range Crucial Bighorn	V	10,213	1970
Lahontan-Cutthroat Trout	V	4,976	1974
Mount Grafton Scenic Area	V	5,898	1967
North Escalante Canyon	V	2,343	1970
Phipps-Death Hollow	V	13,857	1970
Snake River Birds of Prey	V	10,629	1971
Sunrise Mountain	V	4,137	1970
Swamp Cedar	V	1,293	1967
The Gulch	V	1,386	1970
Vermillion Cliffs	V	20,255	1969

Estuarine Sanctuaries/Sanctuaires estuariens

Padilla Bay	IV	12,570	1980

National Forest Wildernesses/Zones nationales
sauvages boisées

Absaroka-Beartooth	III	372,762	1978
Agua Tibia	III	6,439	1974
Aldo Leopold	III	85,576	1980
Alpine Lakes	III	123,687	1976
Anaconda-Pintler	III	63,949	1964
Apache Kid	III	18,225	1980
Beaver Creek	III	1,944	1974
Bell Mountain	III	3,321	1980
Big Blue	III	39,568	1980
Black Elk	III	4,333	1980
Blackjack Springs	III	2,389	1978
Blue Range	III	12,150	1980
Bob Marshall	III	408,807	1978
Boundary Waters Canoe Area	III	321,165	1978
Bradwell Bay	III	9,477	1974
Bridger	III	158,841	1964
Bristol Cliffs	III	1,498	1976
Cabinet Mountains	III	38,191	1964
Cache La Poudre	III	3,807	1980
Caney Creek	III	5,791	1974
Capitan Mountains	III	13,770	1980
Caribou	III	7,614	1964
Chama River Canyon	III	20,371	1978
Chiricahua	III	7,290	1964
Cohutta	III	13,081	1974
Collegiate Peaks	III	64,800	1980
Commanche Peak	III	27,256	1980
Cruces Basin	III	7,290	1980

Cucamonga	III	3,483	1964
Desolation	III	25,717	1969
Devil's Backbone	III	2,754	1980
Diamond Peak	III	14,580	1964
Dolly Sods	III	4,131	1974
Dome Land	III	25,393	1964
Dome	III	2,106	1980
Eagle Cap	III	118,867	1964
Eagles Nest	III	54,189	1976
Ellicott Rock (North Carolina)	III	1,134	1974
Ellicott Rock (South Carolina)	III	1,137	1974
Emigrant	III	42,970	1974
Fitzpatrick	III	77,800	1976
Flat Tops	III	95,215	1975
Galluro	III	21,343	1964
Gates of the Mountain	III	11,583	1964
Gearhart Mountain	III	7,573	1965
Gee Creek	III	1,012	1974
Gila	III	230,688	1980
Glacier Peak	III	188,041	1964
Goat Rocks	III	33,453	1964
Golden Trout	III	122,836	1978
Gospel Hump	III	83,389	1978
Great Bear	III	116,113	1978
Great Gulf	III	2,268	1964
Hell's Canyon (Oregon)	III	43,902	1975
Hell's Canyon (Idaho)	III	33,939	1975
Hercules-Glade	III	49,815	1976
Holy Cross	III	47,223	1980
Hoover	III	19,683	1964
Hunter Fryingpan	III	30,091	1978
Indian Peaks	III	28,552	1980
James River Face	III	3,523	1974
Jarbridge	III	26,203	1964
John Muir	III	202,378	1964
Joyce Kilmer-Slickrock (Tennessee)	III	1,539	
Joyce Kilmer-Slickrock (North Carolina)	III	4,131	1974
Kaiser	III	9,193	1976
Kalmiopsis	III	68,404	1978
Kisatchie Hills	III	3,523	1980
La Garita	III	43,942	1980
Latir Peak	III	8,100	1980
Linville Gorge	III	3,078	1964
Little Wambaw Swamp	III	2,025	1980
Lizard Head	III	16,200	1980
Lone Peak	III	12,190	1978
Lost Creek	III	42,930	1980
Lye Brook	III	5,427	1974
Manzano Mountain	III	14,944	1978
Marble Mountain	III	86,548	1964

Maroon Bells-Snowmass	III	70,470	1980
Mazatzal	III	83,511	1964
Minarets	III	43,497	1964
Mission Mountains	III	29,929	1974
Mokelumne	III	20,047	1964
Mount Adams	III	13,122	1964
Mount Baldy	III	2,835	1970
Mount Evans	III	29,605	1980
Mount Hood	III	18,832	1978
Mount Jefferson	III	40,581	1968
Mount Massive	III	10,530	1980
Mount Sneffels	III	6,561	1980
Mount Washington	III	18,670	1964
Mount Zirkel	III	57,105	1980
Mountain Lakes	III	9,355	1964
Neota	III	4,131	1980
Never Summer	III	5,548	1980
North Absaroka	III	142,114	1964
Otter Creek	III	8,100	1974
Pasayten	III	204,727	1968
Pecos	III	90,436	1980
Pine Mountain	III	8,140	1972
Piney Creek	III	3,402	1980
Presidential Ridge-Dry River	III	8,262	1974
Pusch Ridge	III	23,044	1978
Raggeds	III	27,540	1980
Rainbow Lake	III	2,754	1974
Rattlesnake	III	8,100	1980
Rawah	III	30,739	1980
River of No Return	III	903,271	1980
Rockpile Mountain	III	1,579	1980
San Gabriel	III	14,620	1968
San Gorgonio	III	14,256	1964
San Jacinto	III	8,545	1964
San Pedro Parks	III	16,645	1980
San Rafael	III	60,345	1968
Sandia Mountain	III	12,433	1980
Santa Lucia	III	7,533	1978
Savage Run	III	6,196	1978
Sawtooth	III	87,925	1972
Scapegoat	III	96,916	1972
Selway-Bitterroot (Montana)	III	100,804	1964
Selway-Bitterroot (Idaho)	III	44,104	1980
Shining Rock	III	5,427	1964
Sierra Ancha	III	8,464	1964
Sipsey	III	5,103	1974
South San Juan	III	54,067	1980
South Warner	III	27,702	1964
Strawberry Mountain	III	13,365	1964
Superstition	III	50,260	1964

Sycamore Canyon	III	19,318	1972
Teton	III	225,706	1964
Thousand Lakes	III	6,601	1964
Three Sisters	III	99,346	1978
Upper Buffalo	III	4,131	1974
Ventana	III	64,374	1978
Wambaw Swamp	III	2,065	1980
Washakie	III	278,073	1964
Welcome Creek	III	11,380	1978
Weminuche	III	187,596	1980
Wenaha-Tucannon (Washington)	III	44,955	1978
Wenaha-Tucannon (Oregon)	III	26,892	
West Elk	III	78,730	1980
Wheeler	III	7,978	1980
Whisker Lake	III	2,956	1978
White Mountain	III	19,480	1980
Wild Rogue	III	10,408	1978
Withington	III	7,695	1980
Yolla Bolly-Middle Eel	III	45,319	1964
National Recreation Areas/Aires de loisirs nationales			
Amistad	V	26,260	1965
Arbuckle	V	3,576	1965
Bighorn Canyon (Montana)	V	48,644	1966
Coulee Dam	V	40,424	1946
Curecanti	V	16,985	1965
Cuyahoga Valley	V	12,950	1975
Delaware Water Gap (New Jersey)	V	28,340	1965
Delaware Water Gap (Pennsylvania)	V	11,478	1965
Glen Canyon (Arizona)	V	483,404	1972
Glen Canyon (Utah)	V	580,558	1927
Golden Gate	V	29,611	1972
Lake Chelan	V	25,044	1968
Lake Mead (Arizona)	IV	1,000	1964
Lake Mead (Nevada)	V	606,123	1964
Ross Lake	V	47,582	1968
Sanford	V	16,603	1965
Santa Monica Mountain	V	60,729	1978
Shadow Mountain	V	7,369	1952
Whiskeytown Shasta Trinity	V	17,213	1965
State Natural Area Reserves/Réserves naturelles d'Etat			
Hill Country	I	1,099	
Refuges/Refuges			
Hart Mountain National Antelope Refuge	IV	110,231	1935
National Memorials/Mémoriaux nationaux			
Coronado	V	1,145	1952
Fredericksburg and Spotsylvania Co. Battle	V	1,483	
National Military Parks/Parcs militaires nationaux			
Chickamauga and Chattanooga	V	3,278	1890
Pea Ridge	V	1,729	1961

National Battlefields/Champs de bataille nationaux

Manassas	V	1,101	1940
Petersburg	V	1,103	1926

National Battlefield Parks/Parcs de champs de bataille nationaux

Kennesaw Mountain	V	1,488	1917

Forest Parks/Parcs forestiers

Prince William	III	7,048	1936

Parks/Parcs

Catoctin Mountain	V	2,334	1936
Piscataway	V	1,701	1961

Parkways/Routes touristiques

John D. Rockefeller, Jr	V	9,700	1972
Natchez Trace	V	18,300	1938

National Historic Parks/Parcs historiques nationaux

Chaco Culture	V	13,760	1907
Chesapeake and Ohio Canal	V	50,161	1971
Colonial	V	3,810	1930
Cumberland Gap	V	8,150	1940
Gettysburg	V	1,377	1895
Jean Lafitte	V	3,480	1978
Nez Perce	V	1,212	1965
San Juan Island	III	100	1966
Saratoga	V	2,222	1938

State Parks/Parcs publics

Adirondack	V	2,426,200	1971
Alamo Lake	V	2,279	
Alcova	V	2,488	
Allaire	V	1,199	
Allamuchy Mt.	V	2,329	
Alleghany River	V	1,257	
Andrew Molera	V	1,934	
Annadel	V	1,985	
Anza-Borrego Desert (Arkansas)	V	201,192	
Anza-Borrego Desert (California)	V	211,016	
Babcock	V	1,472	
Bastrop	V	1,418	
Baxter	II	80,800	1940
Beacon Rock	V	1,717	
Bear Brook	V	3,894	
Bear Mountain	V	2,026	
Beavers Bend	V	1,422	
Big Basin Redwoods	V	6,321	
Big Ridge	V	1,360	
Big Sandy	V	3,072	
Big Spring	V	2,334	
Black Moshannon	V	1,477	
Blue Knob	V	2,239	
Bomoseen	V	1,107	
Boysen	V	24,825	
Brown Country	V	6,133	

Bruneau	V	1,212	
Buckhorn	V	1,003	
Bucktail	V	3,100	
Buffalo Bill	V	5,086	
Caballo Lake	V	2,152	
Cacapon	V	2,325	
Caesars Head	V	4,122	
Calaveras Big Trees	V	2,422	
Camden Hills	V	2,211	
Canaan Valley	V	2,434	1968
Cape Henlopen	V	1,227	
Caprock Canyon	I	5,526	
Castle Crags	V	2,512	
Castle Rock	V	1,069	
Catalina	V	2,226	
Catskill	V	99,788	
Cedar Bluff Reservoir	V	5,848	
Cheaha	V	1,098	
Cheraw	V	2,974	
Cimarron Canyon	V	13,332	
Clarence Fahnstock Memorial	V	2,468	
Connetquot	V	1,389	
Cook Forest	V	3,200	
Coolidge	V	6,531	
Coral Pink Sand Dunes	V	1,507	
Crawford Notch	V	2,404	
Croft	V	2,863	
Crow Wing	V	13,130	
Cuivre River	V	2,329	
Cunningham Falls	V	2,000	
Custer	V	29,492	1913
Cuyamaca Rancho	V	9,969	
Dale Hollow	V	1,399	
De Soto	V	2,047	
Dead Horse Point	V	1,869	
Deception Pass	V	1,000	
Deer Creek Lake	V	1,061	
Del Norte Coast Redwoods	V	2,576	
Delaware Canal	V	1,255	
Devils Lake	V	2,988	
Douthat	V	1,815	
Elephant Butte Lake	V	8,287	
F.D. Roosevelt	V	2,017	
Fairy Stone	V	1,846	
False Cape	V	1,745	
Farragut	V	1,912	
Forest of Nisene Marks	V	4,024	
Fort Cobb	V	1,816	
Fort Robinson	V	4,485	
Foss	V	2,816	

Fountainhead	V	1,374	
Franconia Notch	V	2,602	
French Creek	V	2,600	
Galveston Island	I	786	
Gaviota	V	1,122	
Giant City	V	1,220	
Gingko Petrified Forest	V	2,833	1948
Glendo	V	9,614	
Goblin Valley	V	1,315	
Golden Gate Canyon	II	4,048	
Governor Dodge	V	2,032	
Grafton Notch	V	1,257	
Grayson Highlands	V	1,921	
Great Salt Lake	V	10,722	
Greenbo Lake Resort	V	1,322	
Greyson River Lake	V	1,085	
Guernsey	V	4,633	
Gulf	V	2,424	
Gunpowder Falls (Maryland)	V	4,636	
Hale Ranch	I	1,982	
Hard Labor Creek	V	2,345	
Harriman (Idaho)	V	1,899	
Harriman (New York)	V	18,472	
Hartwick Pines	V	3,475	
Hennepin Canal	V	2,527	
Henry Cowell Redwoods	V	1,649	
Henry W. Coe	V	5,300	
Heron Lake	V	1,659	
Heyburn	V	3,161	
Hickory Run	V	6,200	
High Point	V	5,413	
Highland Lakes	V	1,160	
Holly River	V	3,037	
Hudson Highlands	V	1,141	
Humbolt Redwoods	V	22,220	
Hunting Island	V	2,020	
Huntington Beach	V	1,010	
Indian Cave	V	1,212	
Indian Rocks	V	1,438	
Island Beach	V	1,212	
Itasca	IV	12,822	1938
Janes Island	V	1,236	
Jay Cooke	V	3,616	
Jedediah Smith Redwoods	V	3,712	
Joe Wheeler	V	1,030	
John Pennekamp Coral Reef	V	22,684	1961
Julia Pfeiffer Burns	V	1,431	
Kankakee River	V	1,162	
Keyhole	V	5,730	
Kings Mountain	V	2,481	

Lake Barkley Resort	V	1,440	
Lake Cumberland Resort	V	1,200	
Lake Guntersville	V	2,246	
Lake Havasu	V	5,252	
Lake Mineral Wells	V	1,155	
Lake Murray	V	7,362	
Lake Tahoe Nevada	V	5,441	
Lake of the Ozarc	V	6,534	
Laurel Hill	V	1,660	
Laurel Ridge	V	5,300	
Lee	V	1,147	
Letchworth	V	5,738	
Little River (Vermont)	V	4,848	
Lory	V	1,018	
Lost River	V	1,490	
Malibu Creek	V	1,619	
McCalla	V	2,520	
McConnells Mill	V	1,016	
McCroskey	V	1,846	
Meramec	V	2,861	
Mille Lacs-Kathio	V	2,730	
Minnewaska	V	2,798	
Monahans Sand Hills	V	1,554	
Montana de Oro	V	2,961	
Montgomery Bell	V	2,000	
Moran	V	1,860	
Mount Diablo	V	5,073	
Mount San Jacinto	V	5,460	
Mount Spokane	V	6,538	
Mount Tamalpais	V	2,512	
Mt. Blue	V	1,995	
Mustang Island	V	1,499	1964
Natchez Trace	V	18,400	
Navajo Lake (Pine)	V	7,255	
Oak Mountain	V	4,016	
Occoneechee	V	1,087	
Ohiopyle	V	7,480	
Oil Creek	V	2,911	
Oswald West	V	1,000	
Painted Rocks	V	1,131	
Palo Duro Canyon	V	6,638	
Patapsco Valley	V	4,646	
Patuxent River	V	2,576	
Pawtuckaway	V	2,222	
Paynes Prairie	V	7,041	
Pedernales Falls	V	1,967	
Penninsula	V	1,520	
Pere Marquette	V	2,589	
Pettigrew	V	6,731	
Pichacho Peaks	V	1,374	

Pillsbury	V	2,121	
Pine Mountain Resort	V	1,000	
Pipestem	V	1,619	
Pisgah Wilderness	I	5,331	
Plumas-Eureka	V	2,726	
Point Mugo	V	6,052	
Porcupine Mountains Wilderness	II	20,200	1944
Prairie Creek Redwoods	V	5,068	
Presque Isle	V	1,244	
Prince Gallitzin	V	2,671	
Quartz Mountain	V	4,465	
Red Rock Canyon	V	1,610	
Ringwood	V	1,721	
Riverside	V	2,346	
Robbers Cave	V	3,408	
Robert Louis Stevenson	V	1,284	
Rock Cut	V	1,079	
Rocky Gap	V	1,131	
Saddle Mountains	V	1,164	
Saddleback Butte	V	1,162	
Salt Point	V	2,412	
Sam A. Baker	III	2,107	1928
Samuel P. Taylor	V	1,094	
Santa Rosa Lake	V	5,072	
Sea Rim	V	6,115	
Seashore	V	1,039	
Seminole Necklace	V	2,569	
Seminole	V	23,198	
Seneca Creek	V	2,081	
Sequoyah	V	1,161	
Sibam Springs	V	1,273	
Silver Falls	V	3,435	
Snow Canyon	V	2,298	
South Llano River	V	1,065	
St Croix	V	13,453	
Starvation Lake	V	1,337	
Starved Rock	V	1,010	
Steamboat Lake	V	1,120	
Steamboat Rock	V	1,626	
Stephen A. Forbes	V	1,208	
Sumner Lake	V	2,693	
Sun Lakes	V	1,626	
Sunapee, Mount	V	1,102	
Susquehanna	V	1,026	
Swan Marshes	V	5,147	
Table Rock	II	1,239	
Taconic-Rudd Pond-Copake Falls	V	1,878	
Tahquamenon Falls	V	7,197	
The Cove Palisades	V	1,664	
Tobyhanna	V	2,040	

Topanga	V	3,709	
Tuckahoe	V	1,374	
Twin Falls	V	1,530	
Valley of Fire	II	18,584	
Versailles	V	2,325	
Waccasassa Bay	V	10,332	
Wappapello	V	17,038	
Wasatch Mountain	V	8,869	
Watoga	V	6,042	
Wawayanda	V	4,265	
Wildcat Mountain	V	1,335	
Wilderness	V	2,754	
Willard Bay	V	1,080	
Willow River	V	1,118	
Wister	V	1,228	
Wyalusing	V	1,080	
York River	V	1,012	

State Reserves/Réserves publiques

Paynes Prairie	IV	5,656	1961

Alaska

National Parks/Parcs nationaux

Denali	II	1,911,495	1917
Glacier Bay	II	1,304,550	1925
Katmai	II	1,504,774	1980
Kenai Fjords	II	271,255	1980
Kobuk Valley	II	708,502	1978
Lake Clark	II	1,068,805	1978
Wrangell-St Elias	II	3,382,014	1978

National Preserves/Réserves nationales

Aniakchak	IV	248,937	1978
Bering Land Bridge	V	1,125,124	1978
Denali	V	529,800	1980
Gates of the Arctic	V	383,246	1980
Glacier Bay	V	23,385	1978
Katmai	V	151,096	1980
Lake Clark	V	568,546	1980
Noatak	II	2,655,870	1978
Wrangell-St Elias	V	1,962,115	1980
Yukon Charley Rivers	III	915,000	1978

National Wildlife Refuges/Refuges nationaux
de faune et de flore sauvages

Alaska Maritime	IV	1,440,597	1980
Alaska Peninsula	IV	1,417,500	1980
Arctic	IV	7,714,940	1980
Becharof	IV	486,000	1978
Innoko	IV	1,559,250	1980
Izembek	IV	129,961	1960
Kanuti	IV	579,150	1980

Kenai	IV	797,850	1980
Kenai National Moose Range	IV	698,920	
Kodiak	IV	755,325	
Koyukuk	IV	1,437,750	1980
Nowitna	IV	631,800	1980
Selawik	IV	870,750	1980
Tetlin	IV	283,500	1980
Togiak	IV	1,662,525	1980
Yukon Delta	IV	7,947,905	1980
Yukon Flats	IV	3,495,150	1980
National Monuments/Monuments nationaux			
Admiralty Island	IV	387,530	1980
Aniakchak	III	55,514	1978
Bering Land Bridge	II	1,121,457	1980
Cape Krusenstern	III	267,206	1978
Gates of the Arctic	III	2,939,689	1980
Misty Fjords	IV	928,491	1980
National Natural Landmarks/Eléments naturels nationaux marquants			
Alaska Maritime	III	355,000	1980
Aniakchak Crater	III	8,080	
Arrigetch Peaks	III	10,342	
Lake George	III	25,856	
Malaspina Glacier	III	387,840	
Mount Veniaminof	III	323,200	
Unga Island	III	2,586	
Walker Lake	III	73,173	
Yukon Delta	III	760,850	1980
National Forests/Forêts nationales			
Chugach	IV	2,404,000	1907
Tongass	IV	6,708,900	1907
National Forest Wildernesses/Zones nationales sauvages boisées			
Admiralty Island	III	380,376	1980
Coronation Island	III	7,776	1980
Endicott River	III	40,540	1980
Maurelle Islands	III	1,790	1980
Misty Fiords	III	867,510	1980
Petersburg Creek-Duncan Salt Chuck	III	18,994	1980
Russell Fiord	III	141,993	1980
South Baranof	III	153,535	1980
South Prince of Wales	III	36,612	1980
Stikine-LeConte	III	182,128	1980
Tebenkof Bay	III	26,730	1980
Tracy Arm-Fords Terror	III	264,343	1980
Warren Island	III	4,536	1980
West Chicagof-Yakobi	III	107,244	1980
State Parks/Parcs publics			
Chugach	II	198,082	
Kachemak Wilderness	II	47,988	1972

Hawaii/Hawaï

National Parks/Parcs nationaux

Haleakala	II	11,728	1916
Hawaii Volcanoes	II	91,960	1916

Biological Reserves/Réserves biologiques

Kamakou	IV	1,123	1982
Pelekunu	IV	2,332	1987
Waikamoi	IV	2,117	1983

National Wildlife Refuges/Refuges nationaux de faune
et de flore sauvages

Hakalau	IV	16,706	1985
Hawaiian Islands (8 sites)	I	103,068	1945

National Estuarine Research Reserves/Réserves nationales
de recherche estuarienne

Waimanu Valley	IV	1,763	1976

State Natural Area Reserves/Réserves naturelles d'Etat

Hanawi	IV	3,036
Hono O Na Pali	IV	1,275
Kipahoehoe	IV	2,260
Laupahoehoe	IV	3,196
Manuka	IV	10,344
Mauna Kea Ice Age	IV	1,577
Puu Makaala	IV	4,901
Puu O Umi	IV	4,122
West Maui (4 sites)	IV	2,713

National Historic Parks/Parcs historiques nationaux

Kalapapa	II	4,343	1980

American Samoa/Samoa américain

No Areas Listed/pas de sites

Guam

No Areas Listed/pas de sites

Puerto Rico/Porto Rico

Natural Reserves/Réserves naturelles

Laguna Tortuguero	IV	1,000

National Wildlife Refuges/Refuges nationaux
de faune et de flore sauvages

Culebra	IV	633	1909
Desecheo	IV	146	1968

National Estuarine Research Reserves/Réserves nationales
de recherche estuarienne

Jobas Bay	IV	1,371	1981

US Virgin Islands/Iles vierges américaine

National Parks/Parcs nationaux

Virgin Islands	II	7,079	1956

National Monuments/Monuments nationaux
Buck Island Reef	III	356	1961

Other US Pacific Islands/Autres îles americaines du Pacifique

National Wildlife Refuges/Refuges nationaux
de faune et de flore sauvages
Baker Island	I	12,843	1974
Howland Island	I	13,173	1974
Jarvis Island	I	15,183	1974

URUGUAY

Summary/Sommaire		
Category\Catégorie III	2	15,250
Category\Catégorie IV	1	8,000
Category\Catégorie V	5	8,476
Total	**8**	**31,726**

National Parks/Parcs nationaux
Anchorena	V	1,450	1978
Arequita	V	1,000	1964
Franklin Delano Roosevelt	V	1,500	1916
San Miguel	V	1,238	1937
Santa Teresa	V	3,288	1927

Wildlife Reserves/Réserves de ressources sauvages
Laguna Castillos	IV	8,000	1966

Natural Monuments/Monuments naturels
Costa Atlantica	III	14,250	1966
Dunas de Cabo Polonio	III	1,000	1966

VANUATU

No Areas Listed/pas de sites

VENEZUELA

Summary/Sommaire		
Category\Catégorie II	33	8,836,014
Category\Catégorie III	8	33,013
Category\Catégorie IV	3	284,120
Category\Catégorie V	30	11,112,215
Total	**74**	**20,265,362**

National Parks/Parcs nationaux
Aguaro-Guariquito	II	585,750	1974
Archipielago Los Roques	II	225,153	1972
Canaima	II	3,000,000	1962
Cerro El Copey	II	7,130	1974
Cinaruco-Capanaparo	II	584,368	1988
Cueva de la Quebrada del Toro	II	8,500	1969
Dinira	II	42,000	1989

Duida Marahuaca	II	210,000	1978
El Avila	II	85,192	1958
El Guacharo	II	15,500	1975
El Tama	II	139,000	1978
Guaramacal	II	21,000	1988
Guatopo	II	122,464	1958
Henri Pittier	II	107,800	1937
Java Sarisarinama	II	330,000	1978
Laguna de la Restinga	II	10,700	1974
Laguna de Tacarigua	II	18,400	1974
Macarao	II	15,000	1973
Medanos de Coro	II	91,280	1974
Mochima	II	94,935	1973
Morrocoy	II	32,090	1974
Paramos del Batallon y La Negra	II	95,200	1989
Peninsula de Paria	II	37,500	1978
Perija	II	295,288	1978
San Esteban	II	44,050	1987
Santos Luzardo	II	584,368	1988
Serrania de la Neblina	II	1,360,000	1978
Sierra Nevada	II	276,446	1952
Sierra de San Luis	II	20,000	1987
Terepaima	II	18,650	1976
Yacambu	II	14,580	1962
Yapacana	II	320,000	1978
Yurubi	II	23,670	1960
Faunal Reserves/Réserves fauniques			
Cienaga de Juan Manuel	IV	227,795	1975
Cuare	IV	11,825	1972
Estero de Chiriguare	IV	44,500	1974
Natural Monuments/Monuments naturels			
Aristides Rojas	III	1,630	1949
Cerro Santa Ana	III	1,900	1972
Cerros Matasiete y Guayamuri	III	1,672	1974
Laguna de las Marites	III	3,674	1974
Las Tetas de Maria Guevara	III	1,670	1974
Maria Lionza	III	11,712	1960
Morros de San Juan	III	2,755	1949
Platillon	III	8,000	1987
Protective Zones/Zones protectrices			
Area Metropolitana de Caracas	V	84,300	1972
Cuenca Alta de los Rios Maticora y Cozuiza	V	268,000	1974
Cuenca Alta del Rio Cojedes	V	276,000	1974
Cuenca Alta del Rio Tocuyo	V	160,000	1974
Cuencas de los rios Pao y Guarico	V	224,200	1974
Higuerote	V	35,820	1974
La Machiri	V	5,000	1973
Macizo Montanoso del Turimiqire	V	528,750	1974
Piedemonte Andino	V	445,520	1974
Piedemonte Andino San Cristobal	V	10,000	1978

Piedemonte norte de la Cordillera Andina	V	400,000	1974
Region Lago de Maracaibo	V	252,000	1974
Rio Chuspite	V	5,642	1976
Rio Torbes y sus Alrededores	V	12,000	1974
Rio Yacambu	V	40,000	1974
Rubio	V	12,000	1978
San Rafael de Guasare	V	302,000	1973
Sierra Nirgua-Aroa	V	252,000	1974
Sierra de Bobare	V	140,000	1974
Sur del Edo Bolivar	V	4,930,000	1975
Sureste del Lago de Maracaibo Sto. Domingo	V	372,000	1974
Sureste del Lago de Maracaibo Uribante-Caparo	V	444,000	1974
Hydrological Reserves/Réserves hydrologiques			
Burro Negro	V	75,000	1974
Distritos: Maturin, Cedeno, Acosta, Piar	V	187,500	1976
Piedemonte Andino	V	491,280	1974
Region Valle de Quibor	V	72,000	1974
Rio Cupravera	V	3,203	1978
Rio Pedregal	V	195,900	1976
Rio Sanchon	V	8,100	1976
Zona Sur de Lago de Maracaibo	V	880,000	1974

VIET NAM

Summary/Sommaire		
Category\Catégorie II	7	142,387
Category\Catégorie IV	51	749,611
Total	**58**	**891,998**

National Parks/Parcs nationaux			
Ba Be	II	5,000	1977
Ba Vi	II	2,144	1977
Bach Ma Hai Van	II	40,000	1986
Cat Ba	II	27,700	1986
Con Dao	II	6,043	1982
Cuc Phuong	II	25,000	1962
Nam Bai Cat Tien	II	36,500	1978
Nature Reserves/Réserves de nature			
Anh Son	IV	1,500	1986
Ba Mun	IV	1,800	1977
Bana-Nui Chua	IV	5,217	1986
Ben En	IV	12,000	1986
Binh Chan Phuoc Buu	IV	5,474	1986
Bu Gia Map	IV	16,000	1986
Bu Huong	IV	5,000	1986
Chiem Hoa Nahang	IV	20,000	1986
Chu Yang Sinh	IV	20,000	1986
Cu Lao Cham	IV	1,535	1986
Dao Ngoan Muc	IV	2,000	1986
Dao Phu Quoc	IV	5,000	1986

Duoc Nam Can	IV	4,000	1986
Huu Lien	IV	3,000	1986
Kalon Song Mao	IV	2,000	1986
Khu Dao Thac Ba	IV	5,000	1986
Kon Kai Kinh	IV	28,000	1986
Kong Cha Rang	IV	16,000	1986
Langbian Plateau	IV	4,000	1977
Lo Go Sa Mat	IV	10,000	1986
Mom Ray	IV	45,000	
Muong Cha	IV	182,000	1986
Nam Dun	IV	18,000	1986
Nam Lung	IV	20,000	1986
Ngoc Linh	IV	20,000	1986
Nui Ba	IV	6,000	1986
Nui Cam	IV	1,500	1986
Nui Dai Binh	IV	5,000	1986
Nui Hoang Lien	IV	5,000	1986
Nui Pia Hoac	IV	10,000	1986
Nui Yen Tu	IV	5,000	1986
Pa Co Nang kia	IV	1,000	
Quang Xuyen	IV	20,000	1986
Rung Kho Phan Rang	IV	1,000	1986
Sop Cop	IV	5,000	1986
Suoi Trai	IV	19,000	
Tanh Linh	IV	2,000	1986
Tay Bai Cat Tien	IV	10,000	
Thanh Thuy	IV	7,000	1986
Thuong Da Nhim	IV	7,000	1986
Thuong Tien	IV	1,500	1986
Tieu Tao-Easup	IV	20,000	1986
Trung Khanh	IV	3,000	1986
U Minh	IV	2,000	1986
Vu Quang	IV	16,000	1986
Xuan Nha	IV	60,000	1986
Xuan Son	IV	4,585	1986
Yok Don	IV	57,500	1988
Historic-Cultural Sites/Sites historiques-culturels			
Ban dao Son Tra	IV	4,000	1977
Duong Minh Chau	IV	5,000	1986
Nui Tam Dao	IV	19,000	1977

WESTERN SAHARA/SAHARE OCCIDENTALE
No Areas Listed/pas de sites

WESTERN SAMOA/SAMOA OCCIDENTALE
No Areas Listed/pas de sites

YEMEN
No Areas Listed/pas de sites

Since this list was compiled, the Yemen Arab Republic and the People's Democratic Republic of Yemen have combined to form the Republic of Yemen.

Depuis la réalisation de la présente liste, la République arabe du Yémen et la République démocratique du Yémen ont fusionné pour former la République du Yémen.

YEMEN, DEMOCRATIC/YEMEN DEMOCRATIQUE
No Areas Listed/pas de sites

Since this list was compiled, the Yemen Arab Republic and the People's Democratic Republic of Yemen have combined to form the Republic of Yemen.

Depuis la réalisation de la présente liste, la République arabe du Yémen et la République démocratique du Yémen ont fusionné pour former la République du Yémen.

YUGOSLAVIA/YOUGOSLAVIE

Summary/Sommaire		
Category\Catégorie I	7	26,809
Category\Catégorie II	17	405,499
Category\Catégorie III	9	52,265
Category\Catégorie IV	11	68,337
Category\Catégorie V	24	238,339
Total	**68**	**791,249**

National Parks/Parcs nationaux

Biogradska Gora	II	3,400	1952
Brioni	V	4,660	1983
Djerdap	V	63,500	1983
Durmitor	II	33,000	1952
Fruska Gora	V	25,398	1960
Galicica	II	22,750	1958
Kopaonik	II	11,800	1981
Kornati	II	22,400	1980
Kozara	V	3,375	1967
Krka River	II	14,200	1985
Lovcen	II	2,400	1952
Mavrovo	II	73,088	1949
Mljet	II	3,100	1960
Paklenica	II	3,617	1949
Pelister	II	12,500	1948
Plitvice Lakes	V	19,172	1949
Risnjak	II	3,014	1953
Sara	II	39,000	1986
Skadarske jezero	II	40,000	1983
Sutjeska	II	17,250	1965
Tara	II	19,175	1981
Triglav	II	84,805	1981

Nature Reserves/Réserves de nature

Bijele i Samarske Stijene	I	1,175	1985
Deliblatska Pescara	V	29,352	1965
Hajducki i Rozanski Kukovi	I	1,220	1969
Jorgov kamen	IV	1,500	1988
Kopacki Rit	I	7,200	1967
Korab	IV	2,601	1988
Kotorsko Risanski Zaliv	V	12,000	1979
Malostonski Zaljev	I	10,389	1983
Neretva Delta	IV	1,200	
Obedska Bara	V	17,501	1968
Obedska bara Kod Kupinova III	IV	16,133	1968
Ohrid (Ohridsko) jezero	IV	38,000	1958
Otok Cresu	IV	550	1968
Otok Krk Rta Glavine do Uvale Mala Luka	IV	1,000	1969
Planina Vodno	IV	2,840	1970
Prasuma perucica	IV	1,434	1954
Senecka planina	IV	1,953	1988
Veliki i Mali Strbac ra Trajonovum tablom	I	1,124	1975
Zvijezda	V	2,007	1950

Natural Monuments/Monuments naturels

Djalovica Klisura	III	1,600	1968
Djavolja varos	I	1,400	1959
Dojran	III	2,730	1970
Markovi Kuli	III	5,285	1967
Ohridsko jezero	III	23,000	1958
Prespanske jezero	III	17,680	1977
Rugovska klisura	I	4,301	1988
Scedro Island	III	750	1968
Severoistocni dio poluotoka lopara na otoku	III	100	1969
Suma od Krivulj na Jakusici	III	1,000	1970

Landscape Parks/Parcs paysagers

Obalno Podrucje Otaka Hvara	V	200	1963
Otok badija kraj otoka korcule	V	100	1969
Robanov Kot	V	1,580	1987
Topla	V	1,345	1966
Vidova gora	V	1,800	1970
Zvecevo na papuku	V	2,586	1966

Historical Sanctuaries/Sanctuaires historiques

Selo Trsic i okalina marastira	V	1,308	1965

Regional Nature Parks/Parcs naturels régionaux

Biokovo	V	19,550	1981
Gornje Podunavljc	V	10,325	1982
Grmija	IV	1,126	1987
Palic-Ludas	V	6,360	1982
Resava	V	10,000	1957
Stari Begej	V	1,327	1986
Tribevic	V	1,000	1954
Zahorina	V	2,000	1954
Zvijezda na Planini Tara	V	1,893	1971

State Parks/Parcs publics
Titova pecina na otoku visu III 120 1964

ZAIRE

Summary/Sommaire		
Category\Catégorie I	1	250,000
Category\Catégorie II	7	8,544,000
Category\Catégorie IV	1	33,000
Total	**9**	**8,827,000**

National Parks/Parcs nationaux
Garamba	II	492,000	1938
Kahuzi-Biega	II	600,000	1975
Kundelungu	II	760,000	1970
Maiko	II	1,083,000	1970
Salonga	II	3,656,000	1970
Upemba	II	1,173,000	1939
Virunga	II	780,000	1925

Flora Reserves/Réserves de flore
Yangambi	I	250,000

Forest Reserves/Réserves forestières
Luki	IV	33,000	1979

ZAMBIA/ZAMBIE

Summary/Sommaire		
Category\Catégorie II	19	6,359,000
Category\Catégorie III	1	1,900
Total	**20**	**6,360,900**

National Parks/Parcs nationaux
Blue Lagoon	II	45,000	1973
Isangano	II	84,000	1957
Kafue	II	2,240,000	1951
Kasanka	II	39,000	1941
Lavushi Manda	II	150,000	1941
Liuwa Plain	II	366,000	1972
Lochinvar	II	41,000	1972
Lower Zambezi	II	414,000	1983
Luambe	II	25,400	1966
Lukusuzi	II	272,000	1938
Lusenga Plain	II	88,000	1942
Mosi-Oa-Tunya	II	6,600	1972
Mweru-Wantipa	II	313,400	1942
North Luangwa	II	463,600	1939
Nsumbu	II	202,000	1942
Nyika	II	8,000	1972
Sioma Ngwezi	II	527,600	1972
South Luangwa	II	905,000	1938

West Lunga	II	168,400	1951
Natural Monuments/Monuments naturels			
Victoria Falls	III	1,900	1948

ZIMBABWE

Summary/Sommaire		
Category\Catégorie I	1	37,300
Category\Catégorie II	12	2,699,735
Category\Catégorie IV	5	36,314
Category\Catégorie V	3	57,358
Total	**21**	**2,830,707**

National Parks/Parcs nationaux			
Chimanimani	II	17,100	1953
Chizarira	II	191,000	1975
Gonarezhou	II	505,300	1975
Hwange (Wankie)	II	1,465,100	1930
Inyanga	II	28,900	1902
Kazuma Pan	II	31,300	1975
Mana Pools	II	219,600	1963
Matobo (Matopos)	II	43,200	1902
Matusadona	II	137,000	1975
Mtarazi Falls	II	2,495	
Victoria Falls	II	2,340	1979
Zambezi	II	56,400	1979
Wildlife Research Areas/Aires de Recherche sur les ressources sauvages			
Sengwa Wildlife Research Area	I	37,300	
Game Parks/Parcs de gibier			
Imire	IV	1,000	
Iwabe	IV	20,000	
Botanical Reserves/Réserves botaniques			
Bunga Forest	V	1,558	1975
Sanctuaries/Sanctuaires			
Chimanimani Eland	IV	1,200	1975
Mushandike	IV	12,900	1975
Wilderness Areas/Aires de nature sauvage			
Mavuradona	V	50,000	1989
Parks/Parcs			
Gweru Antelope	IV	1,214	
Recreation Parks/Parcs de loisirs			
Ngezi	V	5,800	1956

TOTAL NUMBER OF DESIGNATED SITES/NOMBRE TOTAL DE SITES DESIGNES

Category\Catégorie I	658	50,790,801
Category\Catégorie II	1,392	309,227,406
Category\Catégorie III	316	18,684,639
Category\Catégorie IV	2,944	195,110,966
Category\Catégorie V	1,630	77,653,785
Total	**6,940**	**651,467,597**

Number of areas/Nombre d'aires

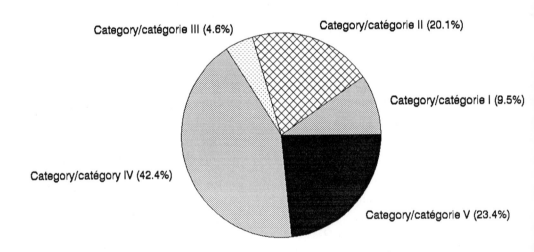

ANALYSIS OF INFORMATION

All of the information provided in this *UN List* is stored within a computer database, and a wide range of other information is held about each site (and about many other sites not covered here). Some of this information will be analysed in publications by WCMC staff and others. As an indication of this analytic capability, two graphs and two tables have been included within the *UN List*.

Growth of the world coverage of protected areas

Two graphs are provided, one illustrating growth in the number and area of protected areas with time (Figure 1), and the other illustrating growth in the number and area within each five year period (Figure 2). It should be noted that establishment of the Northeast Greenland National Park in 1974 (70 million hectares) has a very significant effect on the graphs, as the site is an order of magnitude larger than any other site on the *UN List*.

Biogeography

As in the previous three editions of the list each of the areas has been located within one of the biogeographical provinces defined by Udvardy (1975), although the province concerned is not actually identified within this list. The system of biogeographical provinces of the world defined by Udvardy for IUCN divides the world into eight realms, subdivided into 193 provinces, with each province being characterised by one of 14 biome types. This information is used to provide a crude analysis of coverage both by province, and by biome type.

Table 1 provides a summary of protected area coverage (number of sites and total area) of each of the realms and provinces recognised by Udvardy. However, when analysing this data various limitations of the system must be considered, resulting both from its relative crudity, and, for example, differences in size between provinces. A 5000 hectare protected area in the relatively small Malagasy Thorn Forest province, for example, would protect a much larger section of that province than an equivalent sized reserve in the huge Somalian province. While the results are sufficient to illustrate patchy coverage, more detailed analysis is necessary to determine real needs and priorities.

Table 2 provides a summary of protected area coverage (number of sites and total area) by biome type, indicating the proportion of each biome type protected within each realm. Summarisation of coverage by biome gives a first approximation of how well the major ecological formations are protected, although there is, of course, considerable variation of protection within biomes. It is important to appreciate that biome type does not mean the same as habitat type; a protected area within a tropical humid forest biome may not necessarily contain tropical humid forest, and an area containing tropical humid forest could occur in another biome altogether (such as mixed island systems). Note in this regard that Udvardy identifies all of Indonesia, insular Malaysia and the Philippines as mixed island systems rather than tropical humid forest. Also, as was noted above for provinces, it is important to realise that there are significant differences between the areas covered by different biome types. For example, in the Neotropics there are extensive areas covered by the tropical humid forest biome (about a quarter of the continent), but only a small area covered by the lake systems biome (Lake Titicaca on the Peru/Bolivia border).

ANALYSE DE L'INFORMATION

Toute l'information donnée dans la *Liste des Nations Unies* est stockée dans une base de données informatisée et nous détenons beaucoup d'autres informations sur chaque site (et sur beaucoup d'autres sites ne figurant pas dans la Liste). Une partie de cette information sera analysée dans des publications, par le personnel du CMSC, entre autres. Deux graphiques et deux tableaux présentant cette capacité analytique ont été inclus dans la *Liste des Nations Unies*.

Expansion de la superficie mondiale des aires protégées

Les deux graphiques illustrent, respectivement l'augmentation du nombre et de la superficie des aires protégées dans le temps (Figure 1) et l'augmentation du nombre et de la superficie par période de cinq ans (Figure 2). Il convient de noter que la création du Parc national du Nord-Est du Groenland, en 1974, avec ses 70 millions d'hectares, a eu un effet très marqué car l'ordre de grandeur du site est supérieur à celui de n'importe quel autre site de la *Liste des Nations Unies*.

Biogéographie

Comme dans les trois éditions précédentes de la Liste, chacune des aires a été replacée dans une des provinces biogéographiques définies par Udvardy (1975), même si la province en question n'est pas réellement identifiée dans cette Liste. Le réseau mondial de provinces biogéographiques défini par Udvardy pour l'UICN divise le monde en huit domaines, subdivisés en 193 provinces, chacune étant caractérisée par un des 14 types de biomes. Cette information est utilisée pour donner une analyse brute de la couverture par province et par type de biome.

Le Tableau 1 propose un résumé de la couverture des aires protégées (nombre de sites et superficie totale) de chacun des domaines et provinces reconnus par Udvardy. Toutefois, dans l'analyse de ces données, il convient de prendre en considération diverses limites du système, venant à la fois de sa simplicité relative et, par exemple, de dimensions différentes entre les provinces. Une aire protégée de 5000 hectares dans la province relativement petite de la forêt épineuse malgache, par exemple, protège une plus grande proportion de cette province qu'une réserve de taille équivalente dans l'immense province somalienne. Alors que les résultats sont suffisants pour illustrer une couverture en "patchwork", une analyse plus précise est nécessaire pour déterminer les besoins et les priorités réels.

Le Tableau 2 propose un résumé de la couverture des aires protégées (nombre de sites et superficie totale) par type de biome, et indique quelle proportion de chaque type de biome est protégée dans chaque domaine. Le résumé de la couverture par biome donne un premier aperçu de la protection réelle des principales formations écologiques bien qu'il y ait, naturellement, des variations considérables dans le degré de protection à l'intérieur de chaque biome. Il importe de retenir que "type de biome" n'a pas le même sens que "type d'habitat"; une aire protégée se trouvant dans un biome de forêt humide tropicale ne contient pas nécessairement de forêt humide tropicale et une aire contenant une forêt humide tropicale peut se trouver dans un biome tout à fait différent (par exemple, un système insulaire mixte). A cet égard, il convient de noter qu'Udvardy identifie l'ensemble de l'Indonésie, de la Malaisie insulaire et des Philippines à des systèmes insulaires mixtes et non à des biomes de forêts humides tropicales. De plus, comme nous l'avons déjà mentionné pour les provinces, il importe de savoir qu'il y a des différences importantes entre les aires couvertes par différents types de biomes. Par exemple, en Amérique du Sud, de vastes régions sont couvertes par le biome de forêt tropicale humide (environ un quart du continent) alors qu'une seule région, de faibles dimensions, est incluse dans le biome "système lacustre" (le lac Titicaca, à la frontière du Pérou et de la Bolivie).

Figure 1

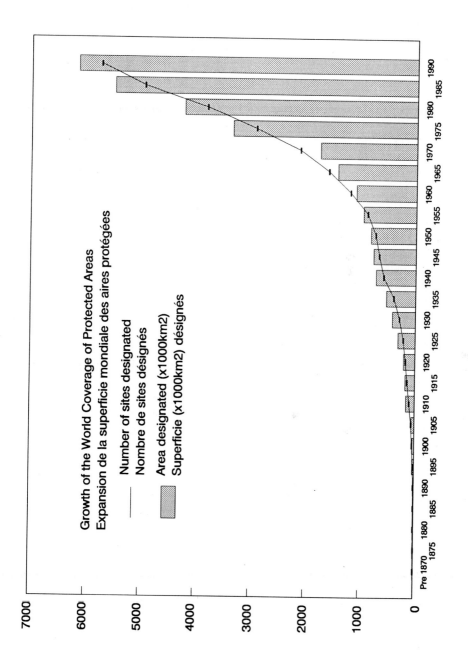

Figure 2

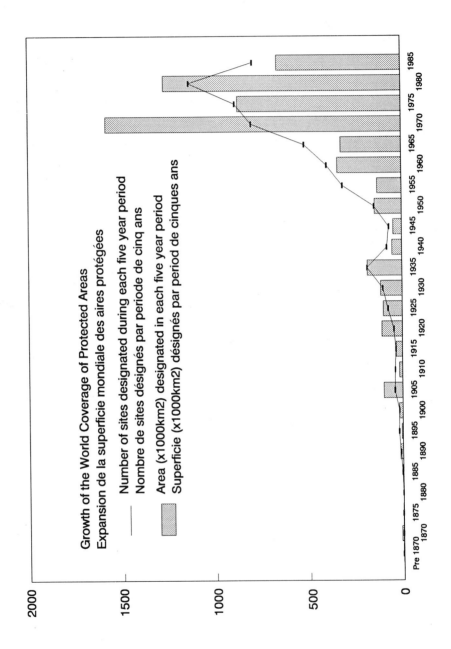

Growth of the World Coverage of Protected Areas
Expansion de la superficie mondiale des aires protégées

— Number of sites designated during each five year period
Nombre de sites désignés par periode de cinq ans

Area (x1000km2) designated in each five year period
Superficie (x1000km2) désignés par period de cinques ans

TABLE 1
Biogeographical Coverage of Protected Areas
Couverture biogéographique des aires protégées

Name of province Nom de la province	Number of areas Nombre (d'aires)	Total area Total (ha)
Neartic		
1 Sitkan	86	17,307,291
2 Oregonian	32	943,317
3 Yukon Taiga	26	19,550,613
4 Canadian Taiga	286	18,030,504
5 Eastern Forest	193	5,196,477
6 Austroriparian	97	1,230,469
7 Californian	12	803,787
8 Sonoran	37	9,572,667
9 Chihuahuan	19	582,187
10 Tamaulipan	3	50,232
11 Great Basin	21	723,283
12 Aleutian Islands	9	7,909,534
13 Alaskan Tundra	25	30,942,068
14 Canadian Tundra	20	19,820,910
15 Arctic Archipelago		0
16 Greenland Tundra		0
17 Arctic Desert and Icecap	2	71,050,000
18 Grasslands	70	787,425
19 Rocky Mountains	144	12,679,666
20 Sierra-Cascade	82	2,838,271
21 Madrean-Cordilleran	76	2,148,636
22 Great Lakes	13	514,048
Total	**1,253**	**222,681,385**
Palaearctic		
1 Chinese Subtropical Forest	41	723,388
2 Japanese Evergreen Forest	41	1,502,452
3 West Eurasian Taiga	122	6,550,893
4 East Siberian Taiga	11	4,574,986
5 Icelandian	23	917,111
6 Subarctic Birchwoods	16	276,699
7 Kamchatkan	1	1,099,000
8 British Islands	100	3,950,888
9 Atlantic	117	4,592,354
10 Boreonemoral	103	1,390,904
11 Middle European Forest	397	6,830,429
12 Pannonian	29	305,754
13 West Anatolian	4	10,691
14 Manchu-Japanese Mixed Forest	33	2,451,539
15 Oriental Deciduous Forest	132	5,213,669
16 Iberian Highlands	115	2,855,488

17	Mediterranean Sclerophyll	230	3,566,135
18	Sahara	14	14,111,100
19	Arabian Desert	29	5,945,691
20	Anatolian-Iranian Desert	43	4,392,285
21	Turanian	15	1,394,217
22	Takla-Makan-Gobi Desert	19	12,957,154
23	Tibetan	2	14,367
24	Iranian Desert	9	980,732
25	Arctic Desert	5	3,491,000
26	Higharctic Tundra	2	2,228,650
27	Lowarctic Tundra	1	1,348,708
28	Atlas Steppe	5	57,698
29	Pontian Steppe	20	712,951
30	Mongolian-Manchurian Steppe	16	2,242,930
31	Scottish Highlands	43	710,928
32	Central European Highlands	325	5,303,245
33	Balkan Highlands	93	852,369
34	Caucaso-Iranian Highlands	66	4,994,114
35	Altai Highlands	6	1,732,136
36	Pamir-Tian-Shan Highlands	30	6,095,916
37	Hindu Kush Highlands	4	142,438
38	Himalayan Highlands	70	4,355,979
39	Szechwan Highlands	44	2,117,646
40	Macaronesian Islands	7	58,822
41	Ryukyu Islands	1	3,680
42	Lake Ladoga	1	40,972
43	Aral Sea	1	18,300
44	Lake Baikal		0
	Total	**2,386**	**123,116,408**

Afrotropical

1	Guinean Rain Forest	25	1,143,729
2	Congo Rain Forest	23	7,897,100
3	Malagasy Rain Forest	14	408,008
4	West African Woodland/Savanna	66	14,087,161
5	East African Woodland/Savanna	49	12,070,261
6	Congo Woodland/Savanna	6	3,820,170
7	Miombo Woodland/Savanna	36	13,876,253
8	South African Woodland/Savanna	99	7,980,891
9	Malagasy Woodland/Savanna	20	624,774
10	Malagasy Thorn Forest	2	44,950
11	Cape Sclerophyll	44	1,769,429
12	Western Sahel	6	1,594,740
13	Eastern Sahel	6	4,155,800
14	Somalian	28	5,815,109
15	Namib	7	9,705,753
16	Kalahari	8	9,643,887
17	Karroo	16	185,557
18	Ethiopian Highlands	13	2,534,000
19	Guinean Highlands	2	335,625

20	Central African Highlands	9	3,391,600
21	East African Highlands	11	267,451
22	South African Highlands	38	432,777
23	Ascension and St Helena Islands		0
24	Comores Islands and Aldabra	1	35,000
25	Mascarene Islands	5	9,392
26	Lake Rudolf		0
27	Lake Ukerewe (Victoria)	1	45,700
28	Lake Tanganyika		0
29	Lake Malawi (Nyasa)	1	9,400
	Total	**536**	**101,884,517**

Indomalayan

1	Malabar Rainforest	44	1,586,806
2	Ceylonese Rainforest	1	7,648
3	Bengalian Rainforest	20	448,121
4	Burman Rainforest	2	20,455
5	Indochinese Rainforest	57	2,606,665
6	South Chinese Rainforest	32	152,915
7	Malayan Rainforest	20	1,103,111
8	Indus-Ganges Monsoon Forest	133	5,636,423
9	Burma Monsoon Forest	29	611,300
10	Thailandian Monsoon Forest	57	2,214,245
11	Mahanadian	29	1,096,956
12	Coromandel	4	156,528
13	Ceylonese Monsoon Forest	42	776,060
14	Deccan Thorn Forest	9	193,975
15	Thar Desert	38	3,868,277
16	Seychelles and Amirantes Islands	3	3,568
17	Laccadives Islands		0
18	Maldives and Chagos Islands		0
19	Cocos-Keeling and Christmas Islands	1	2,370
20	Andaman and Nicobar Islands	42	79,700
21	Sumatra	35	4,573,740
22	Java	39	735,471
23	Lesser Sunda Islands	18	256,606
24	Sulawesi (Celebes)	29	2,148,343
25	Borneo	61	4,090,149
26	Philippines	28	583,999
27	Taiwan	5	288,577
	Total	**778**	**33,242,008**

Oceanian

1	Papuan	31	6,739,286
2	Micronesian	4	2,329
3	Hawaiian	17	266,801
4	Southeastern Polynesian	10	61,929
5	Central Polynesian	3	32,516
6	New Caledonian	14	253,126
7	East Melanesian	2	5,342
	Total	**81**	**7,361,329**

Australian

1	Queensland Coastal	72	8,150,053
2	Tasmanian	22	870,097
3	Northern Coastal	14	1,288,869
4	Western Sclerophyll	125	2,658,858
5	Southern Sclerophyll	66	1,634,342
6	Eastern Sclerophyll	168	3,574,493
7	Brigalow	12	393,932
8	Western Mulga	15	2,260,773
9	Central Desert	17	9,895,645
10	Southern Mulga/Saltbush	14	5,870,350
11	Northern Savanna	8	2,137,666
12	Northern Grasslands	6	669,628
13	Eastern Grasslands and Savannas	51	1,007,736
	Total	**590**	**40,412,442**

Antarctic

1	Neozealandia	150	2,835,022
2	Maudlandia	4	33,545
3	Marielandia	1	250
4	Insulantarctica	10	274,839
	Total	**165**	**3,143,656**

Neotropical

1	Campechean	18	1,093,000
2	Panamanian	9	1,034,857
3	Colombian Coastal	9	1,127,220
4	Guyanan	27	2,629,005
5	Amazonian	28	19,512,899
6	Madeiran	4	1,146,495
7	Serro Do Mar	54	3,587,010
8	Brazilian Rain Forest	58	1,424,412
9	Brazilian Planalto	3	13,922
10	Valdivian Forest	12	4,016,359
11	Chilean Nothofagus	7	3,926,070
12	Everglades	17	767,131
13	Sinaloan	5	296,994
14	Guerreran	6	129,407
15	Yucatecan	3	107,146
16	Central American	54	1,371,642
17	Venezuelan Dry Forest	41	5,121,158
18	Venezuelan Deciduous Forest	17	859,608
19	Equadorian Dry Forest	4	175,897
20	Caatinga	6	250,463
21	Gran Chaco	7	1,192,000
22	Chilean Araucaria Forest	2	45,414
23	Chilean Sclerophyll	8	147,008
24	Pacific Desert	3	383,824
25	Monte	29	1,830,590
26	Patagonian	42	2,732,168
27	Llanos	3	1,718,118

28	Campos Limpos	6	8,531,514
29	Babacu	6	903,050
30	Campos Cerrados	22	3,573,143
31	Argentinian Pampas	10	900,783
32	Uruguayan Pampas	12	1,275,244
33	Northern Andean	19	4,145,579
34	Colombian Montane	23	4,455,969
35	Yungas	18	2,952,885
36	Puna	21	2,398,810
37	Southern Andean	50	11,478,459
38	Bahamas-Bermudean	7	135,590
39	Cuban	31	719,265
40	Greater Antillean	20	562,359
41	Lesser Antillean	10	111,387
42	Revilla Gigedo Island		0
43	Cocos Island	1	2,400
44	Galapagos Islands	2	8,756,514
45	Fernando De Noronja Island	1	36,249
46	South Trinidade Island		0
47	Lake Titicaca	1	36,180
	Total	**736**	**107,615,197**

Biogeographical classification unknown/   **415**   **12,010,655**
Classification biogéographique inconnue

      TOTAL   **6,940**   **651,467,597**

TABLE 2
Ecological Coverage of Protected Areas
Couverture écologique des aires protégées

Biome and Realm Type de biome et domaine	Number of areas Nombre (d'aires)	Total area Total (ha)
Tropical humid forests		
Afrotropical	62	9,448,837
Indomalayan	176	5,925,721
Australian	72	8,150,053
Neotropical	149	30,130,486
Total	**459**	**53,655,097**
Subtropical/temperate rainforests/woodlands		
Nearctic	118	18,250,608
Palaearctic	82	2,225,840
Australian	22	870,097
Antarctic	150	2,835,022
Neotropical	80	9,380,763
Total	**452**	**33,562,330**
Temperate needle-leaf forests/woodlands		
Nearctic	312	37,581,117
Palaearctic	133	11,125,879
Total	**445**	**48,706,996**
Tropical dry forests/woodlands		
Afrotropical	278	52,504,460
Indomalayan	303	10,685,487
Australian	14	1,288,869
Neotropical	160	10,271,446
Total	**755**	**74,750,262**
Temperate broad-leaf forests		
Nearctic	290	6,426,946
Palaearctic	955	27,039,038
Neotropical	2	45,414
Total	**1,247**	**33,511,398**
Evergreen sclerophyllous forests		
Nearctic	12	803,787
Palaearctic	345	6,421,623
Afrotropical	44	1,769,429
Australian	371	8,261,625
Neotropical	8	147,008
Total	**780**	**17,403,472**
Warm deserts/semi-deserts		
Nearctic	59	10,205,086
Palaearctic	43	20,056,791
Afrotropical	71	31,100,846
Indomalayan	38	3,868,277

Australian	46	18,026,768
Neotropical	32	2,214,414
Total	**289**	**85,472,182**
Cold-winter deserts		
Nearctic	21	723,283
Palaearctic	88	19,738,755
Neotropical	42	2,732,168
Total	**151**	**23,194,206**
Tundra communities		
Nearctic	56	129,722,512
Palaearctic	8	7,068,358
Antarctic	15	308,634
Total	**79**	**137,099,504**
Tropical grasslands/savannas		
Australian	14	2,807,294
Neotropical	37	14,725,825
Total	**51**	**17,533,119**
Temperate grasslands		
Nearctic	70	787,425
Palaearctic	41	3,013,579
Australian	51	1,007,736
Neotropical	22	2,176,027
Total	**184**	**6,984,767**
Mixed mountain systems		
Nearctic	302	17,666,573
Palaearctic	681	26,304,771
Afrotropical	73	6,961,453
Neotropical	131	25,431,702
Total	**1,187**	**76,364,499**
Mixed island systems		
Palaearctic	8	62,502
Afrotropical	6	44,392
Indomalayan	261	12,762,523
Oceanian	81	7,361,329
Neotropical	72	10,323,764
Total	**428**	**30,554,510**
Lake systems		
Nearctic	13	514,048
Palaearctic	2	59,272
Afrotropical	2	55,100
Neotropical	1	36,180
Total	**18**	**664,600**
Classification unknown	**415**	**12,010,655**
TOTAL	**6,940**	**651,467,597**

WORLD HERITAGE SITES/BIENS DU PATRIMOINE MONDIAL

The *Convention Concerning the Protection of the World Cultural and Natural Heritage* was adopted in Paris in 1972, and came into force in December 1975. The Convention provides for the designation of areas of "outstanding universal value" as world heritage sites, with the principal aim of fostering international cooperation in safeguarding these important areas. Sites, which must be nominated by the signatory nation responsible, are evaluated for their world heritage quality before being declared by the World Heritage Committee. Only natural sites are considered here.

Article 2 of the World Heritage Convention considers as natural heritage: natural features consisting of physical and biological formations or groups of such formations, which are of outstanding universal value from the aesthetic or scientific point of view; geological or physiographical formations and precisely delineated areas which constitute the habitat of threatened species of animals and plants of outstanding universal value from the point of view of science or conservation; and natural sites or precisely delineated areas of outstanding universal value from the point of view of science, conservation or natural beauty. Criteria for inclusion in the list are published by Unesco.

La *Convention concernant la protection du patrimoine mondial, culturel et naturel* a été adoptée à Paris en 1972 et est entrée en vigueur en décembre 1975. La Convention prévoit la désignation de régions de "valeur universelle exceptionnelle" en tant que biens du patrimoine mondial, dans le but premier d'encourager la coopération internationale pour la sauvegarde de ces régions importantes. Les sites, qui doivent être désignés par l'Etat signataire responsable, sont évalués en fonction de leur qualité de biens du patrimoine mondial avant d'être acceptés par le Comité du patrimoine mondial. Nous ne tenons compte ici que des biens naturels.

L'article 2 de la Convention du patrimoine mondial considère comme patrimoine naturel: les monuments naturels constitués par des formations physiques et biologiques ou par des groupes de telles formations qui ont une valeur universelle exceptionnelle du point de vue esthétique ou scientifique; les formations géologiques et physiographiques et les zones strictement délimitées constituant l'habitat d'espèces animales et végétales menacées, qui ont une valeur universelle exceptionnelle du point de vue de la science ou de la conservation; les sites naturels ou les zones naturelles strictement délimitées, qui ont une valeur universelle exceptionnelle du point de vue de la science, de la conservation ou de la beauté naturelle. Les critères déterminant l'inscription sur la Liste sont publiés par l'Unesco.

Since this list was compiled, the Federal Republic of Germany and the German Democratic Republic have combined to form an enlarged Federal Republic of Germany, and the Yemen Arab Republic and the People's Democratic Republic of Yemen have combined to form the Republic of Yemen.

Depuis la réalisation de la présente liste, la République fédérale d'Allemagne et la République démocratique allemande ont fusionné pour former la République fédérale d'Allemagne, et la République arabe du Yémen et la République démocratique du Yémen ont fusionné pour former la République du Yémen.

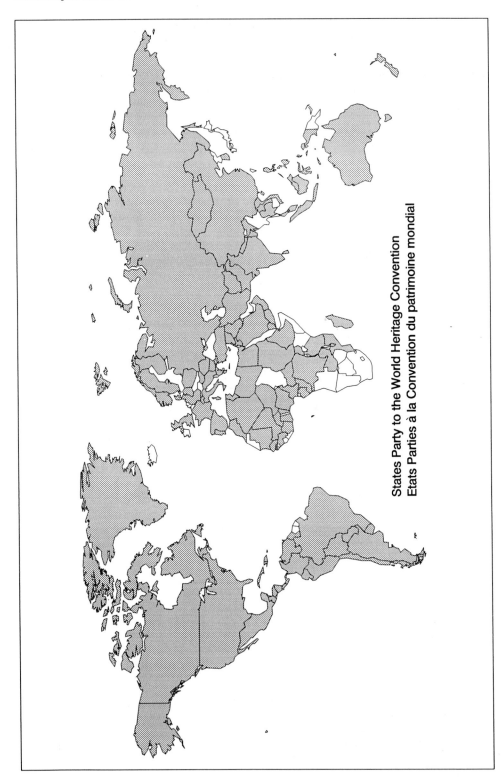

States Party to the World Heritage Convention
Etats Parties à la Convention du patrimoine mondial

WORLD HERITAGE LIST
LISTE DU PATRIMOINE MONDIAL

Natural sites inscribed by the Committee of the Convention concerning the protection of the world cultural and natural heritage

Biens naturels inscrits par la comité de la Convention concernant la protection du patrimoine mondial, culturel et naturel

---

AFGHANISTAN
Ratification 20 March/mars 1979
No sites inscribed/Pas de biens inscrits sur la liste

ALBANIA/ALBANIE
Ratification 10 July/juillet 1989
No sites inscribed/Pas de biens inscrits sur la liste

ALGERIA/ALGERIE
Ratification 24 June/juin 1974
Tassili N'Ajjer (Inscribed/inscrit 1982)

ALLEMAGNE, REPUBLIQUE FEDERAL D'
Voir paragraphe Germany, Federal Republic of

ANTIGUA & BARBUDA
Acceptance/Acceptation 1 November/novembre 1983
No sites inscribed/Pas de biens inscrits sur la liste

ARABIE SAOUDITE
Voir paragraph Saudi Arabia

ARGENTINA/ARGENTINE
Acceptance/Acceptation 23 August/août 1978
Los Glaciares National Park (Inscribed/inscrit 1981)
Iguazú National Park (Inscribed/inscrit 1984)

AUSTRALIA/AUSTRALIE
Ratification 22 August/août 1974
Great Barrier Reef (Inscribed/inscrit 1981)
Kakadu National Park (Stage I Inscribed/inscrit 1981)
(Stage II Inscribed/inscrit 1987)
Willandra Lakes Region (Inscribed/inscrit 1981)
Lord Howe Island Group (Inscribed/inscrit 1982)
Tasmania Wilderness (Inscribed/inscrit 1982)
(Extended/élargie 1989)
Australian East Coast Temperate and Subtropical Rainforest Parks (Inscribed/inscrit 1986)

Uluru (Ayers Rock) National Park (Inscribed/inscrit 1987)
Wet Tropics of Queensland (Inscribed/inscrit 1988)

BANGLADESH

Acceptance/Acceptation 3 August/août 1983
No natural sites inscribed/Pas de biens naturels inscrits sur la liste

BENIN

Ratification 14 June/juin 1982
No natural sites inscribed/Pas de biens naturels inscrits sur la liste

BOLIVIA/BOLIVIE

Ratification 4 October/octobre 1976
No natural sites inscribed/Pas de biens naturels inscrits sur la liste

BRAZIL/BRESIL

Acceptance/Acceptation 1 September/septembre 1977
Iguaçu National Park (Inscribed/inscrit 1986)

BULGARIA/BULGARIE

Acceptance/Acceptation 7 March/mars 1974
Srébarna Nature Reserve (Inscribed/inscrit 1983)
Pirin National Park (Inscribed/inscrit 1983)

BURKINA FASO

Ratification 2 April/avril 1987
No sites inscribed/Pas de biens inscrits sur la liste

BURUNDI

Ratification 19 May/mai 1982
No sites inscribed/Pas de biens inscrits sur la liste

BYELORUSSIAN SSR

Ratification 12 October/octobre 1988
No sites inscribed/Pas de biens inscrits sur la liste

CAMEROON

Ratification 7 December/décembre 1982
Dja Faunal Reserve (Inscribed/inscrit 1987)

CANADA

Acceptance/Acceptation 23 July/juillet 1976
Nahanni National Park (Inscribed/inscrit 1978)
Dinosaur Provincial Park (Inscribed/inscrit 1979)
Wood Buffalo National Park (Inscribed/inscrit 1983)
Canadian Rocky Mountain Parks (Inscribed/inscrit 1984)
Gros Morne National Park (Inscribed/inscrit 1987)

With the UNITED STATES OF AMERICA/avec les ETATS-UNIS D'AMERIQUE
   Kluane-Wrangell/St Elias National Park (Inscribed/inscrit 1979)

CAPE VERDE/CAP-VERT

Acceptance/Acceptation 28 April/avril 1988
   No sites inscribed/Pas de biens inscrits sur la liste

CENTRAL AFRICAN REPUBLIC

Ratification 22 December/décembre 1980
   Parc national de Manovo-Gounda-St Floris (Inscribed/inscrit 1988)

CHILE/CHILI

Ratification 20 February/février 1980
   No sites inscribed/Pas de biens inscrits sur la liste

CHINA, PEOPLES REPUBLIC OF/CHINE, REPUBLIQUE POPULAIRE DE

Ratification 12 December/décembre 1985
   See below/Voir ci-dessous

CHYPRE

Voir paragraphe Cyprus

COLOMBIA/COLOMBIE

Acceptance/Acceptation 24 May/mai 1983
   No natural sites inscribed/Pas de biens naturels inscrits sur la liste

CONGO/REPUBLIQUE POPULAIRE DU CONGO

Ratification 10 December/décembre 1987
   No sites inscribed/Pas de biens inscrits sur la liste

COSTA RICA

Ratification 23 August/août 1977
   Talamanca Range-La Amistad Reserves (Inscribed/inscrit 1983)

COTE D'IVOIRE

Ratification 9 January/janvier 1981
   Taï National Park (Inscribed/inscrit 1982)
   Comoé National Park (Inscribed/inscrit 1983)
With GUINEA/avec la GUINEE
   Mount Nimba Strict Nature Reserve (Inscribed/inscrit 1982)

CUBA

Ratification 24 March/mars 1981
   No natural sites inscribed/Pas de biens naturels inscrits sur la liste

CYPRUS/CHYPRE

Acceptance/Acceptation 14 August/août 1975
  No natural sites inscribed/Pas de biens naturels inscrit sur la liste

DENMARK/DANEMARK

Ratification 25 July/juillet 1979
  Pas de biens inscrits sur la liste/No sites inscribed

DOMINICAN REPUBLIC

Ratification 12 February/février 1985
  No sites listed/Pas de biens inscrits sur la liste

ECUADOR/EQUATEUR

Acceptance/Acceptation 16 June/juin 1975
    Galápagos Islands (Inscribed/inscrit 1978)
    Sangay National Park (Inscribed/inscrit 1983)

EGYPT/EGYPTE

Ratification 7 February/février 1974
  No natural sites inscribed/Pas de biens naturels inscrits sur la liste

EQUATEUR
Voir paragraphe Ecuador

ESPAGNE
Voir paragraphe Spain

ETATS-UNIS D'AMERIQUE
Voir paragraphe United States of America

ETHIOPIA/ETHIOPIE

Ratification 6 July/juillet 1977
    Simien National Park (Inscribed/inscrit 1978)

FINLAND

Ratification 4 March/mars 1987
  No sites inscribed/Pas de biens inscrits sur la liste

FRANCE

Acceptance/Acceptation 27 June/juin 1975
    Cape Girolata, Cape Porto and Scandola Nature Reserve in Corsica (Inscribed/inscrit 1983)
    Also see below/Voir aussi ci-dessous

GABON

Ratification 30 December/décembre 1986
    No sites inscribed/Pas de biens inscrits sur la liste

GAMBIA

Ratification 1 July/juillet 1987
    No sites inscribed/Pas de biens inscrits sur la liste

GERMAN DEMOCRATIC REPUBLIC

Acceptance/Acceptation 12 December/décembre 1988
    No sites inscribed/Pas de biens inscrits sur la liste

GERMANY, FEDERAL REPUBLIC OF

Ratification 23 August/août 1976
No natural sites inscribed/Pas de biens naturels inscrits sur la liste

GHANA

Ratification 4 July/juillet 1975
    No natural sites inscribed/Pas de biens naturels inscrits sur la liste

GREECE/GRECE

Ratification 17 July/juillet 1981
    See below/Voir ci-dessous

GUATEMALA

Ratification 16 January/janvier 1979
    Tikal National Park (Inscribed/inscrit 1979)

GUINEA/GUINEE

Ratification 18 March/mars 1979
With/avec la COTE D'IVOIRE
    Mount Nimba Strict Nature Reserve (Inscribed/inscrit 1981)

GUYANA/GUYANE

Acceptance/Acceptation 20 June/juin 1977
    No sites inscribed/Pas de biens inscrits sur la liste

HAITI

Ratification 18 January/janvier 1980
    No natural sites inscribed/Pas de biens naturels inscrits sur la liste

HOLY SEE

Accession/Adhésion 7 October/octobre 1982
    No natural sites inscribed/Pas de biens naturels inscrits sur la liste

HONDURAS

Ratification 8 June/juin 1979
    Río Plátano Biosphere Reserve (Inscribed/inscrit 1982)

HUNGARY/HONGRIE
Acceptance/Acceptation 15 July/juillet 1985
    No natural sites inscribed/Pas de biens naturels inscrits sur la liste

INDIA/INDE
Ratification 14 November/novembre 1977
    Kaziranga National Park (Inscribed/inscrit 1985)
    Manas National Park (Inscribed/inscrit 1985)
    Keoladeo National Park (Inscribed/inscrit 1985)
    Sundarbans National Park (Inscribed/inscrit 1987)
    Nanda Devi National Park (Inscribed/inscrit 1988)

INDONESIA/INDONESIE
Acceptance/Acceptation 6 July/juillet 1989
    No sites inscribed/Pas de biens inscrits sur la liste

IRAK
Voir paragraphe Iraq

IRAN
Acceptance/Acceptation 26 February/février 1975
    No natural sites inscribed/Pas de biens naturels inscrits sur la liste

IRAQ/IRAK
Acceptance/Acceptation 5 March/mars 1974
    No natural sites inscribed/Pas de biens naturels inscrits sur la liste

ITALY/ITALIE
Ratification 23 June/juin 1978
    No natural sites inscribed/Pas de biens naturels inscrits sur la liste

JAMAHIRYA ARABE LIBYENNE
Voir paragraphe Libya

JAMAICA/JAMAIQUE
Acceptance/Acceptation 14 June/juin 1983
    No sites inscribed/Pas de biens inscrits sur la liste

JORDAN/JORDANIE
Ratification 5 May/mai 1975
    No natural sites inscribed/Pas de biens naturels inscrits sur la liste

LAO PEOPLE'S DEMOCRATIC REPUBLIC
Ratification 20 March/mars 1987
    No sites inscribed/Pas de biens inscrits sur la liste

LEBANON/LIBAN
Ratification 3 February/février 1983
    No natural sites inscribed/Pas de biens naturels inscrits sur la liste

LIBYAN ARAB JAMAHIRIYA
Ratification 13 October/octobre 1978
    No natural sites inscribed/Pas de biens naturels inscrits sur la liste

LUXEMBOURG
Ratification 28 September/septembre 1983
    No sites inscribed/Pas de biens inscrits sur la liste

MADAGASCAR
Ratification 19 July/juillet 1983
    No sites inscribed/Pas de biens inscrits sur la liste

MALAWI
Ratification 5 January/janvier 1982
    Lake Malawi National Park (Inscribed/inscrit 1984)

MALAYSIA/MALAISIE
Ratification 7 December/décembre 1988
    No sites inscribed/Pas de biens inscrits sur la liste

MALDIVES
Acceptance/Acceptation 22 May/mai 1986
    No sites inscribed/Pas de biens inscrits sur la liste

MALI
Acceptance/Acceptation 5 April/avril 1977
    See below/Voir ci-dessous

MALTA/MALTE
Acceptance/Acceptation 14 November/novembre 1978
    No natural sites inscribed/Pas de biens naturels inscrits sur la liste

MAROC
Voir paragraphe Morocco

MAURITANIA/MAURITANIE
Ratification 2 March/mars 1981
    Banc d'Arguin National Park (Inscribed/inscrit 1989)

MEXICO/MEXIQUE
Acceptance/Acceptation 23 February/février 1984
    Sian Ka'an Biosphere Reserve (Inscribed/inscrit 1987)

MONACO

Ratification 7 November/novembre 1978
    No sites inscribed/Pas de biens inscrits sur la liste

MONGOLIA/MONGOLIE

Acceptance/Acceptation 2 February/février 1990
    No sites inscribed/Pas de biens inscrits sur la liste

MOROCCO/MAROC

Ratification 28 October/octobre 1975
    No natural sites inscribed/Pas de biens naturels inscrits sur la liste

MOZAMBIQUE

Ratification 27 November/novembre 1982
    No sites inscribed/Pas de biens inscrits sur la liste

NEPAL

Acceptance/Acceptation 20 June/juin 1978
    Sagarmatha National Park (Inscribed/inscrit 1979)
    Royal Chitwan National Park (Inscribed/inscrit 1984)

NEW ZEALAND

Ratification 22 November/novembre 1984
    Fiordland National Park (Inscribed/inscrit 1986)
    Westland/Mount Cook National Parks (Inscribed/inscrit 1986)

NICARAGUA

Acceptance/Acceptation 17 December/décembre 1979
    No sites inscribed/Pas de biens inscrits sur la liste

NIGER

Acceptance/Acceptation 23 December/décembre 1974
    No sites inscribed/Pas de biens inscrits sur la liste

NIGERIA

Ratification 23 October/octobre 1974
    No sites inscribed/Pas de biens inscrits sur la liste

NORWAY/NORVEGE

Ratification 12 May/mai 1977
    No natural sites inscribed/Pas de biens naturels inscrits sur la liste

NOUVELLE ZELANDE

Voir paragraphe New Zealand

OMAN

Acceptance/Acceptation 6 October/octobre 1981
    No natural sites inscribed/Pas de biens naturels inscrits sur la liste

OUGANDA
Voir paragraphe Uganda

PAKISTAN

Ratification 23 July/juillet 1976
    No natural sites inscribed/Pas de biens naturels inscrits sur la liste

PANAMA

Ratification 3 March/mars 1978
    Darién National Park (Inscribed/inscrit 1981

PARAGUAY

Ratification 28 April/avril 1988
    No sites inscribed/Pas de biens inscrits sur la liste

PERU/PEROU

Ratification 24 February/février 1982
    Sanctuário histórico de Macchu Picchu (Inscribed/inscrit 1983)
    Huascarán National Park (Inscribed/inscrit 1985)
    Manu National Park (Inscribed/inscrit 1987)

PHILIPPINES

Ratification 19 September/septembre 1985
    No sites listed/Pas de biens inscrits sur la liste

POLAND/POLOGNE

Ratification 29 June/juin 1976
    Bialowieza National Park (Inscribed/inscrit 1979)

PORTUGAL

Ratification 30 September/septembre 1980
    No natural sites inscribed/Pas de biens naturels inscrits sur la liste

QATAR

Acceptance/Acceptation 12 September/septembre 1984
    No sites inscribed/Pas de biens inscrits sur la liste

REPUBLIQUE ARABE SYRIENNE
Voir paragraphe Syria

REPUBLIQUE CENTRAFRICAINE
Voir paragraphe Central African Republic

REPUBLIQUE DEMOCRATIQUE ALLEMANDE
Voir paragraphe German Democratic Republic

REPUBLIQUE DEMOCRATIQUE POPULAIRE LAO
Voir paragraphe Lao People's Democratic Republic

REPUBLIQUE DOMINICAINE
Voir paragraphe Dominican Republic

REPUBLIC OF KOREA/REPUBLIQUE DE COREE
Acceptance/Acceptation 14 September/14 septembre 1988
   No sites inscribed/Pas de biens inscrits sur la liste

REPUBLIQUE POPULAIRE DU CONGO
Voir paragraphe Congo

RSS DE BIELORUSSIE
Voir paragraphe Byelorussian SSR

RSS D'UKRAINE
Voir paragraphe Ukrainian SSR

REPUBLIQUE UNIE DE TANZANIE
Voir paragraphe Tanzania

REPUBLIQUE UNIE DU CAMEROUN
Voir paragraphe Cameroon

ROYAUME-UNI
Voir paragraphe United Kingdom

ROMANIA/ROUMANIE
Acceptance/Acceptation 16 May/mai 1990
   No sites inscribed/Pas de biens inscrits sur la liste

SAINT CHRISTOPHER AND NEVIS/SAINT-CHRISTOPHE-ET-NEVIS
Acceptance/Acceptation 10 July/juillet 1986
   No sites inscribed/Pas de biens inscrits sur la liste

SAINT-SIEGE
Voir paragraphe Holy See

SAUDI ARABIA
Acceptance/Acceptation 7 August/août 1978
   No sites inscribed/Pas de biens inscrits sur la liste

SENEGAL

Ratification 13 February/février 1976
    Djoudj National Bird Sanctuary (Inscribed/inscrit 1981)
    Niokolo-Koba National Park (Inscribed/inscrit 1981)

SEYCHELLES

Acceptance/Acceptation 9 April/avril 1980
    Aldabra Atoll (Inscribed/inscrit 1982)
    Vallée de Mai Nature Reserve (Inscribed/inscrit 1983)

SOUDAN

Voir paragraphe Sudan

SPAIN

Acceptance 4 May/mai 1982
    Garajonay National Park (Inscribed/inscrit 1986)

SRI LANKA

Acceptance/Acceptation 6 June/juin 1980
    Sinharaja Forest Reserve (Inscribed/inscrit 1988)

SUDAN/SOUDAN

Ratification 6 June/juin 1974
    No sites inscribed/Pas de biens inscrits sur la liste

SWEDEN/SUEDE

Ratification 22 January/janvier 1985
    No sites inscribed/Pas de biens inscrits sur la liste

SWITZERLAND/SUISSE

Ratification 17 September/septembre 1975
    No natural sites inscribed/Pas de biens naturels inscrits sur la liste

SYRIAN ARAB REPUBLIC

Acceptance/Acceptation 13 August/août 1975
    No natural sites inscribed/Pas de biens naturels inscrits sur la liste

TANZANIA

Ratification 2 August/août 1977
    Ngorongoro Conservation Area (Inscribed/inscrit 1979)
    Serengeti National Park (Inscribed/inscrit 1981)
    Selous Game Reserve (Inscribed/inscrit 1982)
    Mt Kilimanjaro National Park (Inscribed/inscrit 1987)

THAILAND/THAILANDE

Acceptance/Acceptation 17 September/septembre 1987
    No sites inscribed/Pas de biens inscrits sur la liste

TUNISIA/TUNISIE
Ratification 10 March/mars 1975
  Ichkeul National Park (Inscribed/inscrit 1980)

TURKEY/TURQUIE
Ratification 16 March/mars 1983
  Göreme National Park (Inscribed/inscrit 1985)
  Also see below/Voir aussi ci-dessous

UGANDA
Acceptance/Acceptation 20 November/novembre 1987
  No sites inscribed/Pas de biens inscrits sur la liste

UKRAINIAN SSR
Ratification 12 October/octobre 1988
  No sites inscribed/Pas de biens inscrits sur la liste

UNITED KINGDOM
Ratification 29 May/mai 1984
  St. Kilda (Inscribed/inscrit 1986)
  Giant's Causeway (Inscribed/inscrit 1986)
  Henderson Island (Inscribed/inscrit 1988)

UNITED STATES OF AMERICA
Ratification 7 December/décembre 1973
  Yellowstone National Park (Inscribed/inscrit 1978)
  Everglades National Park (Inscribed/inscrit 1979)
  Grand Canyon National Park (Inscribed/inscrit 1979)
  Redwood National Park (Inscribed/inscrit 1980)
  Mammoth Cave National Park (Inscribed/inscrit 1981)
  Olympic National Park (Inscribed/inscrit 1981)
  Great Smoky Mountains National Park (Inscribed/inscrit 1983)
  Yosemite National Park (Inscribed/inscrit 1984)
  Hawaii Volcanoes National Park (Inscribed/inscrit 1987)
With CANADA/avec CANADA
  Kluane-Wrangell/St Elias National Park (Inscribed/inscrit 1979)

USSR/URSS
Ratification 12 Octobre/octobre 1988
  No sites inscribed/Pas de biens inscrits sur la liste

URUGUAY
Acceptance/Acceptation 9 March/mars 1989
  No sites inscribed/Pas de biens inscrits sur la liste

VIET NAM
Acceptance/Acceptation 6 October/octobre 1987
   No sites inscribed/Pas de biens inscrits sur la liste

YEMEN/YEMEN DU NORD
Ratification 25 January/janvier 1984
   No natural sites inscribed/Pas de biens naturels inscrits sur la liste

YEMEN, DEMOCRATIC/YEMEN DEMOCRATIQUE
Acceptance/Acceptation 7 October/octobre 1980
   No natural sites inscribed/Pas de biens naturels inscrits sur la liste

YUGOSLAVIA/YUGOSLAVIE
Ratification 26 May/mai 1975
   Plitvice Lakes National Park (Inscribed/inscrit 1979)
   Durmitor National Park (Inscribed/inscrit 1980)
   Skocjan Caves (Inscribed/inscrit 1986)
   Also see below/Voir aussi ci-dessous

ZAIRE
Ratification 23 September/septembre 1974
   Virunga National Park (Inscribed/inscrit 1979)
   Garamba National Park (Inscribed/inscrit 1980)
   Kahuzi-Biega National Park (Inscribed/inscrit 1980)
   Salonga National Park (Inscribed/inscrit 1984)

ZAMBIA/ZAMBIE
Ratification 4 June/juin 1984
With ZIMBABWE/avec ZIMBABWE
   Victoria Falls/Mosi-oa-Tunya (Inscribed/inscrit 1989)

ZIMBABWE
Ratification 16 August/aot 1982
   Mana Pools National Park, Sapi and Chewore Safari Areas (Inscribed/inscrit 1984)
With ZAMBIA/avec ZAMBIE
   Victoria Falls/Mosi-oa-Tunya (Inscribed/inscrit 1989)

Other mixed natural/cultural sites are inscribed on the list of World Heritage, but on the basis of beauty resulting from the man/nature interaction, rather than natural features alone. These are:

D'autres biens naturels/culturels sont inscrits sur la Liste du Patrimoine Mondial, mais basés sur la beauté émanante de l'action réciproque entre l'homme et la nature plutôt que sur des caractéristiques entièrement naturelles. Ce sont les suivants:

Mont-Saint-Michel and its Bay/et sa baie	**France**	(Inscribed/inscrit 1979)
Kotor	**Yugoslavia/Yougoslavie**	(Inscribed/inscrit 1979)
Ohrid	**Yugoslavia/Yougoslavie**	(Inscribed/inscrit 1979)
Mount Taishan	**China/Chine**	(Inscribed/inscrit 1987)
Mount Athos	**Greece/Grèce**	(Inscribed/inscrit 1988)
Meteora	**Greece/Grèce**	(Inscribed/inscrit 1988)
Hierapolis-Pamukkale	**Turkey/Turquie**	(Inscribed/inscrit 1988)
Bandiagara	**Mali**	(Inscribed/inscrit 1989)

BIOSPHERE RESERVES/RESERVES DE LA BIOSPHERE

The establishment of biosphere reserves is not covered by a specific convention, but is part of an international scientific programme, the Unesco Man and the Biosphere (MAB) Programme. The objectives of the network of biosphere reserves, and the characteristics which biosphere reserves might display, are identified in various Unesco-MAB documents, including the Action Plan for Biosphere Reserves published in 1984.

Biosphere Reserves differ from the preceding types of site in that they are not exclusively designated to protect unique areas or important wetlands, but for a range of objectives which include research, monitoring, training and demonstration, as well as conservation roles. In most cases the human component is vital to the functioning of the biosphere reserve, which does not necessarily hold for either World Heritage or Ramsar sites. A further fundamental difference is the stated aim of developing a biosphere reserve network representative of the world's ecosystems.

La création de réserves de la biosphère ne relève d'aucune convention mais entre dans le cadre d'un programme scientifique international, le Programme de l'Unesco sur l'homme et la biosphère (Programme MAB). Les objectifs du réseau de réserves de la biosphère et les caractéristiques qui doivent être celle des réserves de la biosphère sont définis dans divers documents Unesco-MAB, notamment le Plan d'action pour les réserves de la biosphère, publié en 1984.

Les réserves de la biosphère diffèrent des sites décrits précédemment en ce qu'elles ne sont pas exclusivement désignées afin de protéger des régions uniques ou des zones humides importantes mais pour toutes sortes d'autres raisons, notamment la recherche, la surveillance continue, la formation et la démonstration, sans oublier la conservation. Dans la plupart des cas, l'élément humain est vital pour le fonctionnement des réserves de la biosphère ce qui n'est pas nécessairement le cas pour les biens du patrimoine mondial ou les sites Ramsar. Autre différence fondamentale: un des objectifs fixés consiste à mettre sur pied un réseau de réserves de la biosphère représentatif des écosystèmes de la planète.

Since this list was compiled, the Federal Republic of Germany and the German Democratic Republic have combined to form an enlarged Federal Republic of Germany.

Depuis la réalisation de la présente liste, la République fédérale d'Allemagne et la République démocratique allemande ont fusionné pour former la République fédérale d'Allemagne.

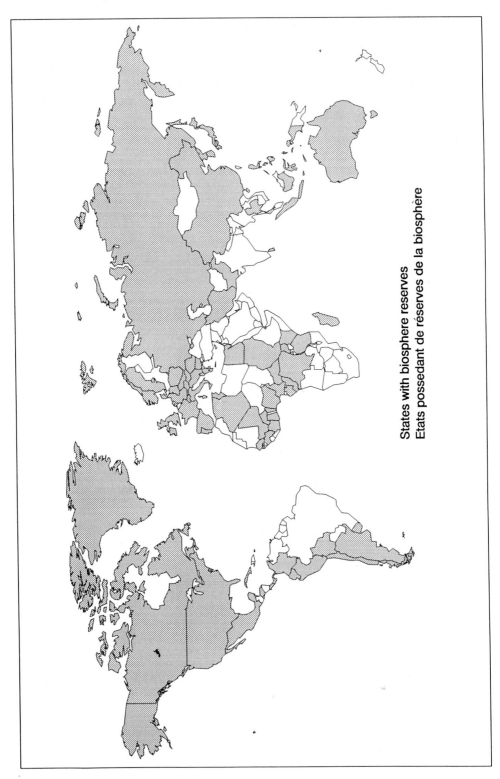

States with biosphere reserves
Etats possedant de réserves de la biosphère

LIST OF BIOSPHERE RESERVES
LISTE DES RESERVES DE LA BIOSPHERE

	Biogeographic province/ Province biogéographique	Area/ Superficie (ha)	Date of approval Date d'approbation

ALLEMAGNE, REPUBLIQUE FEDERALE D'
Voir paragraphe Germany, Federal Republic of

ALGERIA/ALGERIE

Parc national du Tassili	2.18.07	7,200,000	1986

ARGENTINA/ARGENTINE

Reserva de la Biosfera San Guillermo	8.37.12	981,460	1980
Reserva Natural de Vida Silvestre Laguna Blanca	8.25.07	981,620	1982
Parque Costero del Sur	8.31.11	30,000	1984
Reserva Ecológica de Ñacuñán	8.25.07	11,900	1986
Reserva de la Biosfera de Pozuelos	8.37.12	405,000	1990

AUSTRALIA/AUSTRALIE

Croajingolong	6.06.06	101,000	1977
Danggali Conservation Park	6.10.07	253,230	1977
Kosciusko National Park	6.06.06	625,525	1977
Macquarie Island Nature Reserve	7.04.09	12,785	1977
Prince Regent River Nature Reserve	6.03.04	633,825	1977
Southwest National Park	6.02.02	403,240	1977
Unnamed Conservation Park of South Australia	6.09.07	2,132,600	1977
Uluru (Ayers Rock-Mount Olga) National Park	6.09.07	132,550	1977
Yathong Nature Reserve	6.13.11	107,241	1977
Fitzgerald River National Park	6.04.06	242,727	1978
Hattah-Kulkyne NP & Murray-Kulkyne Park	6.05.06	49,500	1981
Wilson's Promontory National Park	6.06.06	49,000	1981

AUSTRIA/AUTRICHE

Gossenkollesee	2.32.12	100	1977
Gurgler Kamm	2.32.12	1,500	1977
Lobau Reserve	2.32.12	1,000	1977
Neusiedler See-Österreichischer Teil	2.12.05	25,000	1977

BIELORUSSIE REPUBLIQUE SOCIALISTE SOVIETIQUE
Voir paragraphe Byelorussian Soviet Socialist Republic

BENIN

Réserve de la biosphère de la Pendjari	3.04.04	880,000	1986

BOLIVIA/BOLIVIE

Parque Nacional Pilón-Lajas	8.06.01	100,000	1977
Reserva Nacional de Fauna Ulla Ulla	8.36.12	200,000	1977
Beni	8.35.12	135,000	1986

BULGARIA/BULGARIE

Parc national Steneto	2.33.12	2,889	1977
Réserve Alibotouch	2.33.12	1,628	1977
Réserve Bistrichko Branichté	2.33.12	1,177	1977
Réserve Boatine	2.33.12	1,281	1977
Réserve Djendema	2.33.12	1,775	1977
Réserve Doupkata	2.33.12	1,210	1977
Réserve Doupki-Djindjiritza	2.33.12	2,873	1977
Réserve Kamtchia	2.33.12	842	1977
Réserve Koupena	2.33.12	1,084	1977
Réserve Mantaritza	2.33.12	576	1977
Réserve Maritchini ezera	2.33.12	1,510	1977
Réserve Ouzounboudjak	2.33.12	2,575	1977
Réserve Parangalitza	2.33.12	1,509	1977
Réserve Srébarna	2.11.05	600	1977
Réserve Tchervenata sténa	2.33.12	812	1977
Réserve Tchoupréné	2.33.12	1,440	1977
Réserve Tsaritchina	2.33.12	1,420	1977

BURKINA FASO

Forêt classée de la mare aux hippopotames	3.04.04	16,300	1986

BYELORUSSIAN SOVIET SOCIALIST REPUBLIC

Berezinskiy Zapovednik	2.10.05	76,201	1978

CAMEROON, UNITED REPUBLIC OF

Parc national de Waza	3.04.04	170,000	1979
Parc national de la Benoué	3.04.04	180,000	1981
Réserve forestière et de faune du Dja	3.02.01	500,000	1981

CANADA

Mont St Hilaire	1.05.05	5,550	1978
Waterton Lakes National Park	1.19.12	52,597	1979
Long Point Biosphere Reserve	1.22.14	27,000	1986
Riding Mountain Biosphere Reserve	1.04.03	297,591	1986
Réserve de la biosphère de Charlevoix	1.04.03	460,000	1988
Niagara Escarpment Biosphere Reserve	1.05.05	207,240	1990

CENTRAL AFRICAN REPUBLIC

Basse-Lobaye Forest	3.02.01	18,200	1977
Bamingui-Bangoran Conservation Area	3.04.04	1,622,000	1979

CHILE/CHILI

Parque Nacional Fray Jorge	8.23.06	14,074	1977
Parque Nacional Juan Fernández	5.04.13	9,290	1977
Parque Nacional Torres del Paine	8.37.12	184,414	1978
Parque Nacional Laguna San Rafael	8.11.02	1,742,448	1979
Parque Nacional Lauca	8.36.12	358,312	1981
Reserva de la Biosfera Araucarias	8.22.05	81,000	1983
Reserva de la Biosfera La Campana-Peñuelas	8.23.06	17,095	1984

CHINA/CHINE

Changbai Mountain Nature Reserve	2.14.05	217,235	1979
Dinghu Nature Reserve	4.06.01	1,200	1979
Wolong Nature Reserve	2.39.12	207,210	1979
Fanjingshan Mountain Biosphere Reserve	2.15.05	41,533	1986
Xilin Gol Natural Steppe Protected Area	2.30.11	1,078,600	1987
Fujian Wuyishan Nature Reserve	2.01.02	56,527	1987
Bogdhad Mountain Biosphere Reserve	2.22.08	217,000	1990

COLOMBIA/COLOMBIE

Cinturón Andino Cluster Biosphere Reserve	8.33.12	855,000	1979
El Tuparro Nature Reserve	8.27.10	928,125	1979
Sierra Nevada de Santa Marta			
(inc. Tayrona NP)	8.17.04	731,250	1979

CONGO

Parc national d'Odzala	3.02.01	110,000	1977
Réserve de la biosphère de Dimonika	3.02.01	62,000	1988

COSTA RICA

Reserva de la Biósfera de la Amistad	8.16.04	584,592	1982
Cordillera Volcánica Central	8.16.04	144,363	1988

COTE D'IVOIRE

Parc national de Taï	3.01.01	330,000	1977
Parc national de la Comoé	3.04.04	1,150,000	1983

CUBA

Sierra del Rosario	8.39.13	10,000	1984
Cuchillas del Toa	8.39.13	127,500	1987
Península de Guanahacabibes	8.39.13	101,500	1987
Baconao	8.39.13	84,600	1987

CZECHOSLOVAKIA

Krivoklátsko Protected Landscape Area	2.11.05	62,792	1977
Slovensky Kras Protected Landscape Area	2.11.05	36,165	1977
Třeboň Basin Protected Landscape Area	2.11.05	70,000	1977
Palava Protected Landscape Area	2.11.05	8,017	1986

Sumava Biosphere Reserve	2.32.12	167,117	1990
Polana Biosphere Reserve	2.11.05	20,079	1990

DENMARK/DANEMARK
North-east Greenland National Park	1.17.09	70,000,000	1977

ECUADOR
Archipiélago de Colón (Galápagos)	8.44.13	766,514	1984
Reserva de la Biosfera de Yasuni	8.05.01	679,730	1989

EGYPT/EGYPTE
Omayed Experimental Research Area	2.18.07	1,000	1981

EQUATEUR
Voir paragraphe Ecuador

ESPAGNE
Voir paragraphe Spain

ETATS-UNIS D'AMERIQUE
Voir paragraphe United States of America

FRANCE
Atoll de Taiaro	5.04.13	2,000	1977
Réserve de la biosphère de la Vallée du Fango	2.17.06	25,110	1977
Réserve nationale de Camargue BR	2.17.06	13,117	1977
Réserve de la biosphère du PN des Cévennes	2.09.05	323,000	1984
Réserve de la biosphère d'Iroise	2.09.05	21,400	1988
Réserve de la biosphère des Vosges du Nord	2.09.05	120,000	1988

GABON
Réserve naturelle intégrale d'Ipassa-Makokou	3.02.01	15,000	1983

GERMAN DEMOCRATIC REPUBLIC
Middle Elbe Biosphere Reserve	2.11.05	17,500	1979
Vessertal Nature Reserve	2.11.05	7,460	1979

GERMANY, FEDERAL REPUBLIC OF
Bayerischer Wald National Park	2.32.12	13,100	1981

GHANA
Bia National Park	3.01.01	7,770	1983

GREECE/GRECE
Gorge of Samaria National Park	2.17.06	4,840	1981
Mount Olympus National Park	2.17.06	4,000	1981

GUINEA/GUINEE

Réserve de la biosphère des Monts Nimba	3.01.01	17,130	1980
Réserve de la biosphère du Massif du Ziama	3.01.01	116,170	1980

HONDURAS

Río Plátano Biosphere Reserve	8.16.04	500,000	1980

HUNGARY/HONGRIE

Aggtelek Biosphere Reserve	2.11.05	19,247	1979
Hortobágy National Park	2.12.05	52,000	1979
Kiskunság Biosphere Reserve	2.12.05	22,095	1979
Lake Fertö Biosphere Reserve	2.12.05	12,542	1979
Pilis Biosphere Reserve	2.11.05	23,000	1980

ILE MAURICE
Voir paragraphe Mauritius

INDONESIA/INDONESIE

Cibodas Biosphere Reserve (Gunung Gede-Pangrango)	4.22.13	14,000	1977
Komodo	4.23.13	30,000	1977
Lore Lindu	4.24.13	231,000	1977
Tanjung Puting	4.25.13	205,000	1977
Gunung Leuser	4.21.13	946,400	1981
Siberut Nature Reserve	4.21.13	56,000	1981

IRAN

Arasbaran Protected Area	2.34.12	52,000	1976
Arjan Protected Area	2.34.12	65,750	1976
Geno Protected Area	2.20.08	49,000	1976
Golestan National Park	2.34.12	125,895	1976
Hara Protected Area	2.20.08	85,686	1976
Kavir National Park	2.24.08	700,000	1976
Lake Oromeeh National Park	2.34.12	462,600	1976
Miankaleh Protected Area	2.34.12	68,800	1976
Touran Protected Area	2.24.08	1,000,000	1976

IRELAND/IRELANDE

North Bull Island	2.08.05	500	1981
Killarney National Park	2.08.05	8,308	1982

ITALY/ITALIE

Collemeluccio-Montedimezzo	2.32.12	478	1977
Forêt Domaniale du Circeo	2.17.06	3,260	1977
Miramare Marine Park	2.17.06	60	1979

Réserves de la biosphère

JAPAN/JAPON

Mount Hakusan	2.02.02	48,000	1980
Mount Odaigahara & Mount Omine	2.02.02	36,000	1980
Shiga Highland	2.15.05	13,000	1980
Yakushima Island	2.02.02	19,000	1980

KENYA

Mount Kenya Biosphere Reserve	3.21.12	71,759	1978
Mount Kulal Biosphere Reserve	3.14.07	700,000	1978
Malindi-Watamu Biosphere Reserve	3.14.07	19,600	1979
Kiunga Marine National Reserve	3.14.07	60,000	1980

KOREA, PEOPLE'S DEMOCRATIC REPUBLIC OF

Mount Paekdu Biosphere Reserve	2.14.05	132,000	1989

KOREA, REPUBLIC OF

Mount Sorak Biosphere Reserve	2.15.05	37,430	1982

MADAGASCAR

Réserve de la biosphère du Mananara Nord	3.03.01	140,000	1990

MALI

Parc national de la Boucle du Baoulé (etc)	3.04.04	771,000	1982

MAURITIUS

Macchabee/Bel Ombre Nature Reserve	3.25.13	3,594	1977

MEXICO/MEXIQUE

Reserva de Mapimí	1.09.07	103,000	1977
Reserva de la Michilía	1.21.12	42,000	1977
Montes Azules	8.01.01	331,200	1979
Reserva de la Biósfera "El Cielo"	1.10.07	144,530	1986
Reserva de la Biósfera de Sian Ka'an	8.16.04	528,147	1986
Reserva de la Biósfera Sierra de Manantlán	8.14.04	139,577	1988

NETHERLANDS

Waddensea Area	2.09.05	260,000	1986

NIGERIA

Omo Strict Natural Reserve	3.01.01	460	1977

NORWAY/NORVEGE

North-east Svalbard Nature Reserve	2.25.09	1,555,000	1976

OUGANDA
Voir paragraphe Uganda

PAKISTAN
Lal Suhanra National Park	4.15.07	31,355	1977

PANAMA
Parque Nacional Fronterizo Darién	8.02.01	597,000	1983

PAYS-BAS
Voir paragraphe Netherlands

PERU/PEROU
Reserva de Huascarán	8.37.12	399,239	1977
Reserva del Manu	8.05.01	1,881,200	1977
Reserva del Noroeste	8.19.04	226,300	1977

PHILIPPINES
Puerto Galera Biosphere Reserve	4.26.13	23,545	1977
Palawan Biosphere Reserve	4.26.13	1,150,800	1990

POLAND/POLOGNE
Babia Gora National Park	2.11.05	1,741	1976
Bialowieza National Park	2.10.05	5,316	1976
Lukajno Lake Reserve	2.10.05	710	1976
Slowinski National Park	2.11.05	18,069	1976

PORTUGAL
Paul do Boquilobo Biosphere Reserve	2.17.06	395	1981

REPUBLIQUE CENTRAFRICAINE
Voir paragraphe Central African Republic

REPUBLIQUE DE COREE
Voir paragraphe Korea, Republic of

REPUBLIQUE DEMOCRATIQUE D'ALLEMAGNE
Voir paragraphe German Democratic Republic

REPUBLIQUE-UNIE DU CAMEROUN
Voir paragraphe Cameroon

REPUBLIQUE-UNIE DU TANZANIE
Voir paragraphe Tanzania, United Republic of

ROMANIA/ROUMANIE
Pietrosul Mare Nature Reserve	2.11.05	3,068	1979
Retezat National Park	2.11.05	20,000	1979
Rosca-Letea Reserve	2.29.11	18,145	1979

ROYAUME-UNI
Voir paragraphe United Kingdom

RWANDA

Parc national des Volcans	3.20.12	15,065	1983

SENEGAL

Forêt classée de Samba Dia	3.04.04	756	1979
Delta du Saloum	3.04.04	180,000	1980
Parc national du Niokolo-Koba	3.04.04	913,000	1981

SPAIN

Reserva de Grazalema	2.17.06	32,210	1977
Reserva de Ordesa-Vinamala	2.16.06	51,396	1977
Parque Natural del Montseny	2.17.06	17,372	1978
Reserva de la Biosfera de Doñana	2.17.06	77,260	1980
Reserva de la Biosfera de la Mancha Humeda	2.17.06	25,000	1980
Las Sierras de Cazorla y Segura BR	2.17.06	190,000	1983
Reserva de la Biosfera de las Marismas del Odiel	2.17.06	8,728	1983
Reserva de la Biosfera del Canal y los Tiles	2.40.13	511	1983
Reserva de la Biosfera del Urdaibai	2.16.06	22,500	1984
Reserva de la Biosfera Sierra Nevada	2.17.06	190,000	1986

SRI LANKA

Hurulu Forest Reserve	4.13.04	512	1977
Sinharaja Forest Reserve	4.02.01	8,864	1978

SUDAN/SOUDAN

Dinder National Park	3.13.07	650,000	1979
Radom National Park	3.05.04	1,250,970	1979

SUEDE
Voir paragraphe Sweden

SWEDEN

Lake Torne Area	2.06.05	96,500	1986

SWITZERLAND/SUISSE

Parc national Suisse	2.32.12	16,870	1979

TANZANIA, UNITED REPUBLIC OF

Lake Manyara National Park	3.05.04	32,500	1981
Serengeti-Ngorongoro Biosphere Reserve	3.05.04	2,305,100	1981

TCHECOSLOVAKIA
Voir paragraphe Czechoslovakia

THAILAND/THAILANDE

Sakaerat Environmental Research Station	4.10.04	7,200	1976
Hauy Tak Teak Reserve	4.10.04	4,700	1977
Mae Sa-Kog Ma Reserve	4.10.04	14,200	1977

TUNISIA/TUNISIE

Parc national de Djebel Bou-Hedma	2.28.11	11,625	1977
Parc national de Djebel Chambi	2.28.11	6,000	1977
Parc national de l'Ichkeul	2.17.06	10,770	1977
Parc national des Iles Zembra et Zembretta	2.17.06	4,030	1977

UGANDA

Queen Elizabeth (Rwenzori) National Park	3.05.04	220,000	1979

UKRAINIAN SOVIET SOCIALIST REPUBLIC/UKRAINE

Chernomorskiy Zapovednik	2.29.11	87,348	1984
Askaniya-Nova Zapovednik	2.29.11	33,307	1985

UNION OF SOVIET SOCIALIST REPUBLICS/UNION DES REPUBLIQUES SOCIALISTES SOVIETIQUES

Chatkal Mountains Biosphere Reserve	2.36.12	71,400	1978
Kavkazskiy Zapovednik	2.34.12	263,477	1978
Oka River Valley Biosphere Reserve	2.10.05	45,845	1978
Repetek Zapovednik	2.21.08	34,600	1978
Sikhote-Alin Zapovednik	2.14.05	340,200	1978
Tsentral'nochernozem Zapovednik	2.10.05	4,795	1978
Astrakhanskiy Zapovednik	2.21.08	63,400	1984
Kronotskiy Zapovednik	2.07.05	1,099,000	1984
Laplandskiy Zapovednik	2.03.03	278,400	1984
Pechoro-Ilychskiy Zapovednik	2.03.03	721,322	1984
Sayano-Shushenskiy Zapovednik	2.35.12	389,570	1984
Sokhondinskiy Zapovednik	2.30.11	211,000	1984
Voronezhskiy Zapovednik	2.11.05	31,053	1984
Tsentral'nolesnoy Zapovednik	2.10.05	21,348	1985
Lake Baikal Region Biosphere Reserve	2.04.03	559,100	1986
Tzentralnosibirskii Biosphere Reserve	2.03/04	5,000,000	1986
West Estonian Archipelago Biosphere Reserve	2.10.05	1,560,000	1990

UNITED KINGDOM

Beinn Eighe National Nature Reserve	2.31.12	4,800	1976
Braunton Burrows National Nature Reserve	2.08.05	596	1976
Caerlaverock National Nature Reserve	2.08.05	5,501	1976
Cairnsmore of Fleet National Nature Reserve	2.08.05	1,922	1976
Dyfi National Nature Reserve	2.08.05	1,589	1976
Isle of Rhum National Nature Reserve	2.31.12	10,560	1976
Loch Druidibeg National Nature Reserve	2.31.12	1,658	1976
Moor House-Upper Teesdale Biosphere Reserve	2.08.05	7,399	1976
North Norfolk Coast Biosphere Reserve	2.08.05	5,497	1976

Silver Flowe-Merrick Kells Biosphere Reserve	2.08.05	3,088	1976
St Kilda National Nature Reserve	2.08.05	842	1976
Claish Moss National Nature Reserve	2.31.12	480	1977
Taynish National Nature Reserve	2.31.12	326	1977

UNITED STATES OF AMERICA

Aleutian Islands National Wildlife Refuge	1.12.09	1,100,943	1976
Big Bend National Park	1.09.07	283,247	1976
Cascade Head Experimental Forest Scenic Research Area	1.02.02	7,051	1976
Central Plains Experimental Range (CPER)	1.18.11	6,210	1976
Channel Islands Biosphere Reserve	1.07.06	479,652	1976
Coram Experimental Forest (incl. Coram NA)	1.19.12	3,019	1976
Denali National Park and Biosphere Reserve	1.03.03	2,441,295	1976
Desert Experimental Range	1.11.08	22,513	1976
Everglades National Park (incl. Ft. Jefferson NM)	8.12.04	585,867	1976
Fraser Experimental Forest	1.19.12	9,328	1976
Glacier National Park	1.19.12	410,202	1976
H.J. Andrews Experimental Forest	1.20.12	6,100	1976
Hubbard Brook Experimental Forest	1.05.05	3,076	1976
Jornada Experimental Range	1.09.07	78,297	1976
Luquillo Experimental Forest (Caribbean NF)	8.40.13	11,340	1976
Noatak National Arctic Range	1.13.09	3,035,200	1976
Olympic National Park	1.02.02	363,379	1976
Organ Pipe Cactus National Monument	1.08.07	133,278	1976
Rocky Mountain National Park	1.19.12	106,710	1976
San Dimas Experimental Forest	1.07.06	6,947	1976
San Joaquin Experimental Range	1.07.06	1,832	1976
Sequoia-Kings Canyon National Parks	1.20.12	343,000	1976
Stanislaus-Tuolumne Experimental Forest	1.20.12	607	1976
Three Sisters Wilderness	1.20.12	80,900	1976
Virgin Islands National Park & Biosphere Reserve	8.41.13	6,127	1976
Yellowstone National Park	1.19.12	898,349	1976
Beaver Creek Experimental Watershed	1.08.07	111,300	1978
Konza Prairie Research Natural Area	1.18.11	3,487	1979
Niwot Ridge Biosphere Reserve	1.19.12	1,200	1979
The University of Michigan Biological Station	1.18.11	4,048	1979
The Virginia Coast Reserve	1.05.05	13,511	1979
Hawaii Islands Biosphere Reserve	5.03.13	99,545	1980
Isle Royale National Park	1.22.14	215,740	1980
Big Thicket National Preserve	1.06.05	34,217	1981
Guanica Commonwealth Forest Reserve	8.40.13	4,006	1981
California Coast Ranges Biosphere Reserve	1.02.02	62,098	1983
Central Gulf Coastal Plain Biosphere Reserve	1.06.05	72,964	1983
South Atlantic Coastal Plain BR	1.06.05	6,125	1983
Mojave and Colorado Deserts Biosphere Reserve	1.08.07	1,297,264	1984
Carolinian-South Atlantic Biopshere Reserve	1.06.05	125,545	1986
Glacier Bay-Admiralty Is. Biosphere Reserve	1.01.02	1,515,015	1986
Central California Coast Biosphere Reserve	1.07.06	404,863	1988

New Jersey Pinelands Biosphere Reserve	1.05.05	445,300	1988
Southern Appalachian Biosphere Reserve	1.05.05	215,596	1988
Champlain-Adirondak Biosphere Reserve	1.05.05	3,990,000	1989
Mammoth Cave Area	1.09.07	83,337	1990

URUGUAY

Bañados del Este	8.32.11	200,000	1976

YUGOSLAVIA/YUGOSLAVIE

Réserve écologique du Bassin de la Rivière Tara	2.33.12	200,000	1976
Velebit Mountain	2.17.06	150,000	1977

ZAIRE

Vallée de la Lufira	3.06.04	14,700	1982
Réserve floristique de Yangambi	3.02.01	250,000	1976
Réserve forestière de Luki	3.02.01	33,000	1979

WETLANDS OF INTERNATIONAL IMPORTANCE (RAMSAR SITES)/ZONES HUMIDES D'IMPORTANCE INTERNATIONALE (SITES RAMSAR)

The Convention on Wetlands of International Importance Especially as Waterfowl Habitat was signed in Ramsar (Iran) in 1971, and came into force in December 1975. This Convention provides a framework for international cooperation for the conservation of wetland habitats. It places general obligations on contracting party states relating to the conservation of wetlands throughout their territories, with special obligations pertaining to those wetlands which have been designated to the List of Wetlands of International Importance.

Each State Party is obliged to list at least one site. Wetlands are defined by the convention as: areas of marsh, fen, peatland or water, whether natural or artificial, permanent or temporary, with water that is static or flowing, fresh, brackish or salt, including areas of marine waters, the depth of which at low tide does not exceed six metres.

La *Convention relative aux zones humides d'importance internationale particulièrement comme habitats des oiseaux d'eau* a été signée à Ramsar (Iran), en 1971 et est entrée en vigueur en décembre 1975. Elle fournit un cadre à la coopération internationale pour la conservation des habitats contenus dans les zones humides. Les Parties contractantes à la Convention ont l'obligation générale de conserver les zones humides se trouvant sur leur territoire et, plus particulièrement, celles qui ont été inscrites sur la Liste des zones humides d'importance internationale.

Chaque Etat Partie a l'obligation d'inscrire au moins un site. La Convention définit les zones humides comme étant des étendues de marais, de fagnes, de tourbières ou d'eaux naturelles ou artificielles, permanentes ou temporaires, où l'eau est stagnante ou courante, douce, saumâtre ou salée, y compris des étendues d'eau marine dont la profondeur à marée basse n'excède pas six mètres.

Since this list was compiled, the Federal Republic of Germany and the German Democratic Republic have combined to form an enlarged Federal Republic of Germany.

Depuis la réalisation de la présente liste, la République fédérale d'Allemagne et la République démocratique allemande ont fusionné pour former la République fédérale d'Allemagne.

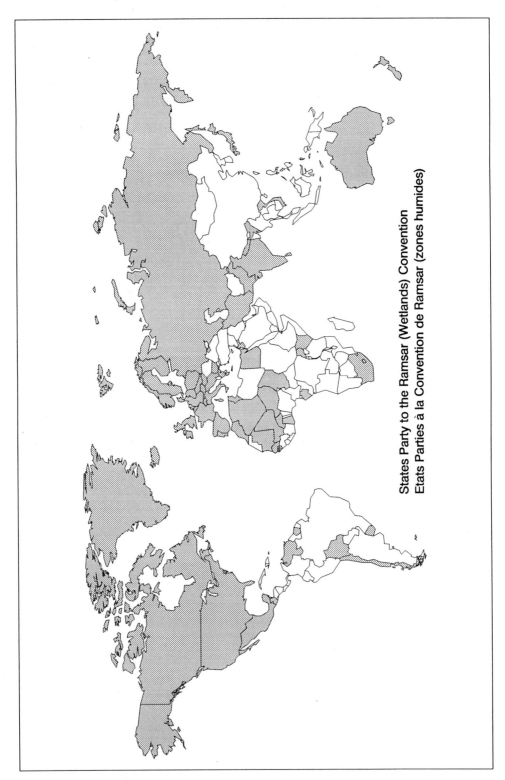

States Party to the Ramsar (Wetlands) Convention
Etats Parties à la Convention de Ramsar (zones humides)

LIST OF WETLANDS OF INTERNATIONAL IMPORTANCE
LISTE DES ZONES HUMIDES D'IMPORTANCE INTERNATIONALE

Designated by the Contracting parties – Convention on Wetlands of International Importance especially as Waterfowl Habitat

Désignées par les Parties contractantes – Convention relative aux zones humides d'importance internationale particulièrement comme habitats des oiseaux d'eau

---

AFRIQUE DU SUD – Voir paragraphe South Africa

ALGERIA/ALGERIE
Accession 4 November 1983/Adhésion le 4 novembre 1983
1. Lac Oubeïra	36°50'N	8°23'E	2,200 ha
2. Lac Tonga	36°51'N	8°30'E	2,700 ha

ALLEMAGNE, REPUBLIQUE FEDERALE D'
Voir paragraphe Germany, Federal Republic of

AUSTRALIA/AUSTRALIE
Signature without reservation as to ratification 8 May 1974/
Signature sans réserve de ratification le 8 mai 1974
1.	Cobourg Peninsula	11°22'S	132°00'E	191,660 ha

Added 12 June 1980/Ajoutée le 12 juin 1980
2.	Kakadu National Park (Stage I)	12°47'S	132°41'E	667,000 ha

Added 16 November 1982/Ajoutée le 16 novembre 1982
3.	Moulting Lagoon	42°05'S	148°10'E	3,930 ha
4.	Logan Lagoon	40°10'S	148°17'E	2,320 ha
5.	Sea Elephant Conservation Area	39°45'S	144°05'E	1,730 ha
6.	Pittwater-Orielton Lagoon	42°47'S	147°30'E	2,920 ha
7.	Apsley Marshes	41°56'S	148°12'E	940 ha
8.	East Coast Cape Barren Is. Lagoons	40°22'S	148°23'E	4,230 ha
9.	Lower Ringarooma River	41°54'S	147°56'E	1,650 ha
10.	Jocks Lagoon	41°21'S	148°18'E	70 ha
11.	Lake Crescent (northwestern corner)	42°09'S	147°10'E	270 ha
12.	Little Waterhouse Lake	40°52'S	147°37'E	90 ha

Added 15 December 1982/Ajoutée le 15 décembre 1982
13.	Corner Inlet	38°45'S	146°32'E	51,500 ha
14.	Barmah Forest	35°55'S	145°08'E	28,500 ha
15.	Gunbower Forest	35°49'S	144°19'E	19,450 ha
16.	Hattah-Kulkyne Lakes	34°41'S	142°26'E	1,018 ha
17.	Kerang Wetlands	35°40'S	143°56'E	9,172 ha
18.	Port Phillip Bay (western shoreline & Bellarine Peninsula)	38°04'S	144°36'E	7,000 ha
19.	Western Port	38°22'S	145°17'E	52,325 ha
20.	Western District Lakes	38°10'S	143°31'E	30,182 ha
21.	Gippsland Lakes	38°00'S	147°36'E	43,046 ha

22. Lake Albacutya	35°46'S	141°58'E	10,700 ha

Added 21 February 1984/Ajoutée le 21 février 1984

23. Towra Point Nature Reserve	34°00'S	151°10'E	281 ha
24. Kooragang Nature Reserve	32°51'S	151°46'E	2,206 ha

Added November 1985/Ajoutée en novembre 1985

25. The Coorong and Lakes Alexandrina and Albert	35°40'S	139°00'E	140,500 ha
26. Bool and Hacks Lagoons	37°08'S	140°41'E	3,200 ha

Added August 1986/Ajoutée en août 1986

27. Macquarie Marshes Nature Reserve	30°45'S	147°33'E	18,200 ha

Added 15 June 1987/Ajoutée le 15 juin 1987

28. Coongie Lakes	27°20'S	140°00'E	1,980,000 ha

Added 23 September 1987/Ajoutée le 23 septembre 1987

29. Riverland	34°02'S	140°51'E	30,600 ha

Added 15 September 1989/Ajoutée le 15 septembre 1989

30. Kakadu National Park (Stage II)	12°21'S	131°53'E	692,940 ha

Added 25 January 1990/Ajoutée le 25 janvier 1990

31. Ord River Floodplain	15°15'S	128°22'E	130,000 ha
32. Lakes Aargyle & Kununurra	16°20'S	128°42'E	150,000 ha
33. Roebuck Bay	18°07'S	122°16'E	50,000 ha
34. Eighty-mile Beach	19°31'S	120°48'E	125,000 ha
35. Forrestdale & Thomsons Lakes	32°09'S	115°52'E	754 ha
36. Peel-Yalgorup System	32°49'S	115°42'E	21,000 ha
37. Lake Toolibin	32°55'S	117°36'E	437 ha
38. Vasse-Wonnerup System	33°37'S	115°25'E	740 ha
39. Lake Warden System	33°48'S	121°56'E	2,300 ha

AUSTRIA/AUTRICHE

Accession 16 December 1982/Adhésion le 16 décembre 1982

1. Neusiedlersee	47°45'N	16°50'E	60,000 ha
2. Donau-March-Auen	48°27'N	16°50'E	38,500 ha
3. Untere Lobau	48°10'N	16°30'E	1,039 ha
4. Lower Inn reservoirs	48°19'N	13°14'E	870 ha
5. Rheindelta, Bodensee	47°30'N	9°45'E	1,960 ha

BELGIUM/BELGIQUE

Signature without reservation as to ratification 4 March 1986/
Signature sans réserve de ratification le 4 mars 1986

1. Les Vlaamse Banken dans les eaux côtières	51°20'N	3°00'E	1,900 ha
2. Les Schorren de l'Escaut à Doel et à Zandvliet	51°19'N	4°15'E	417 ha
3. Le Zwin	51°21'N	3°22'E	550 ha
4. Le Blankaart	50°59'N	2°51'E	2,160 ha
5. Kalmthoutse Heide	51°23'N	4°28'E	4,045 ha
6. Le Marais d'Harchies	50°30'N	3°40'E	535 ha

BOLIVIA
Accession 27 June 1990/Adhésion le 27 juin 1990
1.	Laguna Colorada	22°11'S	67°47'W	5,240 ha

BULGARIA/BULGARIE
Signature without reservation as to ratification 24 September 1975/
Signature sans réserve de ratification le 24 septembre 1975
1.	Srebarna	44°08'N	27°06'E	600 ha
2.	Arkoutino	42°18'N	27°45'E	97 ha

Added 28 November 1984/Ajoutée le 28 novembre 1984
3.	Atanassovo Lake	42°30'N	27°29'E	1,050 ha
4.	Durankulak Lake	43°42'N	28°30'E	350 ha

BURKINA FASO
Accession 27 June 1990/Adhésion le 27 juin 1990
1.	Mare d'Oursi	Description and maps yet to be provided)
2.	Mare aux Hippopotames	Détails et carte à être fournis)
3.	Parc national du "W"	

CANADA
Accession 15 January 1981/Adhésion le 15 janvier 1981
1.	Cap Tourmente	47°05'N	70°45'W	2,200 ha

Added 24 May 1982/Ajoutée le 24 mai 1982
2.	Mary's Point	45°44'N	64°45'W	1,200 ha
3.	Long Point	42°35'N	80°15'W	13,730 ha
4.	Delta Marsh	50°05'N	98°00'W	23,000 ha
5.	Last Mountain Lake (northern part)	51°20'N	105°15'W	15,600 ha
6.	Whooping Crane Summer Range	60°15'N	113°15'W	1,689,500 ha
7.	Peace-Athabasca Delta	58°42'N	111°08'W	321,300 ha
8.	Hay-Zama Lakes	58°30'N	119°00'W	50,000 ha
9.	Alaksen	49°05'N	123°15'W	520 ha
10.	Old Crow Flats	67°34'N	139°50'W	617,000 ha
11.	Polar Bear Pass	75°45'N	98°40'W	262,400 ha
12.	Queen Maud Gulf	67°00'N	102°00'W	6,200,000 ha
13.	Rasmussen Lowlands	68°00'N	93°30'W	300,000 ha
14.	McConnell River	61°07'N	94°03'W	32,800 ha
15.	Dewey Soper	64°14'N	76°32'W	815,900 ha

Added 16 October 1985/Ajoutée le 16 octobre 1985
16.	St Clair	42°22'N	82°22'W	244 ha
17.	Chignecto	45°47'N	64°20'W	1,020 ha

Added 27 May 1987/Ajoutée le 27 mai 1987
18.	Polar Bear Provincial Park	55°00'N	84°00'W	2,408,700 ha
19.	Lac Saint-François	45°02'N	74°29'W	2,214 ha
20.	Baie de l'Ile Verte	48°01'N	69°20'W	1,927 ha
21.	Shepody Bay	45°47'N	64°35'W	12,200 ha
22.	Grand Codroy Estuary	47°50'N	59°18'W	925 ha
23.	Quill Lakes	51°55'N	104°20'W	63,500 ha
24.	Oak-Hammock Marsh	50°10'N	97°06'W	3,600 ha

25.	Southern James Bay Sanctuaries	51°18'N	80°40'W	25,290 ha
26.	Point Pelee	41°47'N	82°31'W	1,564 ha
27.	Musquodoboit Harbour Outer Estuary	44°42'N	63°06'W	1,925 ha
28.	Beaverhill Lake	53°25'N	112°35'W	18,050 ha

Added 5 November 1987/Ajoutée le 5 novembre 1987

29.	Southern Bight-Minas Basin	45°13'N	64°16'W	26,800 ha

Added 28 April 1988/Ajoutée le 28 avril 1988

30.	Malpeque Bay	46°32'N	63°48'W	24,440 ha

CHAD/TCHAD

Accession 13 June 1990/Adhésion le 13 juin 1990

1.	Réserve de la Biosphère du Lac Fitri	12°50'N	17°30'E	195,000 ha

CHILE

Accession 27 July 1981/Adhésion le 27 juillet 1981

1.	Carlos Anwandter Sanctuary	39°41'S	73°11'W	4,877 ha

CZECHOSLOVAKIA/CZECHOSLOVAKIE

Accession 2 July 1990/Adhesion le 2 juillet 1990

1.	Modrava peatbogs	48°59'N	13°25'E	3,615 ha
2.	Třeboň fish ponds	49°03'N	14°43'E	10,165 ha
3.	Novozámecký and Břehyně ponds	50°37'N	14°34'E	923 ha
4.	Lednice fish ponds	48°47'N	16°46'E	552 ha
5.	Šúr	48°15'N	17°13'E	984 ha
6.	Paríž marshes	47°51'N	18°31'E	141 ha
7.	Cicov "dead arm"	47°45'N	17°44'E	135 ha
8.	Senné fish ponds	48°11'N	22°04'E	442 ha

DENMARK/DANEMARK

Accession 2 September 1977/Adhésion le 2 septembre 1977

1.	Fiilsø	55°42'N	8°15'E	4,320 ha
2.	Ringkøbing Fiord	56°00'N	8°15'E	27,240 ha
3.	Stadil and Vestastadil Fiords	56°11'N	8°09'E	7,184 ha
4.	Nissum Fiord	56°21'N	8°14'E	11,600 ha
5.	Nissum Bredning with Harboøre and Agger peninsulas	56°38'N	8°15'E	13,280 ha
6.	Vejlerne and Løgstør Bredning	57°01'N	9°00'E	45,280 ha
7.	Ulvedybet and Nibe Bredning	57°02'N	9°35'E	20,304 ha
8.	Hirsholmene	57°29'N	10°38'E	480 ha
9.	Nordre Rønner	57°22'N	10°56'E	2,923 ha
10.	Læsø	57°12'N	11°10'E	67,840 ha
11.	Randers and Mariager Fiords (part)	56°59'N	10°10'E	41,440 ha
12.	Anholt Island sea area	56°42'N	11°34'E	12,720 ha
13.	Horsens Fiord and Endelave	55°51'N	10°10'E	43,200 ha
14.	Stavns Fiord adjacent waters	55°54'N	10°40'E	16,320 ha
15.	Lillebælt	55°21'N	9°43'E	37,344 ha
16.	Næreå Coast and Æbelø area	55°36'N	10°13'E	13,800 ha
17.	South Funen Archipelago	55°00'N	10°20'E	39,200 ha

18. Sejerø Bugt	55°47'N	11°18'E	42,560 ha
19. Waters off Skælskør Nor and Glænø	55°10'N	11°30'E	17,120 ha
20. Karrebæk, Dybsø and Avnø Fiords	55°10'N	11°45'E	19,200 ha
21. Waters south-east of Fejo and Femo Isles	54°54'N	11°30'E	32,640 ha
22. Præstø Fiord, Jungshoved Nor, Ulfshale and Nyord	55°05'N	12°15'E	25,960 ha
23. Nakskov Fiord and Inner Fiord	54°50'N	11°02'E	8,960 ha
24. Maribo Lakes	54°46'N	11°31'E	4,400 ha
25. Waters between Lolland and Falster, including Rødsand, Guldborgsund, Bøtø Nor	54°14'N	11°45'E	36,800 ha
26. Ertholmene Islands east of Bornholm	55°19'N	15°11'E	1,257 ha
Added 14 May 1987/Ajoutée le 14 mai 1987			
27. Vadehavet (The Waddensea)	55°16'N	8°32'E	140,830 ha

Greenland/Groenland
Added 27 January 1988/Ajoutée le 27 janvier 1988

28. Aqajarua-Sullorsuag	69°40'N	52°00'W	30,000 ha
29. Qinguata Marraa-Kuussuaq	69°56'N	54°17'W	6,000 ha
30. Kuannersuit Kuussuat	69°40'N	53°17'W	4,500 ha
31. Kitsissunnguit	68°50'N	51°50'W	16,000 ha
32. Naternaq	68°20'N	52°00'W	150,000 ha
33. Eqalummiut Nunaat-Nassuttuup Nunaa	67°25'N	50°30'W	500,000 ha
34. Ikkatoq	62°40'N	50°15'W	35,000 ha
35. Ydre Kitsissut	60°45'N	48°25'W	8,000 ha
36. Heden	71°00'N	24°00'W	125,000 ha
37. Hochstetter Forland	75°30'N	20°00'W	140,000 ha
38. Kilen	81°15'N	12°00'W	30,000 ha

EGYPT/EGYPTE
Accession 9 September 1988/Adhésion le 9 septembre 1988

1. Lake Bardawil	31°05'N	33°05'E	59,500 ha
2. Lake Burullus	31°30'N	30°50'E	46,200 ha

ESPAGNE
Voir paragraphe Spain

ETATS UNIS D'AMERIQUE
Voir paragraphe United States of America

FINLAND/FINLANDE
Ratification 28 May 1974/Ratification le 28 mai 1974

1. Aspskär	60°16'N	26°25'E	369 ha
2. a) Söderskär	60°07'N	25°25'E	1,382 ha
b) Langoren	60°09'N	25°38'E	8,250 ha
3. a) Björkör	59°56'N	20°10'E	5,300 ha
b) Lagskär	59°50'N	19°50'E	460 ha
4. Signilskär	60°09'N	19°22'E	11,600 ha
5. a) Valassaaret	63°26'N	21°05'E	11,800 ha
b) Björkögrunden	63°22'N	21°05'E	5,900 ha

6. Krunnit	65°23'N	24°47'E	4,600 ha
7. Ruskis	60°22'N	25°40'E	235 ha
8. Viikki	60°13'N	25°00'E	247 ha
9. Patvinsuo	63°05'N	29°45'E	9,400 ha
10. Maartimoaapa - Lumiaapa	65°49'N	25°15'E	7,400 ha
11. Koitilaiskaira	67°45'N	27°00'E	34,400 ha

FRANCE
Ratification 1 October 1986/Ratification le 1 octobre 1986

1. La Camargue	43°30'N	4°30'E	85,000 ha

GABON
Ratification 30 December 1986/Ratification le 30 décembre 1986

1. Wongha-Wonghé	0°30'S	9°20'E	380,000 ha
2. Petit Loango	2°15'S	9°45'E	480,000 ha
3. Setté Cama	2°50'S	10°15'E	220,000 ha

GERMAN DEMOCRATIC REPUBLIC
Accession 31 July 1978/Adhésion le 31 juillet 1978

1. Rügen/Hiddensee and eastern part of Zingst Peninsula	55°00'N	13°05'E	25,800 ha
2. Krakower Obersee	53°37'N	12°18'E	870 ha
3. Müritz See (eastern shore)	53°27'N	12°49'E	4,830 ha
4. Lower Havel River and Gülper See	52°46'N	12°16'E	5,792 ha
5. Oder Valley near Schwedt	53°04'N	14°20'E	5,400 ha
6. Peitz Ponds	51°51'N	14°25'E	1,060 ha
7. Berga-Kelbra Storage Lake	51°27'N	10°56'E	1,360 ha
8. Galenbecker See	53°38'N	13°44'E	1,015 ha

GERMANY, FEDERAL REPUBLIC OF
Ratification 26 February 1976/Ratification le 26 février 1976

1. Wattenmeer, Elbe-Weser-Dreieck	53°50'N	8°24'E	38,460 ha
2. Wattenmeer, Jadebusen & Western Weser Mouth	53°40'N	8°19'E	49,490 ha
3. Ostfriesisches Wattenmeer & Dollart	53°42'N	7°21'E	121,620 ha
4. Lower Elbe, Barnkrug-Otterndorf	53°47'N	9°07'E	11,760 ha
5. Elbe water-meadows between Schnackenburg and Lauenburg	53°08'N	11°05'E	7,56 0 ha
6. Dümmersee	52°32'N	8°23'E	3,600 ha
7. Diepholzer Lowland Marsh and Peat Bogs	52°34'N	8°48'E	15,060 ha
8. Steinhuder Meer	52°28'N	9°20'E	5,730 ha
9. Rhine between Eltville and Bingen	49°59'N	8°02'E	475 ha
10. Bodensee			1,077 ha
a) Wollmatingen reed-bed with north-eastern part of Ermatingen Basin	47°41'N	9°07'E	
b) Giehren marsh with Bay of Hegne on the Gnadensee	47°42'N	9°06'E	
c) Mindelsee near Radolfzell	47°45'N	9°01'E	

11. Water-meadows and peat-bogs of Donau	48°28'N	10°13'E	8,000 ha
12. Lech-Donau Winkel			230 ha
a) Feldheim Reservoir on the Lech	48°41'N	10°54'E	
b) Bertoldsheim Reservoir on the Donau	48°44'N	11°03'E	
13. Ismaning Reservoir and fish-ponds	48°13'N	11°41'E	900 ha
14. Ammersee	48°01'N	11°08'E	6,517 ha
15. Starnberger See	47°55'N	11°18'E	5,720 ha
16. Chiemsee	47°53'N	12°29'E	8,660 ha
17. Lower Inn between Haiming and Neuhaus	48°20'N	13°09'E	1,955 ha

Added 28 October 1983/Ajoutée le 28 octobre 1983

18. Rieselfelder Münster	52°09'N	7°39'E	233 ha
19. Weserstaustufe Schlüsselburg	52°27'N	8°59'E	1,550 ha
20. Unterer Niederrhein	51°43'N	6°14'E	25,000 ha
21. Nationalpark Hamburgisches Wattenmeer	53°53'N	8°17'E	11,700 ha

GHANA

Accession 22 February 1988/Adhésion le 22 février 1988

1. Owabi	6°44'N	1°41'W	7,260 ha

GREECE/GRECE

Accession 21 August l975/Adhésion le 21 août 1975

1. Evros Delta	40°52'N	26°00'E	10,000 ha
2. Lake Visthonis and Porto Lagos Lagoon	41°00'N	25°00'E	10,000 ha
3. Lake Mitrikou and adjoining lagoons	41°00'N	25°15'E	3,800 ha
4. Nestos Delta and Gumburnou Lagoon	40°57'N	24°44'E	10,600 ha
5. Lakes Volvis and Langada	40°25'N	23°40'E	2,400 ha
6. Lake Kerkini	41°12'N	23°09'E	9,000 ha
7. Axios-Aliakmon-Loudias Delta	40°34'N	22°39'E	11,000 ha
8. Lakes Mikra Prespa and Megali Prespa	40°45'N	21°06'E	8,000 ha
9. Amvrakikos Gulf	39°05'N	20°50'E	25,000 ha
10. Mesolonghi Lagoons	38°20'N	21°26'E	13,900 ha
11. Kotichi Lagoon	38°01'N	21°18'E	3,700 ha

GUINEA BISSAU/GUINEE BISSAU

Accession 14 May 1990/Adhésion le 14 mai 1990

1. Lagoa de Cufada	11°43'N	15°02'W	39,098 ha

GUATEMATA

Accession 26 June 1990/Adhésion le 26 juin 1990

1. Laguna del Tigre	17°27'N	90°52'W	90,562 ha

HUNGARY/HONGRIE

Accession 11 April l979/Adhésion le ll avril 1979

1. Szaporca	45°50'N	18°06'E	250 ha
2. Velence-Dinnyés	47°10'N	18°32'E	1,000 ha
3. Kardoskut	46°30'N	20°28'E	500 ha
4. Kis-balaton	46°40'N	17°15'E	14,745 ha
5. Mártély	46°25'N	20°20'E	2,300 ha

6.	Kiskunság	46°49'N	19°15'E	4,000 ha
7.	Pusztaszer	46°15'N	20°10'E	5,000 ha
8.	Hortobágy	47°37'N	21°05'E	15,000 ha

Added 17 March 1989/Ajoutée le 17 mars 1989

9.	Ócsa	47°18'N	19°14'E	1,078 ha
10.	Tata Old Lake*	47°39'N	18°18'E	269 ha
11.	Lake Fertö	47°45'N	16°45'E	2,870 ha
12.	Lake Balaton*	46°55'N	17°54'E	59,800 ha
13.	Bodrogzug	48°11'N	21°24'E	3,782 ha

* Designations only apply from 1 October to 30 April/Les désignations s'appliquent uniquement pendant la période du 1er octobre au 30 avril

ICELAND

Accession 2 December 1977/Adhésion le 2 décembre 1977

1.	Part of Mývatn-Laxá Region	65°40'N	17°00'W	20,000 ha

Added 20 March 1990/Ajoutée le 20 mars 1990

2.	Thjorsarver	64°40'N	18°40'W	37,500 ha

INDIA/INDE

Accession 1 October 1981/Adhésion le 1 octobre 1981

1.	Chilka Lake	19°42'N	85°21'E	116,500 ha
2.	Keoladeo National Park	27°13'N	77°32'E	2,873 ha

Added 23 March 1990/Ajoutée le 23 mars 1990

3.	Wular Lake	34°16'N	74°33'E	18,900 ha
4.	Harike Lake	31°13'N	75°12'E	4,100 ha
5.	Loktak Lake	24°26'N	93°49'E	26,600 ha
6.	Sambhar Lake	27°00'N	75°00'E	24,000 ha

IRAN

Ratification 23 June 1975/Ratification le 23 juin 1975

1.	Miankaleh Peninsula, Gorgan Bay and Lapoo-Zaghmarz Ab-bandans	36°50'N	53°17'E	40,000 ha
2.	Lake Parishan and Dasht-e-Arjan	29°30'N	52°00'E	6,600 ha
3.	Lake Oroomiyeh	37°30'N	45°30'E	483,000 ha
4.	Neiriz Lakes and Kamjan Marshes	29°40'N	53°30'E	108,000 ha
5.	Anzali Mordab Complex	37°25'N	49°25'E	15,000 ha
6.	Shadegan Marshes and tidal mud-flats of Khor-al Amaya and Khor Musa	30°30'N	48°45'E	190,000 ha
7.	Hamoun-e-Saberi	31°20'N	61°20'E	50,000 ha
8.	Lake Kobi	36°57'N	45°52'E	1,200 ha
9.	South end of Hamoun-e-Puzak	31°20'N	61°45'E	10,000 ha
10.	Shur Gol, Yadegarlu & Dorgeh Sangi Lakes	37°00'N	45°30'E	2,500 ha
11	Bandar Kiashahr Lagoon and mouth of Sefid Rud	37°25'N	49°29'E	500 ha
12.	Amirkelayeh Lake	37°17'N	50°12'E	1,230 ha
13.	Lake Gori	37°55'N	46°42'E	120 ha
14.	Alagol, Ulmagol and Ajigol Lakes	37°23'N	54°35'E	1,400 ha

15. Khuran Straits	26°45'N	55°40'E	100,000 ha
16. Deltas of Rud-e-Shur, Rud-e-Shirin and Rud-e-Minab	27°00'N	56°45'E	20,000 ha
17. Deltas of Rud-e-Gaz and Rud-e-Hara	26°15'N	57°10'E	15,000 ha
18. Gavkhouni Lake and marshes of the lower Zaindeh Rud	32°15'N	52°45'E	43,000 ha

IRELAND/IRLANDE
Ratification 15 November 1984/Ratification le 15 novembre 1984

1. Wexford	52°30'N	6°20'W	110 ha

Added 31 July 1986/Ajoutée le 31 juillet 1986

2. The Raven Nature Reserve	52°20'N	6°19'W	589 ha
3. Pettigo Plateau	54°36'N	7°55'W	900 ha
4. Slieve Bloom Mountains	53°02'N	7°38'W	2,230 ha
5. The Owenduff Catchment	54°03'N	9°40'W	1,382 ha

Added 1 June 1987/Ajoutée le 1 juin 1987

6. Owenboy	54°08'N	9°30'W	397 ha
7. Knockmoyle/Sheskin	54°10'N	9°35'W	732 ha
8. Lough Barra Bog	54°55'N	8°10'W	176 ha

Added 6 September 1988/Ajoutée le 6 septembre 1988

9. North Bull Island	53°17'N	6°05'W	1,436 ha

Added 25 October 1988/Ajoutée le 25 octobre 1988

10. Rogerstown Estuary	53°30'N	6°12'W	195 ha
11. Baldoyle Estuary	53°24'N	6°12'W	203 ha

Added 6 December 1988/Ajoutée le 6 décembre 1988

12. Clara Bog	53°19'N	7°32'W	460 ha
13. Mongan Bog	53°19'N	8°00'W	127 ha
14. Raheenmore Bog	53°20'N	7°20'W	162 ha

Added 10 July 1989/Ajoutée le 10 juillet 1989

15. Tralee Bay	52°16'N	9°48'W	754 ha

Added 30 May 1990/Ajoutée le 30 mai 1990

16. Castlemaine Harbour	52°07'N	9°55'W	923 ha
17. Easkey Bog	54°11'N	8°49'W	607 ha
18. The Gearagh	51°52'N	9°01'W	300 ha
19. Coole/Garryland	53°05'N	8°51'W	364 ha
20. Pollardstown Fen	53°11'N	6°52'W	130 ha
21. Meenachullion Bog	54°55'N	8°07'W	194 ha

ISLANDE
Voir paragraphe Iceland

ITALY/ITALIE
Ratification 14 December 1976/Ratification le 14 décembre 1976

1. Lago di Mezzola – Pian di Spagna	46°13'N	9°26'E	1,740 ha
2. Vincheto di Cellarda	46°01'N	11°58'E	99 ha
3. Sacca di Bellochio	44°38'N	12°16'E	223 ha
4. Valle Santa	44°34'N	11°50'E	261 ha
5. Punte Alberete	44°32'N	12°09'E	480 ha
6. Palude di Colfiorito	43°01'N	12°53'E	157 ha

7.	Palude di Bolgheri	43°14'N	10°33'E	562 ha
8.	Laguna di Orbetello (Northern part)	42°27'N	11°13'E	887 ha
9.	Lago di Burano	42°24'N	11°23'E	410 ha
10.	Lago di Nazzano	42°13'N	12°36'E	265 ha
11.	Lago di Fogliano	41°24'N	12°54'E	395 ha
12.	Lago di Monaci	41°23'N	12°56'E	94 ha
13.	Lago di Caprolace	41°21'N	12°59'E	229 ha
14.	Lago di Sabaudia	41°17'N	13°02'E	1,474 ha
15.	Lago di Villetta Barrea	41°47'N	13°58'E	303 ha
16.	Stagno S'Ena Arrubia	39°49'N	8°34'E	300 ha
17.	Stagno di Molentargius	39°14'N	9°09'E	1,401 ha
18.	Stagno di Cagliari	39°13'N	9°03'E	3,466 ha

Added 6 December 1977/Ajoutée le 6 décembre 1977

19.	Le Cesine	40°20'N	18°23'E	620 ha

Added 10 March 1978/Ajoutée le 10 mars 1978

20.	Valle Cavanata	45°45'N	13°29'E	243 ha

Added 28 March 1979/Ajoutée le 28 mars 1979

21.	Stagno di Cabras	39°53'N	8°28'E	3,575 ha
22.	Corru S'Ittiri Fishery - Stagno di San Giovanni e Marceddi	39°44'N	8°30'E	2,610 ha
23.	Stagno di Pauli Maiori	39°52'N	8°37'E	287 ha
24.	Valle Campotto e Bassarone	44°35'N	11°49'E	1,363 ha

Added 14 May 1979/Ajoutée le 14 mai 1979

25.	Marano Lagunare - Foci dello Stella	45°45'N	13°08'E	1,400 ha

Added 2 August 1979/Ajoutée le 2 août 1979

26.	Salina di Margherita di Savoia	41°24'N	16°05'E	3,871 ha

Added 19 September 1980/Ajoutée le 19 septembre 1980

27.	Lago di Tovel	46°10'N	11°17'E	37 ha

Added 21 July 1981/Ajouté le 21 juillet 1981

28.	Torre Guaceto	40°43'N	17°48'E	940 ha

Added 4 September 1981/Ajoutée le 4 septembre 1981

29.	Valle di Gorino	44°49'N	12°21'E	1,330 ha
30.	Valle Bertuzzi	44°47'N	12°13'E	3,100 ha
31.	Valli residue del Comprensorio di Comacchio	44°30'N	12°07'E	13,500 ha
32.	Pialassa della Baiona	44°30'N	12°15'E	1,630 ha
33.	Ortazzo and adjacent territories	44°21'N	12°19'E	440 ha
34.	Saline di Cervia	44°15'N	12°19'E	785 ha

Added 3 May 1982/Ajoutée le 3 mai 1982

35.	Stagno di Sale Porcus	40°01'N	8°25'E	330 ha
36.	Stagno di Mistras	39°54'N	8°27'E	680 ha

Added 5 December 1984/Ajoutée le 5 décembre 1984

37.	Valli del Mincio	45°03'N	10°46'E	1,082 ha
38.	Torbiere d'Iseo	45°38'N	10°02'E	325 ha
39.	Palude Brabbia	45°44'N	8°40'E	459 ha
40.	Paludi di Ostiglia	45°04'N	11°06'E	123 ha

Added 12 April 1988/Ajoutée le 12 avril 1988

41.	Il Biviere di Gela	37°02'N	14°20'E	256 ha

Added 11 April 1989/Ajoutée le 11 avril 1989

42.	Valle Averto	45°19'N	12°08'E	200 ha

43. Riserva naturale Vendicari	36°48'N	15°07'E	1,450 ha
44. Isola Boscone	45°03'N	11°15'E	201 ha
45. Bacino dell'Angitola	38°46'N	16°13'E	875 ha

JAPAN/JAPON

Accession 17 June 1980/Adhésion le 17 juin 1980
| 1. Kushiro-shitsugen | 43°09'N | 144°26'E | 7,726 ha |

Added 13 September 1985/Ajoutée le 13 septembre 1985
| 2. Izu-numa and Uchi-numa | 38°43'N | 141°06'E | 559 ha |

Added 6 July 1989/Ajoutée le 6 juillet 1989
| 3. Kutcharo-ko | 45°09'N | 142°20'E | 1,607 ha |

JORDAN/JORDANIE

Accession 10 January 1977/Adhésion le 10 janvier 1977
| 1. Azraq Oasis | 31°49'N | 36°48'E | 7,372 ha |

KENYA

Accession 5 June 1990/Adhésion le 5 juin 1990
| 1. Lake Nakuru National Park | 0°24'S | 36°05'E | 18,800 ha |

MALI

Accession 25 May 1987/Adhésion le 25 mai 1987
1. Walado Debo/Lac Debo	15°15'N	4°15'W	103,100 ha
2. Séri	14°50'N	4°40'W	40,000 ha
3. Lac Horo	16°13'N	3°55'W	18,900 ha

MALTA/MALTE

Accession 30 September 1988/Adhésion le 30 septembre 1988
| 1. Ghadira | 35°58'N | 14°21'E | 11 ha |

MAROC
Voir paragraphe Morocco

MAURITANIA/MAURITANIE

Accession 22 October 1982/Adhésion le 22 octobre 1982
| 1. Banc d'Arguin | 20°50'N | 16°45'W | 1,173,000 ha |

MEXICO/MEXIQUE

Accession 4 July 1986/Adhésion le 4 juillet 1986
| 1. Ría Lagartos, Yucatán | 21°30'N | 88°00'W | 47,480 ha |

MOROCCO

Signature without reservation as to ratification 20 June 1980/
Signature sans réserve de ratification le 20 juin 1980
| 1. Merja Zerga | 34°50'N | 6°20'W | 3,500 ha |
| 2. Merja Sidi-Bourhaba | 34°15'N | 6°40'W | 200 ha |

3. Lac d'Affennourir	33°20'N	5°10'W	380 ha
4. Khnifiss Bay or Puerto Cansado	28°00'N	12°25'W	6,500 ha

NEPAL/NEPAL
Accession 17 December 1987/Adhésion le 17 décembre 1987

1. Koshi Toppu	26°37'N	87°00'E	17,500 ha

NETHERLANDS
Accession 23 May 1980/Adhésion le 23 mai 1980

1. De Groote Peel	51°20'N	5°45'E	900 ha
2. De Weerribben	52°37'N	5°59'E	3,400 ha
3. Het Naardermeer	52°17'N	5°07'E	752 ha
4. De Boschplaat	53°27'N	5°30'E	4,400 ha
5. De Griend	53°15'N	5°15'E	23 ha
6. De Biesbosch (part)	51°56'N	4°48'E	1,700 ha

Added 2 May 1984/Ajoutée le 2 mai 1984

13. Wadden Sea	53°15'N	5°15'E	249,998 ha

Added 3 April 1987/Ajoutée le 3 avril 1987

14. Oosterschelde	51°44'N	3°59'E	38,000 ha

Added 15 June 1988/Ajoutée le 15 juin 1988

15. Zwanenwater	52°49'N	4°42'E	600 ha

Added 2 June 1989/Ajoutée le 2 juin 1989

16. Oostvaardersplassen	52°27'N	5°20'E	5,600 ha
17. Engbertsdijksvenen	52°29'N	6°40'E	975 ha

Netherlands Antilles/Antilles néerlandaises
Listed on accession 23 May 1980/Cataloguées sur adhésion le 23 mai 1980

7. Het Lac	12°06'N	68°14'W	700 ha
8. Het Pekelmeer	12°02'N	68°19'W	400 ha
9. Klein Bonaire Island and adjacent sea	12°10'N	68°19'W	600 ha
10. Het Gotomeer	12°14'N	68°22'W	150 ha
11. De Slagbaai	12°16'N	68°25'W	90 ha
12. Het Spaans Lagoen	12°30'N	70°00'W	70 ha

NEW ZEALAND
Signature without reservation as to ratification 13 August 1976/
Signature sans réserve de ratification le 13 août 1976

1. Waituna Lagoon	46°34'S	168°36'E	3,556 ha
2. Farewell Spit	40°33'S	172°56'E	11,388 ha

Added 4 December 1989/Ajoutée le 4 décembre 1989

3. Whangamarino	37°19'S	175°12'E	5,690 ha
4. Kopuatai Peat Dome	37°26'S	175°34'E	9,665 ha

Added 29 January 1990/Ajoutée le 29 janvier 1990

5. Firth of Thames	37°13'S	175°23'E	7,800 ha

NIGER
Signature without reservation as to ratification 30 April 1987/
Signature sans réserve de ratification le 30 avril 1987

1. Parc national du "W"	12°15'N	2°25'E	220,000 ha

NORWAY/NORVEGE

Signature without reservation as to ratification 9 July 1974/
Signature sans réserve de ratification le 9 juillet 1974

1.	Åkersvika	60°50'N	11°08'E	415 ha

Added 24 July 1985/Ajoutée le 24 juillet 1985

2.	Øra	59°10'N	11°00'E	1,560 ha
3.	Kurefjorden	59°30'N	11°00'E	400 ha
4.	Nordre Øyeren	59°53'N	11°09'E	6,260 ha
5.	Ilene and Presterødkilen	59°15'N	10°20'E	177 ha
6.	Jæren	58°50'N	5°34'E	400 ha
7.	Ørlandet	63°42'N	9°35'E	2,920 ha
8.	Tautra and Svaet	63°35'N	10°37'E	2,054 ha
9.	Stabbursneset	70°10'N	24°40'E	1,620 ha
10.	Forlandsøyane	78°20'N	11°36'E	60 ha

Spitzbergen

Added 24 July 1985/Ajoutée le 24 juillet 1985

11.	Dunøyane	77°04'N	15°00E	120 ha
12.	Kongsfjorden	78°55'N	12°10'E	140 ha
13.	Isøyane	77°08'N	14°48'E	30 ha
14.	Gasøyane	78°20'N	11°36'E	100 ha

NOUVELLE-ZELANDE

Voir paragraphe New Zealand

OUGANDA

Voir paragraphe Uganda

PAKISTAN

Ratification 23 July 1976/Ratification le 23 juillet 1976

1.	Thanadarwala	32°35'N	71°05'E	4,047 ha
2.	Malugul Dhand	32°46'N	70°51'E	405 ha
3.	Kandar Dam	33°36'N	71°29'E	251 ha
4.	Tanda Dam	33°35'N	71°29'E	405 ha
5.	Kheshki Reservoir	34°00'N	72°02'E	263 ha
6.	Khabbaki Lake	34°00'N	72°00'E	283 ha
7.	Kinjhar (Kalri) Lake	24°52'N	68°03'E	13,468 ha
8.	Drigh Lake	27°34'N	68°06'E	164 ha
9.	Haleji Lake	24°47'N	67°46'E	1,704 ha

PAYS-BAS

Voir paragraphe Netherlands

POLAND/POLOGNE

Accession 22 November 1977/Adhésion le 22 novembre 1977

1.	Luknajno Lake	53°49'N	21°38'E	710 ha

Added 3 January 1984/Ajoutée le 3 janvier 1984

2.	Slońsk	52°33'N	14°43'E	4,166 ha
3.	Swidwie Lake	53°34'N	14°22'E	382 ha

4. Karaś Lake	53°33'N	19°38'E	816 ha
5. Siedem Wysp	54°20'N	21°36'E	1,016 ha

PORTUGAL
Ratification 24 November 1980/Ratification le 24 novembre 1980

1. Tagus Estuary	38°50'N	8°57'W	14,563 ha
2. Formosa Sound	37°03'N	7°47'W	16,000 ha

REPUBLIQUE DEMOCRATIQUE D'ALLEMAGNE
Voir paragraphe German Democratic Republic

ROYAUME-UNI
Voir paragraphe United Kingdom

SENEGAL
Accession 11 July 1977/Adhésion le 11 juillet 1977

1. Djoudj	16°20'N	16°12'W	16,000 ha
2. Bassin du Ndiaël	16°10'N	16°05'W	10,000 ha

Added 3 April 1984/Ajoutée le 3 avril 1984

3. Delta du Saloum	13°37'N	16°42'W	73,000 ha

Added 29 September 1986/Ajoutée le 29 septembre 1986

4. Gueumbeul	15°57'N	16°28'W	720 ha

SOUTH AFRICA
Signature without reservation as to ratification 12 March 1975/
Signature sans réserve de ratification le 12 mars 1975

1. De Hoop Vlei	34°27'S	20°20'E	750 ha
2. Barberspan	26°33'S	25°37'E	3,118 ha

Added 2 October 1986/Ajoutée le 2 octobre 1986

3. De Mond (Heuningnes Estuary)	34°43'S	20°07'E	1,318 ha
4. Blesbokspruit	26°17'S	28°30'E	1,858 ha
5. Turtle Beaches/Coral Reefs of Tongaland	27°30'S	32°40'E	39,500 ha
6. St Lucia System	28°00'S	32°28'E	155,500 ha

Added 25 April 1988/Ajoutée le 25 avril 1988

7. Langebaan	33°06'S	18°01'E	6,000 ha

SPAIN
Accession 4 May 1982/Adhésion le 4 mai 1982

1. Doñana	36°57'N	6°19'W	49,225 ha
2. Las Tablas de Daimiel	39°10'N	3°39'W	1,812 ha

Added 8 August 1983/Ajoutée le 8 août 1983

3. Laguna de Fuentapiedra	37°07'N	4°46'W	1,355 ha

Added 5 December 1989/Ajoutée le 5 décembre 1989

4. Lagunas de Cadiz			
a) Laguna de Medina	36°37'N	6°02'E	121 ha
b) Laguna Salada del Puerto	36°39'N	6°14'E	37 ha
5. Lagunas del Sur de Cordoba			
a) Laguna de Zóñar	37°30'N	4°45'W	66 ha

b) Laguna Amarga	37°15'N	4°37'W	13 ha
c) Laguna del Rincón	37°27'N	4°38'W	7 ha
6. Marismas del Odiel	37°17'N	6°55'W	7,185 ha
7. Salinas del Cabo de Gata	36°44'N	2°12'W	300 ha
8. S'Albufera de Mallorca	39°49'N	3°07'E	1,700 ha
9. Laguna de la Vega o del Pueblo	39°25'N	2°56'W	34 ha
10. Lagunas de Villafáfila	41°49'N	5°37'W	32,682 ha
11. Complejo Intermareal O Umia-Grove, La Lanzada, Punta Carreirón y Lagoa Bodeira	42°29'N	8°49'W	2,561 ha
12. Rías de Ortigueira y Ladrido	43°42'N	7°47'W	2,920 ha
13. L'Albufera de Valencia	39°20'N	0°21'W	21,000 ha
14. Pantano de el Hondo	38°10'N	0°42'W	2,337 ha
15. Salinas de la Mata y Torrevieja	38°00'W	0°42'W	2,100 ha
16. Salinas de Santa Pola	38°08'N	0°37'W	2,400 ha
17. Prat de Cabanes - Torreblanca	40°10'N	0°11'E	860 ha

SRI LANKA

Accession 15 June 1990/Adhésion le 15 juin 1990

1. Bundala Sanctuary	6°10'N	81°12'E	6,216 ha

SURINAME/SURINAM

Accession 18 March 1985/Adhésion le 18 mars 1985

1. Coppename Rivermouth	5°50'N	55°50'W	12,000 ha

SWEDEN/SUEDE

Signature without reservation as to ratification 5 December 1974/
Signature sans réserve de ratification le 5 décembre 1974

1. Falsterbo-Bay of Foteviken	55°25'N	12°55'E	7,450 ha
2. Klingavälsån-Krankesjön	55°37'N	13°38'E	3,975 ha
3. Helga River			
a) Hammarsjön and Egeside	56°00'N	14°12'E	4,250 ha
b) Araslövssjön	56°03'N	14°07'E	1,200 ha
4. Ottenby	56°12'N	16°24'E	1,600 ha
5. Coastal areas of Öland			
a) Stora Ören - Gammalsbyören	56°27'N	16°36'E	4,800 ha
b) Egby-Kapelludden	56°51'N	16°53'E	2,600 ha
c) Södviken	57°02'N	16°55'E	790 ha

(Prior to 12 June 1989 this site only comprised Södviken/
Avant le 12 juin 1989 ce bien comprenait uniquement Södviken)

6. Getterön	57°08'N	12°14'E	340 ha
7. Store Mosse and Kävsjön	57°18'N	13°57'E	7,450 ha
8. Isles off Gotland			
a) Faludden	57°00'N	18°22'E	1,300 ha

(Faludden was added to this site 12 June 1989/
Faludden était ajoutée à ce bien le 12 juin 1989)

b) Grötlingboholme and Rone Ytterholmen	57°07'N	18°30'E	1,625 ha

c) Laus holmar	57°17'N	18°45'E	540 ha
d) Skenholmen	57°48'N	19°03'E	700 ha
9. Hornborgasjön	58°19'N	13°33'E	6,350 ha
10. Tåkern	58°21'N	14°49'E	5,600 ha
11. Kvismaren	59°10'N	15°23'E	800 ha
12. Hjälstaviken	59°40'N	17°23'E	790 ha
13. Ånnsjön	63°16'N	12°33'E	11,300 ha
14. Gammelstadsviken	65°38'N	22°00'E	440 ha
15. Persöfjärden	65°46'N	22°08'E	3,350 ha
16. Tärnasjön	66°00'N	15°29'E	1,800 ha
17. Tjålmejaure-Laisdalen	66°15'N	16°11'E	22,200 ha
18. Laidaure	67°07'N	17°45'E	4,150 ha
19. Sjaunja-Kaitum	67°17'N	19°49'E	208,000 ha
20. Tavvavuoma	68°30'N	20°45'E	28,400 ha

Added 12 June 1989/Ajoutée le 12 juin 1989

21. Åsnen	56°37'N	14°43'E	16,635 ha
22. Träslövsläga - Morups Tånge	56°59'N	12°20'E	1,920 ha
23. Stigfjorden Bay	58°07'N	11°40'E	5,185 ha
24. Dättern Bay	58°23'N	12°37'E	3,320 ha
25. Lake Östen	58°35'N	13°57'E	1,020 ha
26. Kilsviken Bay	59°03'N	14°04'E	9,100 ha
27. Stockholm Outer Archipelago	59°26'N	19°22'E	14,500 ha
28. River Svartån			
a) Lake Gorgen - Nötmyran	59°57'N	16°17'E	710 ha
b) Fläcksjön - Gussjön	59°53'N	16°20'E	1,280 ha
29. Hovran Area	60°20'N	16°03'E	4,600 ha
30. River Umeälv Delta	63°45'N	20°20'E	1,150 ha

SWITZERLAND/SUISSE

Ratification 16 January l976/Ratification le 16 janvier 1976

1. Fanel Bay and le Chablais	46°59'N	7°03'E	1,155 ha

Added 18 February 1982/Ajoutée le 18 février 1982

2. Bolle di Magadino	46°10'N	8°52'E	661 ha

TUNISIA/TUNISIE

Accession 24 November l980/Adhésion le novembre l980

1. Ichkeul	37°10'N	9°40'E	12,600 ha

UGANDA/OUGANDA

Ratification 4 March 1988/Ratification le 4 mars 1988

1. Lake George	0°07'N	30°02'E	15,000 ha

UNION OF SOVIET SOCIALIST REPUBLICS/UNION DES REPUBLIQUES SOCIALISTES SOVIETIQUES

Ratification 11 October l976/ratification le 11 octobre 1976

1. Kandalaksha Bay	66°57'N	33°18'E	208,000 ha
2. Matsalu Bay	58°48'N	23°22'E	48,634 ha
3. Volga Delta	45°54'N	48°47'E	650,000 ha

4.	Kirov Bay	39°05'N	48°57'E	132,500 ha
5.	Krasnovodsk and North-Cheleken Bays	39°49'N	53°10'E	188,700 ha
6.	Sivash Bay	46°09'N	34°21'E	45,700 ha
7.	Karkinitski Bay	45°51'N	33°33'E	37,300 ha
8.	a) Intertidal Areas of the Dounai	45°25'N	29°40'E	14,851 ha
	b) Yagorlits and Tendrov Bays	46°18'N	32°05'E	113,200 ha
9.	Kourgaldzhin and Tengiz Lakes	50°27'N	69°10'E	260,500 ha
10.	Lakes of the lower Turgay and Irgiz	48°42'N	62°11'E	348,000 ha
11.	Issyk-kul Lake	42°27'N	77°16'E	629,800 ha
12.	Lake Khanka	44°53'N	132°26'E	310,000 ha

UNITED KINGDOM

Ratification 5 January 1976/Ratification le 5 janvier 1976

1.	Cors Fochno and Dyfi	52°31'N	4°00'W	2,497 ha
2.	Bridgwater Bay	51°13'N	3°04'W	2,703 ha
3.	Bure Marshes	52°41'N	1°29'E	412 ha
4.	Hickling Broad and Horsey Mere	52°45'N	1°39'E	892 ha
5.	Lindisfarne	55°41'N	1°48'W	3,123 ha
6.	Lochs Druidibeg, a'Machair & Stilligary	57°21'N	7°24'W	1,780 ha
7.	Loch Leven	56°13'N	3°23'W	1,597 ha
8.	Loch Lomond	56°04'N	4°35'W	253 ha
9.	Lough Neagh and Lough Beg	54°40'N	6°25'W	39,500 ha
10.	Minsmere - Walberswick	52°17'N	1°37'E	1,697 ha
11.	North Norfolk Coast	52°30'N	0°53'E	7,700 ha
12.	Ouse Washes	52°30'N	0°13'E	2,276 ha
13.	Rannoch Moor	56°39'N	4°40'W	1,499 ha

Added 24 July 1981/Ajoutée le 24 juillet 1981

14.	Cairngorm Lochs	58°04'N	3°47'W	179 ha
15.	Loch of Lintrathen	56°41'N	3°11'W	218 ha
16.	Claish Moss	56°45'N	5°44'W	563 ha
17.	Silver Flowe	55°07'N	4°23'W	608 ha
18.	Abberton Reservoir	51°49'N	0°52'E	1,228 ha
19.	Rostherne Mere	53°21'N	2°23'W	79 ha

Added 17 July 1985/Ajoutée le 17 juillet 1985

20.	The Dee Estuary	53°17'N	3°05'W	13,055 ha
21.	The Swale	51°22'N	1°07'W	5,790 ha
22.	Chesil Beach and the Fleet	50°36'N	2°32'W	763 ha
23.	Derwent Ings	53°50'N	0°54'W	783 ha
24.	Holburn Moss	55°37'N	1°57'W	22 ha
25.	Irthinghead Mires	55°04'N	2°22'W	608 ha

Added 28 November 1985/Ajoutée le 28 novembre 1985

26.	Leighton Moss	54°10'N	2°47'W	125 ha
27.	Martin Mere	53°35'N	2°49'W	119 ha
28.	Alt Estuary	53°30'N	3°10'W	1,160 ha

Added 25 September 1986/Ajoutée le 25 septembre 1986

29.	Loch of Skene	57°09'N	2°20'W	125 ha
30.	Loch Eye	57°48'N	3°56'W	195 ha
31.	Rockcliffe Marshes	54°52'N	3°30'W	1,897 ha

Added 4 November 1987/Ajoutée le 4 novembre 1987

32.	Chichester and Langstone Harbours	50°50'N	1°00'W	5,749 ha

Added 5 February 1988/Ajoutée le 5 fèvrier 1988

33.	Upper Severn Estuary	51°46'N	2°23'W	1,437 ha

Added 30 March 1988/Ajoutée le 30 mars 1988

34.	The Wash	52°55'N	0°20'E	63,124 ha
35.	Pagham Harbour	50°46'N	0°46'W	616 ha

Added on 14 July 1988/Ajoutée le 14 juillet 1988

36.	Gruinart Flats	55°50'N	6°20'W	3,170 ha
37.	Eilean Na Muice Duibhe (Duich Moss)	55°42'N	6°15'W	574 ha
38.	Bridgend Flats	55°45'N	6°15'W	331 ha
39.	Gladhouse Reservoir	55°44'N	3°07'W	186 ha
40.	Din Moss - Hoselaw Loch	55°35'N	2°18'W	46 ha

Added 30 April 1990/Ajoutée le 30 avril 1990

41.	Fala Flow	55°49'N	2°54'W	323 ha
42.	Glac-na-Criche	55°51'N	6°27'W	265 ha
43.	Feur Lochain	55°50'N	6°21'W	384 ha
44.	Loch-an-Duin	57°10'N	7°24'W	3,606 ha

Turks & Caicos

Added 27 June 1990/Ajoutéele 27 juin 1990

45.	Turks & Caicos	(Full site details not yet provided/ Détails complets pas encore fournis)

UNITED STATES OF AMERICA/ETATS UNIS D'AMERIQUE

Ratification 18 December 1986/Ratification le 18 décembre 1986

1.	Ash Meadows	36°25'N	116°20'W	9,509 ha
2.	Edwin B Forsythe NWR	39°36'N	74°17'W	13,080 ha
3.	Izembek	55°45'N	162°41'W	168,433 ha
4.	Okefenokee	30°49'N	82°20'W	159,889 ha

Added 4 June 1987/Ajoutée le 4 juin 1987

5.	Everglades	25°00'N	80°55'W	566,143 ha
6.	Chesapeake Bay	38°00'N	76°20'W	45,000 ha

Added 19 October 1988/Ajoutée le 19 octobre 1988

7.	Cheyenne Bottoms	38°29'N	98°40'W	8,036 ha

Added 21 November 1989/Ajoutée le 21 novembre 1989

8.	Cache-Lower White Rivers	34°40'N	91°11'W	145,690 ha

URUGUAY

Accession 22 May 1984/Adhésion le 22 mai 1984

1.	Bañados del Este y Franja Costera	33°40'S	53°20'W	200,000 ha

VENEZUELA

Accession 23 November 1988/Adhésion le 23 novembre 1988

1.	Cuare	10°55'N	68°20'W	9,968 ha

VIET NAM

Accession 20 September 1988/Adhésion le 20 septembre 1988

1.	Red River Estuary	20°10'N	106°20E	12,000 ha

YUGOSLAVIA/YUGOSLAVIE

Accession 28 March 1977/Adhésion le 28 mars 1977

1.	Obedska Bara	44°43'N	20°04'E	17,501 ha
2.	Ludaško Lake	46°04'N	19°48'E	593 ha